THE ENIGMA OF COMPARATIVE LAW

The Enigma of Comparative Law

Variations on a Theme for the Twenty-first Century

ESİN ÖRÜCÜ

SPRINGER-SCIENCE+BUSINESS MEDIA, B.V.

A C.I.P. Catalogue record for this book is available from the Library of Congress.

ISBN 978-90-04-13989-3 ISBN 978-94-017-5596-2 (eBook)
DOI 10.1007/978-94-017-5596-2

Originally published by Martinus Nijhoff in 2004
Softcover reprint of the hardcover 1st edition 2004

http: //www.brill.nl

CONTENTS

OVERTURE

Comparative Law is an enigmatic, paradoxical and elusive subject in that, just as one thinks one has mastered it, another puzzle appears on the horizon. The puzzles start with the name of the subject, continue with its definition, aims, objectives, methodology and its use in practice, and culminate in its value and significance for legal science. Comparative law is at times in accord and at times in discord with other branches of law such as public international law, private international law and legal theory, and with other fields of study such as anthropology, sociology, history, philosophy and economics. It embodies harmony and disharmony, and syncopation. It is stimulating, yet routine. It is enabling, yet frustrating. It is poised to become the 'science of tomorrow', the tool for understanding laws and cultures in the globalizing world of the twenty-first century, and yet it is still not always taken seriously by many scholars. Its functions and malfunctions, conceptions and misconceptions, advantages and disadvantages are under perpetual discussion. This contested subject can only be approached as an enigma and the present study aims to do this.

During the past decade we have witnessed a spreading of interest in all forms of comparative law, international law and transnational law. The character, quality and quantity of work have increased and changed, but the basic problems have remained the same. There is no one single definition of what comparative law and comparative method are. It is true that there is now less concern with 'justifying the practical utility of comparative law', 'making its subject matter manageable' and 'avoiding superficiality'.[1] The emphasis has shifted to regarding comparative law as 'a big tent, encompassing lots of different types of scholarship'[2] or as something which 'there seems little point in trying to specify'[3] and which reveals the inadequacy of the discipline's traditional 'tools, classifications and teaching

---

[1] W. Twining, 'Comparative Law and Legal Theory: the Country and Western Tradition', in I.D. Edge (ed), *Comparative Law in Global Perspective* (New York, Transnational Publishers, 2000), p. 51.

[2] D. Kennedy, 'The methods and the politics', in P. Legrand and R. Munday (eds), *Comparative Legal Studies: Traditions and Transitions* (Cambridge, Cambridge University Press, 2002), pp. 345-433.

[3] R. Cotterrel, 'Seeking Similarity, Appreciating Difference: Comparative Law and Communities', in A. Harding and E. Örücü (eds), *Comparative Law in the 21st Century* (London, Kluwer Law International, 2002), p. 36.

techniques' for 'the analysis of modern legal problems'.[4] It has even been said that, 'Few experienced comparatists compare - and for good reason.'[5] Maybe it is the case that comparison has become more implicit.

The theme 'Comparative Law' can be approached from three standpoints: that of the educator, the critic or the comparative lawyer. The present work is a book by an educator, a critic and a comparative lawyer combined. The educator should be detached, the critic objective, but for the comparative lawyer there is something vital at stake. She is working towards the spreading of comparative culture.

This work aims to be a preparation for true comparison. No comparative lawyer worthy of the name would be content to prepare the reader for acquaintance with only a partial view of her subject. That is why I have tried to unravel the enigma of the theme 'Comparative Law' through a number of its sub-themes.[6] One genuinely interested in comparative law would be unwilling to confine her perusal to a single version of the theme or one version of its sub-themes. There must be the possibility of a richer synthetic understanding.

Though the book is written primarily with comparative lawyers and law students in mind, it is my hope that legal practitioners may also profit from it. No one should lose sight of comparative law as a whole. Here is an attempt to tie up the loose ends, juxtapose different views and present this enigma in its polyphonic texture. Listening polyphonically or approaching contrapuntal textures enables a listener to hear separate strands of melody simultaneously.[7] The parts need not be of equal importance but they must be sensed independently. Contrapuntal textures are not confined to any one specific form, so a listener must be ready 'to listen polyphonically at any moment.'[8] Of course, one cannot develop one's appreciation of anything by just reading a book about it. If one wants to understand comparative law better one has to undertake it. It is experience that really counts.

I have been researching and teaching comparative law for over twenty-five years and one of the questions addressed to me which has always astonished me, is

---

[4] B. Markesinis, *Foreign Law and Comparative Methodology* (Oxford, Hart Publishing, 1998), p. 36.

[5] Twining, above note 1, at p. 47.

[6] 'Enigma Variations' by Sir Edward Elgar inspired the title of this work in the choice of the two words, 'enigma' and 'variation', but beyond that there is no relationship between this Enigma and variations and Elgar's 'Enigma Variations'. 'Variations on an original theme, the Enigma' was composed in 1899 as a set of 14 orchestral variations on an undisclosed theme. The 'original theme' is said to represent Elgar himself, this being the 'enigma' of the title. The sub-enigma is 'another and larger theme' which Elgar said 'goes' through and over the whole set 'but is not played'. Through the eyes of the 'original' theme, Elgar, the listener sees his wife and 12 of his friends, and Elgar in the finale. A third enigma lies in the asterisks of the 13th variation. If there had been a relationship between my work and that of Elgar's, I would have taken all the comparative lawyers I know one by one and written a chapter on each titled with the initials of each!

[7] I am indebted to Aaron Copland for all musical references. See A. Copland, *What to Listen for in Music*, Revised ed. (New York, Toronto, London, McGraw-Hill Book Co., 1957)

[8] *Ibid.*, p. 162.

the second question after the question, 'What is your specialism?' has been answered. The answer: 'I am a comparative lawyer', invariably gives rise to variants of a second questions: 'What do you compare?', 'What is your substantive area of law?' or better still: 'Yes, but what is your specialism?' One could of course repeat the first answer or try something like, 'I am a generalist', or 'I am a methodologist'. This usually brings a rather blank look and an 'Ah!' Were one to respond: 'I am a comparative contract lawyer' or 'a comparative family lawyer' or even more fashionable today, 'a comparative human rights lawyer', then the possibility of some communication and lively discussion might ensue.

It was this experience that first inspired me to approach comparative law under the name 'Critical Comparative Law',[9] and pointed to the need for a book on the enigma of comparative law, variations on a theme with sub-themes, having come to the conclusion that even when comparative lawyers do agree on some aspects of their subject they never agree on all. The approach I take here does not in any way mean that I regard the theme 'Comparative Law' as a musical theme, apart from coincidentally treating it as an 'enigma with variations', and proposing the term 'transposition', as in music, to replace the term 'transplantation'. Otherwise, the musical allegories are reserved for the form to be followed. Nevertheless, some clarification of the musical terms may be called for now, as the reader will be asked to transpose these into the handling of Comparative Law for her own understanding.

Let me start with the term 'theme'. A theme is an idea that returns in one form or another throughout a composition. It is one of the main parts out of which a piece is made.

> A theme is a succession of notes. Merely by changing the dynamics, that is by playing loudly and bravely or softly and timidly one can transform the emotional feeling of the very succession of notes. By a change of harmony a new poignancy may be given the theme, or by a different rhythmic treatment the same notes may result in a war dance instead of a lullaby.[10]

A simple theme can be repeated many times, each time with changes, that is, variations. When variations become more elaborate the theme may be completely ignored and one aspect of it concentrated on; this could even be the first few notes or a particular rhythm, wandering away and yet still 'related'.

> The variation forms well exemplify what the listener is expected to hear and what he is not expected to hear, as regards form in music… No listener, when hearing a variation form for the first time, hears it with any degree of exactitude as regards each separate variation. Nevertheless, it is of considerable value to

---

[9] E. Örücü, Critical Comparative Law: Considering Paradoxes for Legal Systems in Transition (Deventer, Kluwer Law International, 1999) and also in (2000) 4 Electronic Journal of Comparative Law 2.

[10] Copland above note 7, p. 25.

> him to know the general outlines, even though he is unable to follow the working out of each individual variation in detail.[11]

The variation form – a technique of changing and modifying a chosen theme – has been a particular favourite with composers of music. At first, variations were decorations of the melody, with rhythm and harmony untouched; later, the romantic composers went further and changed the melody and the rhythm with only the harmonic scaffolding remaining which provided a basis for free improvisation. The metro and the tempo also changed; change of key however, had not yet been thought of. Later still, that principle itself was overridden and eventually the variation technique reached its limits, variations being stimulated by the theme in some way but becoming almost free fantasies. Nearly all classical sets of variations are 'harmonic variations' in which an unchanging harmony forms the basis and the variations are generally arranged in contrast to one another or form groups.

Thus, the first aspect of a variation is one in which any element in the music may be varied – any harmony, any melody, any rhythm – as well as any form – sectional, sonata, fugal etc;. The second aspect is one in which a variation is the sole and exclusive formal principle.[12] It is in this sense that the theme 'Comparative Law' is treated here.

Variations can be harmonic,[13] melodic,[14] rhythmic[15] or contrapuntal[16] - possibly the extraction of a single phrase from the original theme treated contrapuntally.[17] The reader may see one of these variations in this book or a combination of all four.

One type of variation I am particularly interested in is the 'passacaglia'. In this type, the theme can be seen in a new light with the addition of each new variation,[18] and beyond the effect of any one variation taken alone, the variations together gathering 'cumulative momentum', the form as a whole becoming more satisfying.[19]

---

[11] Ibid., p. 142.

[12] *Ibid.,* p. 143.

[13] Here there are four possibilities. The first is where the melody is retained literally, but the accompanying harmonies are completely transformed; the second is where the texture becomes enriched though the melody is kept; the third is where the melody is lost but the underlying harmonic skeleton is kept; and in the extreme fourth case, the chordal skeleton itself is varied – thus it is not so much a variation of the theme as a variation of the accompanying chords of the theme.

[14] Here there are three possibilities. The first is where the melody itself is varied, the outer contours are kept but the line is more florid; the second is where the melodic line becomes less florid by concentrating on the barest essential notes; and the third is where the theme is retained but its position is changed.

[15] Here all types of rhythmic variations can be seen where the theme is completely transformed by rhythmic changes.

[16] Here a simple type is achieved by adding a new theme to the original, retaining the original in the background.

[17] For musical examples see Copland, above note 7, pp. 276-282.

[18] *Ibid.,* p. 151.

[19] *Ibid.*

When different variations are bound into a coherent whole, several variations on a similar pattern are customarily grouped together;[20] hence the different ways in which I approach the Chapters.

The 'theme and variation' is the most important variation form. This also reflects the overall plan of the present work. The musical theme adopted for variations could be original or borrowed. The theme here is 'Comparative Law'. In music, the theme is generally simple at the start. This work also starts by asking some simple but fundamental questions such as: What does the term comparative law mean? Why compare? What should be compared? How does one compare? Gradually the theme and its variations become more complex, and the variations loosely strung together, gain a general sense of balance and contrast out of which an attempt is made to build some structural unity.

This work can be read in a number of ways. Each Chapter presents a sub-theme with two Variation sections. The Chapters can be read in sequence and the book from beginning to end. In this way one can indulge in a discussion comprising at times diametrically opposed views. The second possibility is that the first Variations of each Chapter can be read in sequence or the second Variations in the same manner. Thus this study approaches comparative law as a grand divide. This divide enables the author to adopt a two-pronged approach. To this end, each of the Chapters is divided into the two Variation sections, each section being a Variation on the sub-theme covered in that Chapter. The sub-themes are not 'contrasting themes' but the variations on them are. The two exceptions to the scheme, as is appropriate, are Chapters six, the Intermezzo, and ten, the Cadenza where I use the freedom to extemporize. These two chapters should be read whether one is following Variations one or two.

If the reader chooses to read the whole book from page one to the end, she will be confronted by two opposing challenges in each of the Chapters and thus become immersed in the paradoxes of comparative law. In this way, a discursive, contrastive and argumentative texture would emerge: fertile ground for communication and conversation. On the other hand, the reader may prefer to follow either one or the other stream, and thereby read two slimmer books.

The first Variation of each Chapter takes the reader along one integrative path, to one conclusion and one view of the subject. The second Variation of each carries her along another path to another view and to another conclusion. Minor overlaps are inevitable, even though the way the issues are dealt with is not the same. The last Chapter, the Finale, is the end of the piece but not the end of the story! However, the reader by following the separate streams or by reading the whole may come to her own conclusions. A closing Coda section terminates the work. This Coda is not quiet and reminiscent in mood, but reaches a climax left to be pondered upon.

It will also become apparent to the reader familiar with the author's work and ideas, that some trends, concepts and frameworks alluded to in earlier works are here expanded into theories of comparative law.

---

[20] *Ibid.*, p. 152.

Depending on one's own personal stance on comparative law, one Variation will have a positive, the other a negative tonality. But this tone is there only because the reader's approach to, and appreciation of the topic reflects her expectations of the contents of one chain of Variations. Perchance, the reader may find that in the chain of Variations she is following, there is a Variation in a sub-theme that she is not happy to listen to. Then I suggest that she glance at the other Variation to see whether that is more satisfying.

Depending on the density of the paradox looked at, some Chapters and Variation sections are shorter than others. Half way through the book there is an Intermezzo - a short pause in which to take stock and to note the relationship of, and common ground shared by, the two approaches thus far. Further on, the Cadenza provides an opportunity for improvization without Variations, where a number of complex examples and cases are discussed, the meeting of law and culture is analysed, a de-construction of systems classification and a 'family trees model' is offered, the reality of mixing systems is re-visited and limits of comparativism are considered. The Finale, an integrative Chapter, looks towards our destination and indicates trends and horizons. The tail-piece Coda, in which the shifts ahead are indicated, brings the work to a close

I suggest that the subject be approached not as a monophonic or not even a homophonic texture, but as the polyphonic texture that it is. The question then is, where do we begin? Begin at the beginning, with the theme. So, now is the time to introduce the Theme, 'Comparative Law'.

Chapter 1

THE THEME COMPARATIVE LAW: WHAT IS IT? WHAT IS IN A NAME?

'...... O! be some other name:
What's in a name? that which we call a rose
By any other name would smell as sweet;'[1]

Comparative law as we know it today can be regarded as a child of the nineteenth century which has reached adolescence in the twentieth.[2] During this period, their subject seems to have given comparative lawyers total freedom and provided them with the seemingly endless pastime of discussing the true meaning, historical development, dangers, virtues, scope, functions, aims and purposes, uses and misuses, and the method of their subject. This has not only been the favourite pastime of comparative lawyers but of others also. Neither did this pastime lose its attraction when comparative law was accepted as part of the undergraduate curriculum in most universities in most legal systems, albeit as an elective course. In our century comparative law will reach maturity.

Although the twenty-first century has been heralded as 'the age of comparative law', amazingly, it is still open to question whether comparative law is indeed an independent discipline at all.[3] Only recently, comparative lawyers have been called upon to re-think their subject[4] and it has also been suggested that the healthiest path for comparative law to secure its future is to penetrate other subjects[5] and to present itself in integrated courses.

---

[1] W. Shakespeare, Romeo and Juliet, Act II Sc. 2, Lines 42-44.
[2] The history of comparative law is not to be discussed in this work, but see K. Zweigert and H. Kötz, *An Introduction to Comparative Law,* 3rd. edn., trans. T. Weir (Oxford, Clarendon Press, 1998) and the bibliography provided there, pp. 48-62.
[3] G. Samuel, 'Comparative Law and Jurisprudence' (1998) 47 *International and Comparative Law Quarterly*, 817; and J. Gordley, 'Is Comparative Law a Distinct Discipline?' (1998) 46 *American Journal of Comparative Law*, 607.
[4] B. Markesinis, 'Comparative law – A Subject in Search of an Audience' (1990) 53 *Modern Law Review*, 1.
[5] *Ibid.,* p. 21.

Objectives as varied as aiding law reform and policy development, providing a tool of research to reach a universal theory of law, a critical perspective to students and an aid to international law practice, facilitating international unification and harmonization of laws, helping courts in filling gaps in the law and even working towards the furthering of world peace and tolerance have been attributed to comparative law. These objectives have been grouped as practical, sociological, political and pedagogical. The findings of comparative lawyers could be utilized for any of these objectives. However, unanswered questions remain: Are these the true objectives of comparative lawyers and if so, are they fully taken advantage of?

Other categorizations have also been made and attached to the name 'comparative law' such as descriptive, dogmatic, applied, contrasting, integrative, legislative, scholarly, scientific, formal, historical, macro, mezzo and micro. The terms 'traditional comparative law', 'conventional comparative law' and 'critical comparative law' have also become popular.

One thing is certain. There is a growing interest in comparative law. For example even a cursory survey of legal journals shows that there is an increase in the number of journals either dedicated to Comparative Law or with Comparative Law in their titles. Additionally, the number of articles with a comparative element published in these journals has quadrupled within the past ten years.[6] It has recently been observed that, 'Comparative law is an odd discipline. Long considered to be exotic and irrelevant to real issues, today it is a required component of university curricula and legal practice'.[7] Not only that, but it has become indispensable for all doctoral research, and judges and legislators consult foreign material as a matter of routine.[8]

Of course diversity and popularity are to be welcomed. 'However, comparative law is not just experiencing the pleasure of the ageing movie star suddenly becoming a cult figure: it is also fraught with internal contradictions, uncertainty, and a sense of mid-life crisis.'[9]

It has been said that in the UK, 'Comparative law may have been the hobby of yesterday, but it is destined to become the science of tomorrow. We must welcome, rather than fear, its influence.'[10] On the European continent it is said that:

> For a long time it looked as though comparative law was a matter for academic research, difficult and, surely, very interesting, beautiful to know something

---

[6] See P.G. Monateri, 'Everybody's Talking'; The Future of Comparative Law' (1998) 21*Hastings International and Comparative Law Review,* 825.

[7] O. Pfersmann, 'Le droit comparé comme interprétation et comme théorie du droit', (2001) *Oxford University Comparative Law Forum* 4 , p. 1 at ouclf.iuscomp.org; also in (2001) 53 *Revue international de droit comparé*, 275-288.

[8] *Ibid.*

[9] A. Harding and E. Örücü, 'Preface' in id. (eds) *Comparative Law in the 21st Century* (London, Kluwer Law International, 2002), p. xii.

[10] Lord Goff, 'The Future of the Common Law', (1997) 46 *International andComparative Law Quarterly*, 745, at p. 748.

> about, but not immediately relevant to the daily life of the law. Over the last ten or fifteen years the legal climate seems to be changing. This evolution may be influenced by the process of European integration; it may also result from the fact that we are living closer together (the 'global village' situation); it may finally be an autonomous process, occasioned by the lawyer's search for fresh perspectives, in particular when completely new legal problems are to be solved.[11]

It is certainly true that 'if comparative law did not exist it would have to have been invented'.[12] Yet the two fundamental questions related to comparative law remain, 'What is it?' and, 'Is the name "comparative law" appropriate?' This is remarkable. What is even more remarkable is that the attempts to answer both these questions are so varied.

Although Harold Gutteridge once observed that, 'the essential problem is not – What is comparative law? The question of real importance is – What is its purpose?',[13] most works on comparative law start with the question, 'What is Comparative Law?' and then try to define it. As pointed out by Alan Watson, who himself starts by asking the same question, 'the range of replies is startling',[14] even including a rather circular, vague and open-ended definition telling us that 'the words suggest an intellectual activity with law as its object and comparison as its process.'[15]

We as comparative lawyers may rejoice in the knowledge that the more complete a theme appears to be, the less possibility there is of seeing it in its various aspects, so we can say that the less complete the theme, the more likely it is to be open to new connotations. Hence the pleasure in dealing with an 'incomplete theme' such as Comparative Law.

The first Variation below regards comparative law as an autonomous branch of social science, a science of legal knowledge, an end in itself, as a high level analytical subject. The second Variation considers the subject comparative law, if it exists at all, as merely a way of looking at the normative world and trying to discover similarities and differences between legal systems and legal rules, and for a practical purpose.

---

[11] T. Koopmans, 'Comparative Law and the Courts' (1996) *45 International and Comparative Law Quarterly*, 545, at p. 545.

[12] H.J. Ault and M.A. Glendon, 'The Importance of Comparative Law in Legal Education: United States – Goals and Methods of Legal Comparison', in N.J. Hazard and W.J. Wagner (eds) *Law in the USA in Social and Technological Revolution* (Brussels, Bruylant, 1974) p. 69.

[13] H.C. Gutteridge, *Comparative Law* 2nd. ed., (London, Cambridge University Press, 1949; reprint, Wildy & Sons, London, 1974) p. 5.

[14] A.Watson, *Legal Transplants: An Approach to Comparative Law* (Edinburgh, Scottish Academic Press, 1974) pp. 171-172.

[15] Zweigert and Kötz, above note 2, p. 2.

VARIATION I

Is Comparative law to be defined merely as the juxtaposing, contrasting and comparing of legal systems or parts thereof with the aim of finding similarities and differences? For the purposes of this Variation, the reply must surely be much wider than that. The appropriate reply here is: 'Comparative Law' is a science of knowledge with its own separate sphere. Comparative law is an independent science, producing theoretical distillate. The enabling of the comparative lawyer to extract new knowledge with diverse applications, makes even comparative law methodology a method of acquiring knowledge. Comparative law can be regarded as the 'critical method of legal science'.[16]

Obviously, this does not mean to say that there are no other aspects to it. Indeed comparative law is a very broad field and the fruits gained by comparative study can be put to many uses. Comparative study can have many objectives: sociological, political, practical and pedagogical. It has developed in a number of well-established disparate directions. However, it can never be justified by its uses or objectives. As Rodolfo Sacco points out 'the use to which scientific ideas are put effects neither the definition of a science nor the validity of its conclusions.'[17] According to him, the reason why 'those who compare legal systems are always asked about the purpose of such comparison'[18] is not because comparative law has to justify its existence by its uses, but because the inquirers are of the 'common sense' or 'utilitarian' ilk. 'Comparative law remains a science as long as it acquires knowledge and regardless of whether or not the knowledge is put to any further use',[19] though obviously this does not mean that the knowledge gained should not be put to practical use. For example, my inaugural lecture at Erasmus University Rotterdam, 'Symbiosis between Comparative Law and Theory of Law',[20] at no point denied the uses to which knowledge gained by comparative legal research can be put, yet saw comparative law as intertwined with legal theory in the quest for knowledge. In this way comparative law gives deep understanding and insight. The initial thesis of the Trento group is to be endorsed: 'Comparative law, understood as a science, necessarily aims at the better understanding of legal data. Ulterior tasks such as the improvement of the law or interpretation are worthy of the greatest consideration but nevertheless are only secondary ends of comparative research.'[21]

---

16 *Ibid.,* p. 33.

17 R. Sacco, 'Legal Formants: A Dynamic Approach to Comparative law (Installment I of II)' (1991) 49 *American Journal of Comparative Law*, 1.

18 *Ibid.*

19 *Ibid.,* p. 4.

20 See E. Örücü, *Symbiosis Between Comparative Law and Theory of Law – Limitations of Legal Methodology* (Mededelingen van het Juridisch Instituut No 16, 1982, Erasmus Universiteit Rotterdam), pp. 1-25.

21 Sacco above note 17, pp. 4-5.

Comparison is the essence of understanding. Comparison is for logical abstraction. Comparison is the juxtaposing of the unknown to the known in order to glean legal knowledge. Comparative law is essentially for scholars.

The everyday process of thinking involves the making of a series of comparisons, that is, it is a process of contrasting and comparing. We comprehend the phenomena around us by observing differences and similarities, by juxtaposing the unknown and the known. 'Just as the qualities of a yellow, its hue, brilliance and tone are perceived and sharpened most truly by placing it first on or beside another yellow and secondly by placing it in contrast to purple, so we explore the world around us.'[22] One cannot appreciate darkness till one has seen light or light till one has seen darkness. All research which aims at explanatory generalizing involves comparison.

> Many terms have been used to designate the methods of scholarly investigation: *a priori, a posteriori*, deductive, inductive, analogical, historical, artistic, genetic, statistical, scientific, intuitive, observation, experiment, classifying, hypothesizing, empirical, logical, ethical, quantitative, qualitative, descriptive, narrative, dialectical, codifying and so on. Comparison is involved in all these methods. It is characteristic of all intellectual functions whose purpose is the discovery of sameness and difference.[23]

It is in this way that we also understand the legal world around us.

Comparative law is the name of the most sophisticated analysis of law. It looks at the world of law and the environment in which it lives, provides knowledge about law as rules, law in context and law as culture, thus enabling us to have comprehensive and deep knowledge of the legal phenomena and their interactions in society. The subject works towards total understanding of law. Although traditional legal doctrine does engage in comparative law through the 'law as rules approach', here law is approached in context and not merely as 'sets of rules'. Any other way of looking at law and at comparative law bears the prejudices of positivism and of national legal cultures. It is important to regard comparative law 'as an indispensable international component of a "*culture juridique*"'.[24]

Comparative law gives us a tool of communication. Indeed it is the vital tool for this. Therefore, one must study comparative law with its vast subject matter, as a separate topic in undergraduate studies and as a sophisticated tool in postgraduate studies. This can only be done in an autonomous general comparative law course.[25]

---

[22] A.E. Örücü, ' Method and object of comparative law' in: H.W. Blom and R.J. de Folter (eds.), *Methode en Object in de rechtswetenschappen* (Zwolle, W.E.J. Tjeenk Willink, 1986) pp. 57-72, at p. 57.

[23] J. Hall, *Comparative Law and Social Theory* (Louisiana, Louisiana State University Press,1963), p. 20.

[24] Zweigert and Kötz, above n. 2 p. 54.

[25] This subject will be considered again in Variation I in Chapter 7.

Comparative law is the ultimate in sophistication in legal research; it has the generality of legal theory but also the specificality of drawing its examples from the pool of models which it can use to illustrate the general points it is making. Comparative law, like legal theory, legal history and legal sociology, brings to the lawyer additional perspectives, and not only that, it is indispensable for these other fields as well. It can even be claimed that, 'comparative law, properly pursued, is an essentially philosophical activity.'[26] However, it has also been pointed out that unfortunately traditional comparative law has failed by paying insufficient attention to context and ignoring the context of ideas.[27] This is the failure of comparative lawyers not the inadequacy of comparative law. To regard comparative law purely as the comparison of laws has been rejected as, 'incompetence masquerading as jurisprudential expertise.'[28] These observations must be noted and the situation reviewed, and where necessary, remedied in our new century.

Of course, all can avail themselves of the fruits of comparative law research. But for the academic comparative lawyer the prime function of comparative law, sometimes called 'scholarly comparative law', is to provide access to legal knowledge which can be used not only for the purposes of law reform, or as a research tool, or to promote international understanding, but above all to fulfil the essential task of a comparative law scholar proper, that is, to further the universal knowledge and understanding of the phenomenon of law. Such extraction of knowledge also breeds scepticism, this being the starting point of intellectual freedom. Comparative law is concerned with the overall problems which influence the legal, social and cultural systems in society rather than with rules of a particular field of law. It belongs as a theoretical subject, with legal history, sociology of law and jurisprudence or legal theory. As pointed out earlier, the findings often do, but need not have practical value

Hence, 'Global systematic legal comparison is essential for an accurate definition of law as a social phenomenon and for the understanding of the nature of law and its function in society generally. Comparative law is indispensable to the legal theorist or legal philosopher ... for the formulation of general theories of law ... for the testing of these general theories.'[29]

As Harry Lawson observed:

---

[26] W. Ewald, 'Comparative Jurisprudence (1): What Was It Like to Try a Rat?' (1995) 143 *Pennsylvania Law Review*, 1889 at p. 2145.

[27] *Ibid.*, p. 1889; and also M. van Hoeke and M. Warrington, 'Legal Cultures and Legal Paradigms: Towards a New Model for Comparative Law', (1998) 47 *International and Comparative Law Quarterly*, 495.

[28] R.H.S. Tur, 'The Dialectic of General Jurisprudence and Comparative Law' (1977) *Juridical Review*, p. 238.

[29] W.J. Kamba, 'Comparative Law: A Theoretical Framework', (1976) 23 *International and Comparative Law Quarterly*, p. 494.

> The jurist who approaches legal theory by way of comparative law, not only becomes sceptical of facile generalisations about law, but refuses to be exclusively interested in definitions or theories which squeeze out of the law of any country the peculiarities that give it life. To adopt a mathematical metaphor, he is more interested in discovering the least common multiple of law than its highest common factor.[30]

A succinct view formulated by Richard Tur summarises the ultimate position:

> The unity of general jurisprudence and comparative law consists in the unity of form and content; they are essential moments of legal knowledge, different sides of the same coin. General jurisprudence without comparative law is empty and formal: comparative law without general jurisprudence is blind and non-discriminating. General jurisprudence with comparative law is real and actual: comparative law with general jurisprudence is selective and clear-sighted.[31]

This Variation fully endorses the view expressed by the highly respected American comparative lawyer Hessel Yntema who equated legal research with comparative law, saying that, comparative law was another name for legal science being 'an integral part of the more comprehensive universe of social and human science.'[32] It has lately been claimed that macro-comparativism is being pursued as an alternative to jurisprudence.[33] If this is the case, then why not regard this as a worthy aim? Comparative lawyers would be well advised to strive towards this goal. Comparative law is also in competition with legal history. It has been said that, 'ten lively lectures on the Persian or Chinese conception of law would do more to stimulate true jurisdic intelligence than a hundred addresses on the pitiful bunglings of the law of intestate succession between Augustus and Justinian.'[34]

Reading this Variation the reader might be led to the conclusion that comparative lawyers are undertaking an ambitious, delicate and infinitely difficult task, but then: 'Who ever claimed that comparative legal studies should be easy? Who ever asserted that comparative legal studies should be for everyone?'[35] .

---

[30] F.H. Lawson, 'Comparative Law as an Instrument of Legal Culture' in F.H. Lawson, *The Comparison, Selected Essays*. V. II (Amsterdam, New York, Oxford,North-Holland Publishing Co., 1977) p. 75.

[31] Tur, above note 28, p. 249.

[32] H. Yntema, 'Comparative Law Research – Some Remarks on Looking out of the Cave', (1956) 54 *Michigan Law Review*, p. 902.

[33] I. Ward, 'The limits of Comparativism: Lessons from UK-EC Integration', (1995) 2 *Maastricht Journal of European and Comparative Law*, 23 at p. 31.

[34] Zweigert and Kötz, above n. 2 p. 53 from Thibaut supported by Feurbach. (Thibaut,'Über die Nothwendigkeit eines allgeeminen bürgerlichen Rechts fur Deutschland', in Thibaut, *Civilistische.Abhandlungen* (1814) 433)

[35] P. Legrand, 'How to compare now' (1996) 16 *Legal Studies*, 232 at p. 239.

In addition to the question of 'What is comparative law?', a second concern is with the name of the subject itself. This concern is voiced mostly in the English speaking world and for the term in the English language. However, and most interesting, though in Turkish, '*Mukayeseli Hukuk*' or '*Karşılaştırmalı Hukuk*' - an exact translation of 'comparative law'- is the term used, discussion related to the name has never arisen among Turkish comparative lawyers and the name is well established. But then, in Turkey, as on the European continent, law is regarded to be a branch of social science. This is not so in the English speaking world. In the English speaking world we are constantly asked: Is comparative law an appropriate name? Is it not a misleading term? It has been said that the term 'comparative law' is misleading since it is not a specific area of law as is family law, property law or administrative law. Many, especially those who regard comparative law as a non-subject void of a content of its own, as will be seen in 'Variation II', point to the term as it appears in some other languages where, as translated, the subject is either called 'Comparison of Laws' (*Rechtsverglichung*, *Rechtsverkelijking*) or 'Law Compared' or 'Compared Law' (*droit comparé*) and suggest that 'comparative law' as a term be abandoned.

However, this Variation regards the name 'Comparative Law' to be appropriate as comparative law has its own specific sphere, is the central element in all comparative work, is the critical subject for the study of law in context which increases our knowledge of law in society. It has recently been stated that, 'Because law is not only a reference but is the very field of our study, the traditional term of comparative law is fully justified and suitably reflects the field of our scholarly endeavours.'[36] Not only law, but comparison are the central elements here. If there were a serious call for a change of name, then 'Comparative Study of Law' or better still, 'Comparative Legal Studies', another name that is now often used, would be apt, as this has a generality beyond the normative approach dominant among black-letter-law comparatists and implies a wider approach to law. In a recent work for example, carrying the title 'Comparative Legal Studies: Traditions and Transitions', it is stated that the term 'Comparative Legal Studies' in the title was chosen deliberately to avoid 'this academic quagmire'.[37]

Comparative law is an independent theme. As a branch of social science it is based on positive observation rather than philosophical speculation. Nevertheless, as earlier stated, even the philosophy of law which aims at true knowledge of law must exist in symbiosis with comparative law as it cannot afford to be merely speculative if it intends to serve the purpose of the furtherance of legal knowledge by answering questions about law. Hence:

---

[36] K.D. Karameus, 'Comparative Law and Comparative Lawyers: Opening Remarks', (2001) 75 *Tulane Law Review*, 859-870, at p. 867.

[37] R. Munday, 'Accounting for an Encounter', in P.Legrand and R. Munday (eds), *Comparative Legal Studies: Traditions and Transitions* (Cambridge, Cambridge University Press, 2002), p. 10.

> To regard theory of law as a theory of legal knowledge establishing a specific science of law and to regard comparative law as the critical extraction of this legal knowledge from individual instances by translating the inquiry into conceptual equivalents and thus to verifiable hypothesis through an active analytical exercise, indicates that legal knowledge can be accrued only by a symbiosis between comparative law and theory of law.[38]

Michael Bogdan states that, 'It appears to be clear that highly qualified work in comparative law has a scientific character, even if there is no generally accepted definition of "scientific"'.[39] However, answering the question as to whether comparative law is an independent science, Michael Bogdan is more doubtful and says, 'There are no generally accepted criteria for what constitutes an independent field of scientific research'.[40] Nevertheless the conclusion he reaches is that, 'comparative legal research is normally of such degree of difficulty and has to deal with so many unique tasks that its independent treatment ... is well justified.'[41]

VARIATION II

Comparative law 'has by common consent the somewhat unusual characteristic that it does not exist'.[42] 'Legal definitions are notoriously unsatisfactory and apt to lead to controversies which are often barren of result. This, in particular, is the case when any attempt is made to define "comparative law", since the subject-matter, being non-existent, is one which defies definition.'[43] Comparative law is not just another branch of law, it is certainly not independent of the subject area it is investigating. As Harold Gutteridge observed:

> The process of comparing rules of law taken from different systems does not - result in the formulation of any independent rules for the regulation of human relationships or transactions. Not only are there no "comparative" rules of law but there are no transactions or relationships which can be described as comparative.[44]

---

[38] Örücü, above note 20, p. 6.
[39] M. Bogdan, *Comparative Law* (Kluwer Tano, Göteborg, 1994), pp. 24-25.
[40] *Ibid.*, p. 25.
[41] *Ibid.*
[42] O. Kahn-Freund, 'Comparative Law as an Academic Subject', (1966) 82 *Law Quarterly Review*, pp. 40-41.
[43] H.C. Gutteridge, *Comparative Law, An Introduction to the Comparative Method of Legal Study and Research*, 2nd. edn. (London, Cambridge University Press, 1949; reprint, Wildy & Sons, London, 1974), p. 2.
[44] *Ibid.*, p.1.

Thus, as comparative law has no subject matter, it does not exist and is not a category of law at all: it has no subject as contract law, tax law or administrative law have. One could at best talk of a comparative family law, a comparative constitutional law or a comparative contract law. Here the comparison is not the central element of the comparative work but the focus is on fields of law which are inquired into comparatively for specific purposes such as law reform, harmonization or offering solutions to problems of domestic law. There must always be specificity and a purpose in comparative law research. One cannot fruitfully talk of 'theoretical' comparative law but only of 'applied' comparative law.

William Twining very aptly remarks that 'there is a lingering yearning to maintain that comparative law is an autonomous discipline or sub-discipline which has a distinctive method if not a distinct subject matter.'[45] He then puts forward three reasons for questioning this idea. According to William Twining the first is that such an idea is philosophically dubious, the second that since all legal scholarship involves comparison, 'it is misleading, indeed dangerous', to set comparative law apart, and the third that comparative law has no defined subject matter. He is of the opinion that, if one abandons the idea that comparative law is an autonomous discipline, then 'it is easier to accept the plurality of approaches as legitimate without giving up on basic standards of scholarly vigour.'[46]

In essence, comparative law is a term with many meanings. 'The term "comparative law" can mean so much or so little that it is only by examining particular methods, aims, approaches and the consequent utilisation that we can glean from "comparative law" substance and purpose'.[47] As comparative law has no specific content, the content of any particular comparative endeavour will depend entirely on what is being compared and the purpose of comparison. If it is anything, comparative law is merely a method or technique of looking at law.

Comparative law is the technique used by those who call themselves comparative lawyers to collect information on foreign law, present foreign law, contrast the findings and make comparisons, that is, identify similarities and differences. This means that by comparative law research, one finds and establishes foreign laws, juxtaposes them and then adapts these findings to the domestic legal system or to each other. Thus, comparative law as a method or technique of legal research is used to contrast, juxtapose and compare entire legal systems, legal institutions or legal rules from different legal systems with the view of discerning similarities and differences, and it is the purposes or objectives of this method that give comparative law meaning. However, a serious question remains: Does one need to be a comparative lawyer in order to do that?

---

[45] W. Twining, 'Comparative Law and Legal Theory: The Country and Western Tradition', in I.D. Edge (ed), *Comparative Law in Global Perspective* (New York, Transnational Publishers, 2000) p. 45.

[46] *Ibid.*

[47] C.M. Campbell, 'Comparative Law: Its Current Definition', (1966) *Juridical Review*, p. 151.

In addition, comparative law is only one of the ways of looking at the legal world, one of the methods of research; just one way of approaching legal phenomena. It is a facilitator. However it is in good company as it belongs to a group of facilitators which includes history, sociology, economics and others.

As to the name, indeed the name given to the subject, or the non-subject, is entirely misleading. This misconception is created by the English version of the name. Precise translations from French, German or Dutch would render something like 'Comparison of Laws', 'Compared Law', 'Law Compared', or 'Legal Comparison'. 'Legal Comparison' as used in Germany may be the most appropriate term to be used here. At least 'Legal Comparison' indicates clearly that there is no interest in the extrinsic factors in the comparisons to be undertaken which should remain normative. Many writers today find the terms 'comparative analysis of law' or 'comparative study of law' more suitable. The preferred approach in this Variation is not to use the term 'Comparative Law' at all but talk of Comparative Family Law, Comparative Property Law or Comparative Civil Procedure, as the field of inquiry demands.

The recently coined and widely used title, 'Comparative Legal Studies', also has a confusing aspect in that it indicates studies beyond the law as conventionally understood. Surely, a degree obtained in Legal Studies would not have the same weight as a degree in Law. Lawyers compare law and should continue to do only that.

Having no subject matter and the wrong name, comparative law should not even appear on the curriculum for a law degree as an independent autonomous subject but be subsumed in others. After all, in our day all courses should contain some contrasting and comparing of domestic law with laws in other legal systems, and we do not need 'comparative lawyers' to do that. At best comparative law should be specific, maybe a method, and at its worst it is nothing. 'Comparative lawyers', who claim to be a special kind of academic with a deeper insight into law in context, are in essence superficial and mediocre; they claim to be generalists but in reality they are not real lawyers nor do they effectively add to information about foreign law. They should juxtapose the functionally equivalent rules they find in various jurisdictions and identify differences and similarities with a specific purpose in mind.

'Because "comparative law" is in a sense a subject without a constituency, a clear appreciation of its objectives is especially vital. ...unless the subject does discover a meaningful sense of purpose, it will find itself without an audience.'[48] In Chapter 3 a more comprehensive coverage will be found as to the 'why' of comparative law.

As a method, comparative law could be applied to domestic problems or transactions across international boundaries. In this sense it has close connections

---

[48] Munday, above n. 37, p. 10; also B. Markesinis, 'Comparative Law – A Subject in Search of an Audience', (1990) 53 *Modern Law Review*, 1.

with international private law, or the so-called, conflict of laws. In any case, comparative law has been superseded today by Transnational Law.

Chapter 2

COMPARABILITY: THEORIES AND PRESUMPTIONS

'Shall I compare thee to a summer's day?'[1]

Is it not true that any one thing can be compared with any other thing if they either both belong to the same category, or if one belongs to it and the other does not? When translated into law terms, what is meant by comparability? Is an element of similarity necessary for comparability? Since the existence of comparative law indicates that there is a plurality of legal systems, legal institutions and legal rules, can the comparative lawyer compare the seemingly 'incomparable'? What is the so-called 'meaningful' comparison? Now, we know that the term 'comparative law' itself is by no means free from ambiguity; the factor of 'comparability' is even less so.[2]

Below, the first Variation of this Chapter, in line with the first Variation of the foregoing Chapter, deals with the question of comparability in its widest sense inclusive of comparability of differents both at macro and micro level; whereas the second Variation approaches this sub-theme through functionality and the comparability of similars. However, it must be remembered that 'similar' indicates a lack of difference and 'difference' a lack of similarity, both ever present unless two things are identical, which state also can only be discovered by comparison.

VARIATION I

All things are comparable even if unique. Understanding the phenomena around us necessitates such comparison. Even identicals must be compared in order to determine that they are in fact identical. How would we know and decide on the issue except by placing them side by side?
The sea and a blue slipper can be compared if the aim is to determine the blueness of one as against the other, or an apple to a table if the aim is to test whether our teeth

---

[1] Shakespeare Sonnet XVIII.
[2] I discuss some of the issues of comparability in Chapter 3 of M. Aitkenhead, N. Burrows, R. Jagtenberg and E. Örücü, *Law and lawyers in European integration: A compareative analysis of the education, attitudes and specialisation of Scottish and Dutch Lawyers* (Medelingen van het Juridisch Instituut van de Erasmus Universiteit Rotterdam No: 43, 1988), pp. 40-64.

would break or not upon biting these two objects. Thus 'thee' can very easily be compared to 'a summer's day' and it may be discovered that 'thou art more lovely and more temperate' and that though there is no eternal summer in the seasons, 'thy eternal summer shall not fade'. 'Thee' is comparable to 'a summer's day', the slipper to the sea, an apple to a table, and darkness to light. How else can we develop understanding?

Now, how is this to be transposed to law? Can we not, for example, compare a divorce case with an eviction case if our intention is to find out how courts deal with cases in general and develop an understanding of, for example, how long cases take in court or how decisions are written? Could we not compare, for example, an English statute on taxation, town and country planning or matrimonial causes with three pieces of German legislation on entirely different topics if we were trying to establish how such documents are prepared and how long or detailed they are in order to develop an understanding of such a source of law? The examples could be infinite.[3]

Nevertheless, the fact that any thing can be compared with any other thing has not prevented wide and varied discussion of the concept of 'comparability' by comparative lawyers. The discussion actually arises from another basis, namely, that 'things to be compared must be comparable', and usually revolves around the words 'like' and 'similar'. It is stressed that 'like must be compared with like' and '*similia similibus*', these being two well-established maxims of comparative law. What is 'like' in law? Even if what 'like' means is determined, how 'like' do things have to be to be 'comparable'? May we not compare diverse legal systems, legal institutions or legal rules and come to the conclusion that they are not 'like'? Would this not be 'meaningful' or 'fruitful'?

It is claimed that 'comparison is possible only if the instances are comparable and the results interpretable'. By 'comparability' is meant a requirement that 'there be a variable common to each instance and that the variable have the same meaning for each instance'.[4] It is further claimed that, 'comparisons can be useful only if the legal institutions under investigation are naturally or functionally comparable'.[5] In 1900 the assumption underlying the Paris Congress, presented as the starting point of methodological and scientific comparative law proper, might have been that only 'similar' things could be compared. But is this the approach we want to take today? Might it be that the reason why, for example, socialist comparative lawyers rejected the possibility of comparison between their legal systems and bourgeois legal systems was partly based on a misunderstanding of the word 'comparable': in many

---

[3] See also M. Bogdan, *Comparative Law* (Göteborg, Kluwer Tano, 1994), p. 58.

[4] J.H. Merryman, 'Comparative Law and Scientific Explanation' in J.N. Hazard and W.J. Wagner (eds), *Law in the U.S.A. in Social and Technical Revolution* (Brussels, Bruyand, 1974), p. 92, and also in id., *The Loneliness of the Comparative Lawyer* (The Hague/London/Boston, Kluwer Law International, 1999), 478-502 at p. 489 where he discusses Zelditch's views on comparability, referring to Zelditch, 'Intelligible Comparisons', in Vallier (ed) *Comparative Methods in Sociology* (1971) pp. 267-307.

[5] K. Zweigert and H. Kötz, *An Introduction to Comparative Law*, 3rd. edn., trans. T. Weir (Oxford, Clarendon Press, 1998), p. 34.

languages the word 'comparable' 'can also mean "approximately similar" or "not too different".'[6] Thus to talk of 'comparability' evokes an intellectual activity of juxtaposing somewhat similar systems, institutions or rules. Is this correct? As rightly put though, 'to accept comparability is, however, not the same as accepting similarity: the comparison can of course demonstrate great fundamental differences.'[7] However, even then, it is not clear whether this means that to accept comparability means to accept that different things can be compared or that only similars can be compared but we may of course discover differences.

Comparative law is said to be a comparison of 'comparable' legal institutions or of the solutions to 'comparable' legal problems in different systems.[8] This statement does not contribute significantly to the meaning of the concept of 'comparability'; neither does recognition that the topics under examination must be 'comparable' or 'meaningfully comparable'. So, what is meant by the seemingly tautological sentence 'only comparables can be meaningfully compared' or by concepts such as 'sufficiently comparable', 'reasonably comparable' or 'fruitfully comparable'?

Many scholars use the term *tertium comparationis*, a common comparative denominator which could be the third unit besides the two legal *comparanda*, that is the elements to be compared, the *comparatum* and the *comparandum*. Here, comparability is seen to be closely related to *tertium comparationis* and to depend on the presence of common elements which render juridical phenomena 'meaningfully comparable': thus comparability is equated with *tertium comparationis*. It is said that the objects of comparison must share common characteristics which serve as the common denominator, the *tertium comparationis*. What must the comparative lawyer look at as *tertium comparationis*? Should this be the common function between institutions and rules, or the common goal they are set out to achieve, or the problem, or the factual situations they are created to solve or the solutions offered?

To give further substance to this discussion it is necessary to look at 'comparability' on two distinct levels: macro-comparability and micro-comparability.

Comparability at the level of macro-comparison, or macro-comparability materializes at the level of legal systems. Therefore, the definition of a legal system may be the first task to tackle.[9] What is a legal system? From a theoretical starting point 'a legal system exits if, and only if, it reaches a certain minimum degree of efficacy',[10] the efficacy of the system being a function of the efficacy of its laws which is determined by the obedience to them, reinforced by the application of sanctions. Also a 'normative system is a legal system only if it has a certain

---

[6] See Bogdan, above note 3.
[7] *Ibid.*, p. 67.
[8] Zweigert and Kötz, above note 5, p. 34.
[9] This is re-visited in the sub-theme in Chapter 4.
[10] J. Raz, *The Concept of a Legal System: An Introduction to the Theory of Legal Systems*, (Oxford, Oxford University Press, 1973), p. 93.

minimum degree of complexity',[11] that is, every legal system should at least possess a court structure of some kind and lay down sanctions. These are normative analyses. For one comparative lawyer, a legal system means, 'the complex of legal institutions, actors and processes in the context of a legal culture and the secondary legal rules'.[12] Furthermore, a legal system 'has a vocabulary used to express concepts, its rules are arranged into categories, it has techniques for expressing rules and interpreting them, it is linked to a view of the social order itself which determines the way in which the law is applied and shapes the very function of law in that society'.[13]

To analyze comparability at the level of the legal system then, it is necessary to choose an accepted definition of the term 'legal system' and test this definition in macro-units regarded in actuality as legal systems. Above are four such definitions. In addition to these four, other definitions could be so tested. Two of the above are the result of normative analysis, and two are supplied by comparative lawyers and therefore indicate a wider context. Hans Kelsen's normative analysis, elaborated by Joseph Raz, depends on the criterion of efficiency which means obedience to the laws and application of sanctions as a reinforcement for them. The second normative approach, again elaborated by Joseph Raz, requires a minimum degree of complexity for the existence of a legal system which demands some kind of court structure and sanctions. John Merryman's definition stresses the legal institutions, actors and processes in the context of a particular legal culture. René David and John Brierley provide a more extensive definition of a legal system requiring the existence of a specific vocabulary, rules arranged into categories and techniques for interpreting these rules. In this definition, the legal system is also linked to a view of the social order itself which determines the way in which law is applied.

Although it is difficult to assess how far any legal system is linked to a specific social order, it can be said that in most societies laws are deeply imbedded in political and social cultures. It is essential for the purpose of later attempts at explaining differences and similarities encountered in the legal systems under comparison, that the notion of a system as a macro-unit combines the legal system with the societal, cultural, political and economic systems. Most of the differences that cannot be explained in terms of the legal system can more easily be explained in terms of the societal, political or economic systems. Social systems may determine the content of the corresponding legal systems and vice versa. Therefore, for a true understanding and evaluation it is necessary to establish the link between the legal systems under comparison and the social systems in which they live. This interrelationship is striking whether legal systems at the same level of legal development are surveyed, or legal systems at the same level of socio-cultural background. The same could be said of the economic systems.

---

[11] *Ibid.*, p. 141.

[12] Merryman, above note 4, p. 101.

[13] R. David and J.E.C. Brierley, *Major Legal Systems in the World Today* 3rd. edn., (London, Stevens, 1985), p. 193.

At the level of macro-comparison, the issue of 'comparability' has been resolved by many comparative lawyers with the argument that the comparison must extend to the same evolutionary stage of different legal systems under comparison. For example, Harold Gutteridge understands from 'compare like with like', that 'concepts, rules or institutions under comparison must relate to the same stage of legal, political and economic development.' That is to say, that at the macro-level also the legal systems under comparison should be at the same stage of development, whether, economic, social or legal. Harold Gutteridge also introduces the provision of 'the subject matter lending itself to comparison'. Only when this is realised the 'nature and the extent of the comparison may be left to the discretion of the investigator.'[14] However, are these really requirements of 'comparability'?

There is nothing in the logic of comparative inquiry dictating that comparison be limited to any specific level or unit. Hence it must be argued that at the macro-level, 'comparability' may be relative to the interests of the comparative lawyer. It is the aims of the specific comparative study that should determine the choice of legal systems to be compared. Whether such systems have reached the same degree of development, legal or otherwise, may be a secondary consideration when the purpose of the comparative lawyer points to a preferred selection.[15] Nor need one carry out comparative research only in groups of legal systems with broadly shared attributes. Even if one were to think the reverse, history shows otherwise, and the overlapping systems and the 'family trees' approach suggested below regarding legal systems as sitting on family trees with intertwining branches,[16] expand the scope of the comparative field to legal systems grouped in different ways and at different level of development.

Yet, can a comparative lawyer use her discretion as to the extent and nature of the comparison and then generalize from, for example, two legal systems? Here a distinction must be made between specific results and methodology. While it is true that the degree of generality of the findings in a piece of research considering but two legal systems can only be limited, the methodological grid carefully worked out in the process is of far more general application. For example, in a survey covering Scotland and the Netherlands, the findings may be limited to Scotland and the Netherlands, but the methodological grid can be applied elsewhere, to obtain a general understanding of the similar factual problems in, for example, other Member States of the European Union.[17] However, it should also be remembered that the findings themselves would probably be valid for a number of other Member States. Naturally, the degree of probability would have to be verified by further research. In addition to this, the findings would be useful as a working hypothesis for possibly a large number of additional countries.

---

[14] H.C. Gutteridge, *Comparative Law*, 2nd ed. (London, Cambridge University Press, 1949; reprint., Wildy & Sons, London, 1974), p. 73.
[15] W.J. Kamba, 'Comparative Law: A Theoretical Framework', (1976) 23 *International and Comparative Law Quarterly*, 494 at pp. 507-508.
[16] See Chapter 10 below.
[17] See our research, above note 2.

Ideally, macro-comparison and micro-comparison should merge since the micro-comparative topic must be placed within the entire legal system. Hence the totality of the legal system in context, the macro-comparative unit, is the frame within which all else is contained and evaluated. From such analysis, it should be possible to offer ideal types, determine the level of permeability of specific legal systems and make conjectures about cross-fertilization between systems. Within the context of a supra-legal system, such as the European Union for example, the comparative lawyer has an even wider frame within which to evaluate her findings. From such analysis it is possible to venture into suggesting common denominators, be they at the level of the lowest, the average or the highest. Common core studies also can be pursued after such exploration. In this context, the 'better law' approach must also be analyzed and evaluated.[18]

At the level of micro-comparison, it has been widely argued that the true basis of comparative law is functional equivalence. According to Michele Graziadei, functionalism represents two distinct currents: the 'functionalist method' which is 'one of the best-known working tools in comparative legal studies', and 'functionalism' in the sense 'that law responds to society's needs'.[19] Though the 'functionalist method' does not represent 'the sole or even the dominant approach' in comparative law research, and though today it is being challenged, it has gained new life 'under the flag' of common core studies in Europe.

Now, if by 'law' we meant a body of rules only and comparison at the micro-level was directed at these rules, then the functional approach would be useful, since a body of rules is created for the purpose of solving human problems most of which are shared. Thus, in the context of the European Union for example, where comparative law is a driving force and has a decisive role in the harmonization process, the 'functional comparative analysis method' shifts the focus from the 'vertical' to the 'horizontal' and provides the potential for convergence of both the legal systems and the legal methods of the Member States of the Union, this leading to gradual and eventual legal integration. In this, to build on similarities may be desirable and decisive. However, the scope is narrow. A considerable number of areas are left out of the range of the 'functional equivalence' approach because of history, mores, ethics, religion, politics, ideology and cultural difference. Not only that, but the question of whether each rule or each institution has only one function has not been satisfactorily addressed. In addition, though law can be seen as 'a body of rules', it is much wider than that. Therefore, this Variation, though not totally opposed to employing 'functional equivalence' as a tool of comparability at the micro-level for specific projects, supports the use of a multiplicity of approaches.

---

[18] This is considered more fully in Chapter 3.

[19] M. Graziadei, 'The Functionalist Heritage', Chapter 5 in P. Legrand and R. Munday (eds), *Comparative Legal Studies: Traditions and Transitions* (Cambridge, Cambridge University Press, 2003), p. 100; also see for a useful discussion of functionalism with a capital (F) and a small (f), W. Twining , 'A Post-Westphalian Conception of Law' (2003) 37 *Law and Society Review*, pp. 213-217 and 238-243.

This Variation also supports the comparison of differents and contexts and therefore the extension of comparison beyond functionally equivalent rules.

The problem-solving, sociological approach is the other side of the coin. It is an alternative to the functional-institutional approach or a variation of it. This problem-solving basis answers the question, 'How is a specific social or legal problem encountered both in society A and society B resolved by their respective (legal or other) systems?' that is, 'What legal or other institutions have developed to cope with it?' This approach, similar to the 'functionalist' approach, springs from the belief that similar problems have similar solutions across legal systems, though reached by different routes. For example, how is the problem of supporting a wife who would otherwise be destitute after the termination of marriage, resolved in society A and B? This problem may be tackled in various ways: by alimony, by state social security or by care within the traditional family of the needy spouse. Again, how is an individual represented in court in Scotland and the Netherlands respectively? This matter may be tackled differently and handled by different bodies in the two societies. In this connection it is said that, 'the fact that the problem is one and the same warrants the comparability'.[20]

The functional-institutional approach, though a useful and elegant understanding of comparability, does not solve the issue of comparability as between a western legal system and a religious system or a developing legal system. In addition, if a problem arises in one legal system but has no counterpart in another, this approach faces another dilemma, and yet this is when comparative law research becomes most fruitful. Legal systems pertaining to societies that are socio-culturally and legal-culturally different from each other can also be compared even if for the purpose of establishing diversity and in this case the functional-institutional approach cannot be the basis. Legal systems of 'ordinary' places and of 'extraordinary'[21] places must be compared by comparative lawyers of our day if our knowledge of the law is to be enhanced, not in one place or in another place, but law as a social phenomenon. This functional-institutional approach has also been challenged as not working between capitalist and socialist legal systems, in spite of the fact that basic human needs are largely universal. There are other fundamental criticisms of this approach on grounds such as the limitation of subject areas that can be compared by using this method and the fact that many areas of law are left out of the scope of comparison since they are regarded as 'not lending themselves to comparison', being determined by specific histories, ethical values, political ideologies, cultural differences or religious beliefs. As pointed out above, there is also the problem of 'one institution or rule with many functions'.

Should all this lead the comparative lawyer to abandon the task because no functionally comparable solution can be found and come to the conclusion that

---

[20] M. Schmitthoff, ' The Science of Comparative Law' (1939) 7 *The Cambridge Law Journal*, 94-110 at p. 96 where he refers to M. Salomon's work, *Grundlegung zur Rechtsphilosophie* (1925).

[21] I discuss the meanings of 'extraordinary' place in E. Örücü, 'Comparatists and extraordinary places' Chapter 13 in Legrand and Munday above note 19, pp. 467-489.

comparisons are impossible, or, does it only raise a serious problem of comparability which should lead the comparative lawyer away from functional terms? Is a certain degree of similarity of content a basic requirement for a 'meaningful comparison' of forms, or is similarity of forms a presupposition for comparison? Do structural differences between the basic systems preclude comparability? The answer to these questions in this Variation is 'no'. Surely, it would be odd to allow comparative law research but one methodology, functional inquiry, which has only a technical perspective.

In fact, recently, many other bases have been presented as being more appropriate. As Michele Graziadei notes, 'no one could have foreseen the plurality of methods which are currently being practised when comparative law was thought to be a method in itself'.[22] It would be reductivist to view 'comparative law' as a method since there are indeed a number of methodological options. Most of these are contextual approaches such as analysis of existing rules and institutions in 'historical context', 'economic context', 'political context' or in 'cultural context'. Some of these approaches are now dubbed as post-modernist, intermingled with legal realism. The functional method was built to do away with 'the local dimensions' of rules and to reduce the rules to their operative description 'freed from the context' of their own systems; whereas, the contextual approaches specifically stress the 'local dimension'.

Surely a seasoned comparative lawyer could not be guided by the following advice given by Konrad Zweigert and Hein Kötz:

> ...if we leave aside the topics which are heavily impressed by moral views or values ... we find that as a general rule developed nations answer the needs of legal business in the same or in very similar ways. Indeed it almost amounts to a "presumptio similitudinis"... At the end of the study the same presumption acts as a means of checking our results: the comparatist can rest content if his researches through all the relevant material lead to the conclusion that the systems he has compared reach the same or similar practical results, but if he finds that there are great differences or indeed diametrically opposite results, he should be warned and go back to check again whether the terms in which he posed the original question were indeed purely functional, and whether he has spread the net of his researches quite wide enough.[23]

Other words of caution seem called for:

> Functionalism has led us unwittingly to a precipice where we can almost think that all institutions which perform equivalent functions are essentially the same, that any pattern of change which achieves developmental goals is equal to any other on grounds of cultural relativism, and that the significance of

---

[22] Graziadei above note 19, p. 101.

[23] Zweigert and Kötz, above note 5, p. 40.

> institutions can be discovered exclusively in their social or economic consequences, not in their intrinsic characteristics.[24]

'The proliferation or diffusion of structurally similar institutions over much of the globe is true' and legal systems possess strikingly similar institutions. But, 'there is no reason for assuming that functionalism provides a better guide to the subtleties of the (legal) process'[25].

It has been suggested that 'the post-modern critique of functionalism, coined as "better-solution-comparativism" is primarily directed against its implied or outspoken universalism, its "agenda of sameness".'[26] In that critique functional-equivalence is seen to be useful for yielding results of similarity and to be avoiding 'challenging questions about the role of law in society'. Anne Peters and Heiner Schwenke assert that claims that the functional approach underestimates differences flows from cultural 'framework-relativist' thinking, 'according to which legal thought, language and judgements are determined by greatly differing and ultimately irreconcilable frameworks'.[27] They reject this theory which they call 'framework-theory'.

Vivian Curran who is cited by them as one of the post-modernist 'framework-relativist' however, has also said that 'hypersentivity to differences, and hesitation in the face of cross-cultural judgments, may make good sense as a component of comparative law methodology, but may be detrimental in developing a legal order for the European Union'.[28] Furthermore, 'this hypersensitivity to difference, so useful to the conduct of comparative legal analysis, can become a liability when the comparatist also is a law-maker or is preparing to advise law-makers.'[29] Moreover, 'Our globalized world of encounter is unlikely to preserve the cultural differences that have been'. Vivian Curran goes on to say that 'Deference to national tradition, culture and distinctiveness should remain a point of departure for the comparatist, but as an absolute mandate beyond discussion or modification, one of the costs it can carry, and has carried, is death'. This warning must be taken to mean that the post-modernist approach to comparability is softening and becoming more realistic.

In any case, even the so-called functionally equivalent institutions are what they are because they reflect the structure of the legal and social system within which they exist. Thus, legal, social, cultural, economic, religious and political backgrounds cannot be neglected. Indeed, in the explanation of results this background is vital. Legal systems and legal institutions in countries socio-culturally and legal-culturally different from one another must be comparable, especially for a

---

[24] F.W. Riggs, 'The Comparison of Whole Political Systems' in R.T. Holt and J.E.Turner (eds), *The Methodology of Comparative Research* (New York, The Free Press, 1970), p. 77.
[25] J. LaPalombara, 'Parsimony and Empiricism in Comparative Politics' in ibid., p. 131.
[26] A. Peters and H. Schwenke, 'Comparative Law Beyond Post-modernism' (2000) 49 I*nternational and Comparative Law Quarterly*, 800 at p. 827.
[27] *Ibid*., pp. 827-828.
[28] V.G. Curran, 'On the Shoulders of Schlesinger: The Trento Common Core of European Private Law Project' (2002) 2 *Global Jurist Frontiers*, p. 8.
[29] *Ibid.*

comparative lawyer who wants to study 'extraordinary' places, to leave the shores of Eurocentrisism and to investigate 'localisms' in our 'globalizing' world. This Variation suggests that nets be cast as wide as possible to include the comparison of the 'ordinary', the 'extraordinary', the 'similar' and the 'different', and bases this on the assumption that 'everything is comparable'.

Although the comparison of 'thee' to a 'summer's day' presents no problems of comparability, it does create a problem of functional equivalence. No umbrella would be large enough to shelter the comparatist here and yet comparison can always take place depending on the comparatist's strategy. So also in law.

VARIATION II

To compare 'thee' to a 'summer's day' is totally and solely poetic and even then, absurd; and such comparison can never be transposed to the realm of comparative law. The motto in any comparison must be 'compare that which is comparable', 'compare like with like'. In comparative legal method this must be an absolute. Topics selected, and the rules, concepts or institutions under comparison must be comparable. It is at this level, that is comparability at the level of micro-comparison, or micro-comparability, that problems emerge. It can be asked: In what sense should the topics selected be comparable? It becomes more difficult to determine this when the systems, that is, the units of macro-comparison, belong to different levels of legal development or have entirely different socio-cultural backgrounds. Can one speak of comparability in such cases? The answer is 'no'. Thus, at the macro-level fruitful comparisons can only be carried out between systems that share the same degree of economic, political and social development and also are within groups of legal systems broadly sharing similar attributes. In any event, the comparative lawyer's proper role is to establish the basic similarity of legal systems. This is one of the assumptions of the functionalist method - the main method of comparative legal research.

What is the meaning then of 'compare like with like'? Harold Gutteridge for example, understands from 'compare like with like' that 'concepts, rules or institutions under comparison must relate to the same stage of legal, political and economic development.' He also introduces the provision 'the subject matter lending itself to comparison'.[30] Based on this starting point we can move on.

One method that works in comparative law research is functionalism, to be taken as both the 'functional method' and the understanding that law responds to human needs and therefore all rules and institutions have the purpose of answering these needs. Then there is the universalist approach to human needs. Social problems are universal. Laws respond to these needs in various ways but the end results are comparable. Hence we start with a 'concrete problem'. As noted, 'It is possible to compare the incomparable provided that the focus is on the same facts'.[31]

---

[30] Gutteridge, above note 14, p. 73.

[31] Graziedei, above note 19, p. 105.

The 'factual approach' is the starting point. If facts are not the same there is no comparability. In the universalist approach the similarity of solutions is paramount. If this were not so there would be no place for comparisons. That is why certain areas such as family law, where moral and religious values are prominent, should be left out of comparisons. Comparability benefits from the findings of similarity as it can then develop further on '*praesumptio similitudinis*'. Functional inquiry also suits the utilitarian approach to comparative law.

It is essential that topics selected be comparable in the sense that they relate to functionally equivalent rules, provisions or institutions, since the true basis of comparative law is this functional-institutional approach The functional-institutional approach, answers the question, 'Which institution in system B performs an equivalent function to the one under survey in system A?' From the answer to this question, the concept of 'functional equivalence' emerges. For example, if an institution called 'divorce' is under survey in system A, the comparative family lawyer looks for an institution in system B performing an equivalent function, that of freeing an individual from an unsatisfactory marital relationship within which he or she does not want to remain. Again, if the institution of 'solicitor' is under survey in Scotland, the comparative private lawyer looks for an institution performing an equivalent function, that of preparing documents for litigation and also dealing with non-contentious matters, representing the client, and so on, in another system, for example, the Netherlands. [32]

The problem-solving approach - the other side of the same coin - asks the question, 'How is a specific social or legal problem encountered both in society A and society B, resolved?' that is, 'Which legal or other institutions cope with this problem?' For example, how are children in need of a home and caring parents catered for in society? By fostering, adoption, or institutionalization? Or, 'how is an individual protected from human rights abuses perpetrated by the State in Scotland and the Netherlands respectively?' This legal problem may be handled differently and by different bodies in the two societies. Here it can be said that, 'the fact that the problem is one and the same warrants the comparability'.[33] According to the functionalist-institutionalist approach the above questions once answered, are immediately translated into functional questions.

Thus one either starts with a social problem or need in one society, discovers the institution that deals with it and then looks to other societies for institutions, legal, or otherwise, which deal with the same problem or need, that is functional equivalents, or, one starts with an institution in one society, asks the question, 'what is the purpose or function of this institution in that society?', and having ascertained it, looks for a functionally equivalent institution in the second and then, if so wished, in a third society. The underlying assumptions are that there are shared problems or needs in all the societies under comparison, that they are met somewhere in the society and that the means of solving these problems are different but comparable, their functions being equivalent.

---

[32] See our research, above note 2.

[33] Schmitthoff, above note 20, p. 96.

At the level of micro-comparison, 'functional equivalence' is the answer to the question of 'comparability' or 'similarity'. Comparative lawyers should seek out institutions that have the same role, that is, have functional comparability, or solve the same problem, that is, similarity of solutions. Konrad Zweigert and Hein Kötz regard this issue as finite and say:

> the basic methodological principle of all comparative law is that of functionality. From this basic principle stem all the other rules which determine the choice of laws to compare, the scope of the undertaking, the creation of a system of comparative law. Incomparables cannot be usefully compared and in law the only things which are comparable are those which fulfil the same function.[34]

Hence the comparative lawyer searches for functionally equivalent rules, concepts and institutions in societies that have reached comparable levels of development.

It must be admitted that it is difficult to answer ongoing questions of comparability without resorting to terms such as 'sufficiently comparable', 'reasonably comparable', 'fruitfully comparable' or 'meaningfully comparable'. The problem can sometimes be dealt with by separating those legal institutions in a legal system that are system-conditioned from those that are not.[35]

It has already been pointed out above that the starting point can be the 'factual' one. That is, for example, the consideration of recourse to the Court of Justice of the European Community in matters of Community law in Scotland and the Netherlands or the Community Law cases encountered in the work-loads of lawyers in the respective systems would point to the existence of common factual problems. The comparative lawyer choosing the 'factual approach' may also discover functional comparability or similarity of solutions through observing accidental divergences of facts. Again, similarity of factual needs answered by different legal systems makes them comparable, and 'different legal systems can be comparable only if they solve the same factual problem, that is answer the same legal need ... institutions can be meaningfully compared if they serve the same function'.[36] However, would this approach be satisfactory when institutional facts encountered in one legal system have no comparable counterpart in the other legal system? The answer must lie in comparisons being carried out between legal systems of some similarity. If the countries under comparison have social orders that are different to one another then legal rules that regulate situations specific to only one of the societies must be separated from the legal rules that regulate shared situations. Those in the first

---

[34] Zweigert and Kötz, above note 5, p. 34.

[35] See solution offered by E.K. Banakas, 'Some Thoughts on the Method of Comparative Law:
The Concept of Law revisited', (1981) LXVII *Archiv fur Rechts- und Sozialphilosophie*, 289; and a suggestion by R.P. Schlesinger (ed) *Formation of Contracts: a Study on the Common Core of Legal Systems* (Dobbs Ferry, Oceana, 1981), p. 70.

[36] Zweigert and Kötz, above note 5, pp. 44-45.

category are not comparable, whereas those in the second are. Thus comparative lawyers must work in systems that are in some way related.

Some other problems must be tackled. One such is that even when subject-areas are broadly comparable, categories can be imprecise and open to different interpretations. For example, certain areas of law, such as law relating to transport or competition have a narrower scope in Scottish law than in Dutch law, thus direct translations or synonyms do not suffice. Here the crucial questions are: Should the classificatory scheme of one or the other national system be adopted? Or should one try to create a new system of classification by merging or making compromises between some of the divergent categories found in the various systems? Or, is it preferable to create a brand new set of categories for comparative purposes?[37] If the chosen path is the second, then an effort must be made from the outset to redefine or delineate existing concepts, in order to achieve communication across the barriers. Here, functional equivalents would have to be looked for. Areas of law which perform the same task, that is, institutions that serve the same function in relation to problems and needs, would to be looked at. Thus 'meaningful' comparisons could be carried out. Care must be taken to identify functions in terms of system-relevance.

At the level of the concepts, when problems arise that create doubt as to the suitability of synonyms or taxonomies, one approach could be, as suggested earlier, to abandon existing concepts and create totally new ones to encompass the variations and nuances.[38] This might be called 'the ultimate path'. On this path umbrella concepts must be created for use as a problem solving technique. Having studied what the existing institutions comprise, a definition can be elaborated which does not involve concepts exclusive to one or the other of the legal systems. For example, if an umbrella concept were sought to cover the notions of advocates and solicitors in Scotland and *advocaten* and *notarissen* in the Netherlands, as none of the existing terms can be used, a definition might be arrived at with the label 'lawyer'. This is still a functional definition but is wider than the existing individual concepts. If the four professions in the two societies were individually examined, then a determination could be made on the overall comparability. Since all the institutions are sufficiently comparable, a meaningful umbrella concept to cover all could be formed.

Konrad Zweigert and Hein Kötz[39] advocate developing a special syntax and vocabulary, with concepts large enough to embrace the quite heterogeneous institutions, which are functionally comparable; the higher concept or heading being related to the function common to all. Using the umbrella term 'lawyer' in the example above, a net wider than those of the national systems is cast to catch solicitors in private practice, including trainees and advocates in Scotland; *advocaten*, trainees and *notarissen* in private practice in the Netherlands.[40] If,

---

[37] *Ibid.*, p. 76.
[38] *Ibid.*
[39] Zweigert and Kötz, above note 5, pp. 37-38.
[40] See our research, above note 2.

however, the functions of two institutions with the same label, such as 'advocates' and '*advocaten*' were totally different in the two systems, then a serious problem of comparability in functional terms would arise. How is this to be resolved? One may have to come to the conclusion that the two institutions are not comparable.

A final word of advice is offered by Konrad Zweigert and Hein Kötz:

> ...if we leave aside the topics which are heavily impressed by moral views or values ... we find that as a general rule developed nations answer the needs of legal business in the same or in very similar ways. Indeed it almost amounts to a "*presumptio similitudinis*"... At the end of the study the same presumption acts as a means of checking our results: the comparatist can rest content if his researches through all the relevant material lead to the conclusion that the systems he has compared reach the same or similar practical results, but if he finds that there are great differences or indeed diametrically opposite results, he should be warned and go back to check again whether the terms in which he posed the original question were indeed purely functional, and whether he has spread the net of his researches quite wide enough.[41]

Let us reiterate. This Variation takes legal systems as the units of macro-level inquiry and legal rules as the units of micro-level inquiry. However, if legal cultures are taken as determinants of legal systems and if the comparison is not to be carried out at the normative level and the intention is to go beyond the rules, the picture changes altogether. In total opposition to Variation I, where there seem to be no incomparables, this Variation may go so far as to say that 'everything is incomparable', since cultural frameworks are incommensurable. Therefore, comparison is futile. This futility is the consequence of what has been called 'framework-relativism'.[42]

[41] Zweigert and Kötz, above note 5, p. 40.
[42] See Peters and Schwenke, above note 26.

Chapter 3

WHY COMPARE?

Can there be one simple answer to the question: What is the purpose of carrying out comparative legal research? Is this purpose the same for all involved in comparative law or should a distinction be made between scholarly activities and the activities of the legislatures, the practitioners of the law and the judiciary? In other words, is there one identifiable purpose or is there a multiplicity of purposes? Comparative law research has moved in a number of disparate clear directions. What are they? Do these studies serve only the interests of national laws particularly when there are weaknesses or gaps in the home legal system? To what extent are legal solutions derived from comparative analysis useable in the domestic scene? Should the interest rather be directed towards satisfying curious minds of scholars? Why do we engage ourselves in this enigmatic subject?

In the past it was claimed that comparative law could only be defined and justified by its purposes such as to facilitate legislation and the practical improvement of the law or unification of private law. Has anything changed?

Below, Variation I considers the wider aims of comparative law and answers the question 'why' in this broad perspective. Variation II approaches the question from several practical standpoints. Both Variations pave the way to the discussion related to the sub-themes to be covered in Chapters 7 and 8.

VARIATION I

Comparative law research is undertaken to improve and consolidate knowledge of the law and knowledge and understanding of the law in context. As mentioned in the previous discussion on the nature of comparative law, this branch of legal science gives us insight into law and legal texture as no other branch can do. We understand the legal world around us by juxtaposing the unknown to the known and thereby analyzing and assessing legal phenomena, domestic or foreign, and do this in a wider ambit than the rules and institutions of law provide. An attempt to create a science of universal law would be too ambitious. This would also ignore the fact that there is no universality even in a globalizing world and that localisms coloured by different social, cultural, political and economic conditions help our understanding of human phenomena. The aim is to sharpen awareness and cognition of the legal, social and cultural environments in which we live.

This is best done not just by discovering resemblances between similars or even similarities between differents, but more fundamentally by finding and explaining similarities among differents, and differences and divergences among similars. It is not only similarities but often differences that help us to develop theories.[1] Comparative law thrives on differences. It is a fact that comparisons complicate rather than facilitate research; yet this enhances the quality of research. Therefore, scholarly comparative law research, by increasing detailed understanding of legal phenomena will point in the direction of diverse systems: the more diverse the systems, the more rewarding the findings. Choice is open-ended and it is advisable to look for extreme positions, remembering that there are no 'incomparables'.[2] 'Extraordinary' systems must be considered beside those regarded as the 'ordinary'.[3]

The aim is not romantic: it is not to create one law for the whole world. Neither is it utopian: a dictionary of legal terms in all languages. Far from it. The aim is to discover and understand differences between legal systems and legal institutions and explain the reasons for these in order to enhance knowledge and at the same time to discover similarities between different and diverse legal systems and find explanations for these. This reflects a wide approach to comparative law rather than the positivistic and nationalistic approach. Hypotheses must be tested, concepts refined, differences uncovered, sameness pinpointed, underlying assumptions critically investigated and syntheses drawn. Comparative law is conversation on and about law.

As early as 1938 it was said by Harold Gutteridge that:

> The isolation of legal thought in national watertight compartments has always seemed to me to be one of the factors which is most prolific in producing that frame of mind which leads to a spirit of national egotism. We have much to learn from one another in legal as well as other departments of human activities, and it is, in a sense, a reproach to the lawyers of all nations that they

---

[1] See for example P. Legrand, 'The same and the different', Chapter 9 in P. Legrand and R. Munday (eds), *Comparative Legal Studies: Traditions and Transitions* (Cambridge, Cambridge University Press, 2003), pp. 240-311.

[2] For a fruitful discussion of 'incommensurability' seen as equivalent to 'incomparability' see H.P. Glenn 'Are Legal Traditions Incommensurable?' (2001) 49 *American Journal of Comparative Law*, 133; and also see R. Chang, 'Comparison and the Justification of Choice' (1998) 146 *University of Pennsylvania Law Review*, 1569 who regards 'competing systems' as 'comparative alternatives' and asks the question of whether, if two alternatives were incomparable, would it follow that there could be no justified choice between them. (pp. 1569, 1573). Additionally, this issue of the Review is reserved to the papers given at a Symposium 'Law and Incommensurability'.

[3] See for an understanding of 'ordinary' and 'extraordinary E. Örücü, 'Comparatists and extraordinary places', Chapter 13 in above note 1, pp. 467-489.

> have been unable, up to the present, to arrive at the free interchange of knowledge and ideas which has been attained in other branches of learning.[4]

It goes without saying that one of the main pursuits of comparative law is the creation of groupings of legal systems. This objective can be regarded even as the starting line of all comparative law activity. Legal systems, legal cultures and legal traditions are classified for the purpose of comparison.

Where scholarly comparative law research is also concerned in tracing relationships, legal systems historically related by colonization, imposition and borrowing, and systems related in other ways must be studied. In order to understand the changes that take place during the moving of institutions, the emphasis must be placed on the institutions that have moved. Explanations for the changes have to be sought, and therefore, social and cultural as well as political contexts must be understood. Choice of systems here is pre-determined by historical connections. The systems will be related systems for one of the above reasons. This is the kind of comparative law research that attracts many legal historian comparatists.

An often-claimed virtue of scholarly comparative law is that it serves the purpose of broadening the mind of the law student and helps in the development of tolerance. In this context, the most valuable course to be offered to undergraduates is not comparative family law, comparative contract law, comparative civil procedure or even comparative private law or comparative public law, but an autonomous general comparative law course providing the breadth necessary for the development of critical minds. A Comparative Jurisprudence component in a Jurisprudence course would also be highly desirable.[5]

Recently there has been increasing interest in comparative law among the judiciary, an interest not confined to the filling of gaps in domestic law by reference to foreign solutions but an active search for a universal language in areas such as human rights.[6] It may soon become possible to talk of a 'common law or a *ius commune* of human rights'. This 'common law' is now being developed by domestic judges in conversation with judges from other jurisdictions and from the European Court of Human Rights. This may even be regarded as the new natural law. The comparative lawyer is active in this creation.[7] This search for 'commonality' can be seen as connected to 'common core' research, comparative law being geared towards discovering 'common cores', and further, creating 'better law'.

Today, in the context of the European Union, a number of Commissions are working on projects to produce at least 'General European Principles' in a number of fields. Most of these are 'common core' based Principles. However, it has been

---

4 H.C. Gutteridge, 'The comparative aspects of legal terminology' (1938) 12 *Tulane Law Review*, 401-411, at p. 410.

5 These issues will be re-visited in the course of Chapter 7.

6 See contributions in E. Örücü (ed), *Judicial Comparativism in Human Rights Cases*, United Kingdom Comparative Law Series Vol: 22, (London, UKNCCL/BIICL, 2003).

7 These issues will be considered in depth in Chapter 8.

suggested, that General Principles could be drafted 'with a low level modernity and innovation using the common core methodology', or such Principles could be drafted 'based upon the highest standard or modernity achieved ... using the "better law" method.'[8] Though harmonization suggests that the new rules should be 'derived from existing laws rather than invented by the drafters', in practice what is done is to 'make use of a rule that is common for all or most of the relevant jurisdictions, or a rule selected 'that represents a minority or even one jurisdiction'. Of course, it would be possible to formulate a brand new rule invented, or inspired from some other source. The last two options correspond to the 'better law' approach.[9]

Obviously the 'common core' approach is the easiest to use as it makes justification more straightforward by restating what represents the majority. However, as one tries to move closer to the majority of the jurisdictions, the value of the exercise diminishes. Also, gathering the rules that achieve the same end may prove to be difficult in practice. Even when a 'common core' is found, this may not correspond to a 'satisfactory' solution. Another problem concerns similar legal concepts which conceal fundamentally different understandings. Therefore a move towards the 'better law' approach becomes attractive.

However, in the selection of the 'better law', justification of the choice made can be taxing as it is difficult to decide what is 'modernity' and what is 'progressive'. Also the 'better law' approach entails a comparative evaluation of all the legal systems or legal solutions involved. This could prove to be an impossible task. Even if a quantitative measurement were possible, the 'data' relied on would not answer the question, 'Why?'. It is also difficult to secure total agreement on the necessity and desirability of the 'better law' in all localisms involved.

It is inevitable that by making choices, drafters take up positions and express value judgements. It may have to be admitted that 'no objective criteria can be found in order to justify the choice as to why the drafters consider the rule they have selected to be the "better" one.'[10] Especially in areas politically and ideologically coloured, justification would have to be subjective 'depending on the conviction of the drafters'.[11] When courts adopt this approach in search of commonality, then the same considerations must be faced.

This Variation supports the use of 'better law' solutions even in such politically and ideologically coloured areas as long as the solutions serve as models only. The comparative lawyer's co-operation and contribution is essential in this search if European legal integration is to be one of the main-roads on the map of the twenty-first century.

---

[8] M. Antokolskaia, 'The "Better Law" Approach and the Harmonisation of Family Law' in K. Boele-Woelki (ed*) Perspectives for the Unification and Harmonisation of Family Law in Europe* (Answerp-Oxford-New York, Intersentia, 2003), p. 160.

[9] *Ibid.*

[10] *Ibid.*, p. 181.

[11] *Ibid.*

VARIATION II

As comparative law does not exist independently and is but a method of research, its being can only be justified by the purposes for which the method is used. In addition, as comparative law has no substance in itself, the methodology that it professes should be for the use of other disciplines. Comparative law research must be an instrument for the realization of certain aims. The utilitarian view presented in this Variation considers comparative law research as justified only if it is undertaken for specific purposes, either having direct value for the legislature and the courts, or having indirect value by the contribution it makes to legal education and the training of lawyers.

The answer to why one undertakes comparative law work and what is one trying to achieve can be found in the works of many comparative lawyers. If one surveys the bulk of work undertaken to date the following objectives stand out: law reform and policy development by the legislature, an aid to international practice of law, international harmonization and unification – common core research, and a gap filling device in law courts. The findings arrived at by comparative lawyers can be utilized for any one of these. However, three other objectives that can be observed are more controversial for this Variation. One is 'giving students perspective', the other 'being a tool of research to reach a universal theory of law' and another 'aiding world peace'. Such vague purposes as these cannot be valid reasons for undertaking comparative law research.

For instance, one purpose that can justify the use of comparative law research is legislative law reform, when the comparative lawyer works *de lege ferenda*. So, if the purpose of employing the comparative law method is law reform as an aid to the legislature, then comparative law research should provide a pool of models to choose from. Using foreign law to modernize and improve domestic law may occasionally be necessary though essentially this Variation regards internal modernization the more suitable. Nevertheless, when law reform is the purpose, then this will dictate the choice of models. The reformer will be looking for legal systems preferably in socio-cultural and legal cultural affinity, systems which share the same problem and systems which deal with the same problem in different ways, better ways or more efficient ways, from whose solutions the reformer can learn and derive answers.

Harmonization of law, and as a further step, unification of law are other areas in which comparative law research is useful. The activity envisaged might either be harmonization only or unification with prior harmonization. Here the choice of the legal systems and subjects to be comparatively researched is pre-determined by political considerations. Systems to be studied will be those whose laws will be harmonized or unified. The comparative law researcher's work is to provide ideas for the necessary changes to the legal systems or institutions to be harmonized, to smooth the process or suggest the creation of a model law or a unified law. A thorough knowledge of all the systems involved in the process is required before an approximation is suggested. More problems will be encountered if the two or more systems involved are socio-culturally and/or legal culturally diverse. Here comparative lawyers' advice will be, to confine the process to legal systems that are similar.

Yet another area where comparative law is of use as a method is in the drawing up of international conventions and agreements. The function of the method here is crucial in that the terminology to be used in international documents must be distilled from the laws of the legal systems of the target audience. Additionally, comparative law is indispensable in the interpretation of international instruments. Comparative lawyers' work is essential in discovering the 'general principles of law recognized by civilised nations' or by 'member states' and in determining the customary rules of public international law.

Comparative law research can also provide a tool for judges by making them aware of foreign solutions to similar problems when there are none at home, that is, act as a gap filling device, *de lege lata*. This method obviously should not be frequently used as, where possible, domestic problems deserve domestic answers. Judges may have to refer to foreign law out of necessity when the case they are dealing with involves a foreign element, these would either be cases where private international law rules apply or cases involving the application of, for example, European directives or regulations where a knowledge of cases from Luxembourg or the decisions of the courts of other Member States related to that instrument must be looked at. Apart from this, it is not legitimate for judges to create new law by using foreign solutions. They are not in the business of creating law but applying it.

The same criticism applies to the search for 'better law'. How can the selection of the 'better law' be justified? There are no criteria to tell us what is the 'ideal law', if it exists. We cannot tell what is 'modernity' or what is 'progressive'. There are further considerations. Inherent in the 'better law' approach, is the serious issue of evaluation. Who is entitled to make comparative evaluations of legal systems or legal solutions? Even if such an evaluation were feasible, then quantitatively this should rely on 'data'. In any case, there can seldom be total agreement on the necessity and desirability of the 'better law' in all the localisms involved.

In addition, in the 'better law' approach, drafters make choices, take positions and express value judgements. There are no objective criteria 'to justify the choice as to why the drafters consider the rule they have selected to be the "better" one.'[12] Any possible justification would be subjective 'depending on the conviction of the drafters, especially in areas which are politically and ideologically coloured.'[13] 'Better law' solutions should not be used even as models and comparative lawyers should not involve themselves in such projects.

Another area in which comparative law method can be used is in legal education. The aim here is not to use comparative law for the purpose of broadening the mind - a rather vague claim with no substance - but to use it for practical purposes. Education in comparative law enables students to have a taste of things to come if

[12] *Ibid.*
[13] *Ibid.*

they are taking part in international exchange programmes; however these courses should be courses on foreign law such as French law, German Law or English law. Apart from this, there is not much space for comparative law in already crammed curricula. An autonomous general comparative law course would prove useless. There could be courses such as comparative contract law or comparative tort law to give the students a broader outlook in specific areas, but comparative law should be taught in integrated courses, if taught at all.[14]

[14] This subject will be re-visited in Chapter 7.

Chapter 4

WHAT TO COMPARE?

Here, 'What to compare?' is dealt with at two levels: the macro-comparative and the micro-comparative. These levels are complementary, since the second presupposes the first. The Variations will consider respectively, the units of macro-comparison taking two different stances as to what should be handled by comparative lawyers at this level and then consider the micro level. The first Variations, regarding law in context, look beyond the legal system and are uncomfortable with the notion of legal families and indeed with statutory rules as units of inquiry; whereas the second Variations consider legal systems alone as the macro-comparative units and deal with them within legal families and approach statutory rules as the micro-comparative units.

1. MACRO-COMPARATIVE LEVEL: LEGAL SYSTEMS - LEGAL FAMILIES - LEGAL CULTURES - LEGAL TRADITIONS?

Traditionally, at the macro level, comparative law has been concerned with comparing 'the legal systems of different nations'. This is the starting point for writers such as René David and John Brierley or Konrad Zweigert and Hein Kötz. At the macro-comparative level then, it is legal systems that are to be studied. However, are these two hundred or so legal systems to be studied one by one by comparative lawyers? Or are they to be grouped into the so-called 'legal families' and if so, should only the parent or the dominant systems in each family be studied to give insight into the family as a whole? Is this satisfactory?

William Twining indicates that 'mainstream' comparative law has two approaches. At the macro-level, the approach is what he calls the very broad '*Grands Systèmes*' approach, and at the micro-level, the 'Country and Western' tradition, a 'conspicuously' narrow approach which 'concentrates on some aspects of private law doctrine in the official legal systems of the Western nation-states.'[1]

---

[1] W. Twining, 'Comparative Law and Legal Theory: The Country and Western Approach' in I.D. Edge (ed), *Comparative Law in Global Perspective* (New York, Transnational Publishers, 2000), p. 32.

Logic necessitates moving the focus from legal system and legal family to legal culture or legal tradition. What a legal culture is may be more difficult to determine than determining what a legal system is however. It has been said that 'the center of gravity of legal development lies not in legislation, nor in jurisdic science, nor in judicial decisions, but in society itself.'[2] This observation takes us into the mysteries of the interaction of social norms and legal rules. For instance, Henry Ehrmann looks at legal culture as a link and says that, 'the attitudes, beliefs, and emotions of the operators as well as of the users (and victims) of the legal system have much to do with the way in which it functions.'[3] Is it this link that should be studied? Are comparative lawyers then to look into what is called by Henry Ehrmann 'legal culture', but by John Merryman, the 'legal tradition', the two definitions given being the same? Then we see Patrick Glenn, who challenges the very notion of culture and insists on the word 'tradition', the term 'tradition' taking on a different meaning (the presence of the past) from that used by John Merryman.[4]

How do comparative lawyers align themselves?

In the usual manner, the first Variation takes the broader approach and the second, the narrower.

VARIATION I

The comparative lawyer must understand the relationship between legal systems, legal cultures and legal traditions as well as find rules which are not necessarily within the formal framework of the legal system but are held by the people to be valid. Both the 'bottom-up' and the 'top-down' models of law must be understood and appreciated. In addition, her approach must be broad and inclusive of both 'ordinary' and 'extraordinary' legal systems. Today a new approach is called for - maybe a 'family trees' approach, which regards all legal systems as overlapping. If a classification is needed, then it must accord with the ingredients; interrelationships must be given their due weight.[5] A new understanding of what has to be studied, understood, interpreted and re-presented must be developed.

In such comparative research, accidental and changeable factors may have to be ignored. That said, differentiation between the accidental and the necessary, the changeable and the constant must rely on sound criteria. For this, one must know the cultures under consideration with their different ethical theories and techniques of social control, and the values and attitudes which bind the systems together. The changeable, irrelevant or accidental can be determined only as a result of empirical survey. So what should we study and what should we compare?

---

[2] E. Ehrlich, *Fundamental Principles of the Sociology of Law*, trans. W.L. Moll, (Cambridge, Mass., Harvard University Press, 1912, 1936), p. xv.

[3] H.W. Ehrmann, *Comparative Legal Cultures* (New Jersey, Prentice Hall, 1976), p. 9.

[4] See H.P. Glenn, *Legal Traditions of the World* (Oxford, Oxford University Press, 2000).

[5] See Chapter 10.2 for this.

A broad approach to comparative law would certainly move us away from 'legal systems and the law as rules' attitude, as law cannot be understood or represented unless regarded within broad historical, political, socio-economic and psychological contexts. John Merryman starts one of his works by stating that there are three 'highly influential legal traditions' in the world today and then draws the attention of the reader to the term he uses - not 'legal system' but 'legal tradition'. He subsequently defines both terms. For him a legal system is 'an operating set of legal institutions, procedures and rules', legal systems being frequently classified into groups or families.[6] He hastens to add however, that being grouped together does not suggest that the legal systems within a group 'have identical legal institutions, processes and rules.' In fact 'there is great diversity among them.'[7] That they are grouped together signified that they have something else in common. This 'something else' is what distinguishes them from legal systems differently classified, and that is legal tradition which relates the legal system to the 'culture of which it is a partial expression .. and puts the legal system into cultural perspective.'[8] A legal tradition is 'not a set of rules of law about contracts, corporations, and crimes, although such rules will almost always be in some sense a reflection of that tradition.'[9] Instead, it

> is a set of deeply rooted, historically conditioned attitudes about the nature of law, about the role of law in the society and the polity, about the proper organisation and operation of a legal system, and about the way law is or should be made, applied, studied, perfected, and taught.[10]

Indeed, many contemporary comparative lawyers abide by his definition. Henry Erhmann for one, takes the very same definition offered by John Merryman for 'legal tradition' and uses it as his preferred term, 'legal culture', at the same time claiming that the two concepts have been used in 'much the same way.[11]

John Bell gives his definition of legal culture as 'a specific way in which values, practices, and concepts are integrated into the operation of legal institutions and the interpretation of legal texts',[12] thus presenting 'legal culture' as a configuration of values, concepts, practices and institutions through which individuals interpret and apply legal norms; legal culture being rooted in general culture. Mark van Hoecke and Mark Warrington go on to say that 'understanding law implies a knowledge and an understanding of the social practice of its legal

---

[6] J.H. Merryman, *The Civil Law Tradition: An Introduction to the legal Systems of Western Europe and Latin America*, 2nd ed. (California, Stanford University Press, 1985), p. 1.
[7] *Ibid.*
[8] *Ibid.*, p. 2.
[9] *Ibid.*
[10] *Ibid.*
[11] Ehrmann, above note 3, p. 8.
[12] J.S. Bell, 'English Law and French Law – Not So Different?', (1995) 48 *Current Legal Problems* (Oxford, Oxford University Press, 1995) 63-101, at p. 70.

community',[13] which presupposes an understanding of the general culture of that society since the legal community is embedded in that society. Therefore, to distinguish legal systems one must locate them and their cultures 'within the broader context of the societal culture to which they belong'.[14]

It has been suggested that it may be more appropriate therefore, to talk of 'cultural families' rather than legal families. 'Legal families' suggests regarding legal systems as isolated from the culture within which they are embedded and also corresponds to the 'law as rules' approach.[15] Rather, the approach should be 'law as culture'. When this approach is assumed, differences as to world-views held, the concept of law, the role of law in society and the way conflicts are handled become central. These cannot be understood by merely comparing rules, legal institutions or even processes. This issue is of greater relevance when the comparative lawyer is looking cross-culturally rather than intra-culturally.[16] It is also true that cross-cultural comparisons are more valuable in enhancing knowledge about law in context than intra-cultural comparisons.

As basic elements of legal culture the following have also been suggested: a concept of law, a theory of valid legal sources, a methodology of law, a theory of argumentation, a theory of legitimation of law and a common basic ideology.[17] David Nelken admits that, 'Like any fruitful theoretical term, the meaning of legal culture is far from settled',[18] and that 'Clearly, legal culture is something which is both hard to pin down and, at the same time, difficult to escape.'[19] On the one hand it is used in relation to sociology of law, on the other as a catch-all. David Nelken calls Lawrence Friedman's distinction between 'internal legal culture', that is, ideas and practices of legal and political actors, and 'external legal culture', that is, the type and level of expectations of people from law, a classical understanding. This distinction seems to be reduced sometimes to 'supply' and 'demand'.[20] Talking of 'boundary problems', David Nelken tells us that, 'Disagreements in approaches to legal culture may simply reflect the different purposes which these definitions are intended to serve.'[21] However, it is also noted that the definition of legal culture itself depends on 'the culture from which it emerges.'[22]

---

[13] M. van Hoeke and M. Warrington, 'Legal Cultures and Legal Paradigms: Towards a New Model for Comparative Law', (1998) 47 *International and Comparative Law Quarterly*, 495, at p. 498.
[14] *Ibid.*
[15] *Ibid.*, p. 502.
[16] Van Hoecke & Warrington, above note 13, pp. 508-509.
[17] *Ibid.*, pp. 514-515.
[18] D. Nelken, 'Disclosing/Invoking Legal Culture: An Introduction' (1995) 4 *Social and Legal Studies*, 435-452 at p. 437.
[19] *Ibid.*, p. 443.
[20] *Ibid.*, p. 437.
[21] *Ibid.*, p. 438.
[22] *Ibid.*

It has been aptly questioned: Where should we go to look for legal culture and, how should we investigate it?[23] What is the impact of the economy, politics, social control, institutional structures, practices and ideas on legal systems? Can we measure their impact? We need to show how concepts both reflect and constitute culture. We as comparative lawyers see the need for such understanding and yet require the help of others such as economists, political scientists, sociologists and psychologists in order to grasp true meanings, even when we are looking at our own legal system. Nevertheless, we must undertake this task in order to get at the true picture, though 'we must also beware of the danger of artificially presupposing too high a degree of internal coherence within a culture, or exaggerating its separateness from other cultures or from global trends.'[24] Culture is never a homogenous whole, neither is law.

However, Patrick Glenn rejects the concept of a legal system conclusively and of a legal culture tangentially, and talks of 'legal traditions' instead, stating that 'the notion of tradition, after two or three centuries of neglect and opprobrium in the western world, has recently received renewed attention', the result of a 'postmodern shift' from 'rational-legal authority' to 'self-expression'.[25] He recognises that tradition is not an uncontroversial process and therefore, does not offer a definition, but rather, talks of the elements of tradition, 'pastness' and 'presence', tradition involving 'the extension of the past to the present' representing legal civilizations.[26] The whole journey is related to the question of 'How do we validate our knowledge of the law?'.

William Twining tells us that, 'Legal orders are made up of complexes of social relations, ideas, ideologies, norms, concepts, institutions, people, techniques and traditions.' Quoting from Italo Calvino, he defines the concern as 'to portray the diversity and at the same time universality of human experience.'[27] These legal orders have been placed in geographical levels by William Twining thus: global, international, inter-communal, territorial state, sub-state, non-state, sometimes all impacting the same relationships.[28] This understanding also has a bearing on the micro-comparative level below.

All the above shows us two things. The first is that we cannot talk of legal systems as the sole units of macro comparative inquiry and the second, that there is no clear cut definition of legal culture and legal tradition or any obvious reasons for preferring one concept to the other. What is certain however is that it is context that counts. Macro-comparison must be carried out in context, legal systems – at present the hallmark of the nation State - must be approached within their social, cultural, economic and political environment if we are to reach a deep understanding of law

[23] *Ibid.*, p. 440.
[24] *Ibid.*, p. 444.
[25] Glenn, above note 4, p. xxi.
[26] *Ibid.*, p. 11.
[27] W. Twining, *Globalisation and Legal Theory* (London, Butterworths, 2000) p. 172.
[28] *Ibid.*, p. 139.

as it actually unfolds. Interrelationships between legal systems must also be considered.

VARIATION II

Comparative law must be involved only in the 'top-down' model, that is the legal system as laid down by the formal law-maker, and elaborated upon by the appropriate high courts. A broader approach is dangerous and beyond the comparative lawyer's competence. Comparative lawyers can only rely on normative inquiry; this is all that is needed. To resort to 'legal culture' only confuses the issues as the following questions cannot be answered: Can differences between legal systems be explained by 'national character'? Can legal cultures faithfully mirror national character and overall culture? Can two legal cultures be more alike but the overall cultures more divergent? Is national character the effect or the cause of differences? Comparative lawyers should keep clear of such discussion.

Comparison should be limited to civil law/common law since the ordinary world is clearly divided between 'the heirs of Rome and Westminster'. Interest in other regions of the world or 'extraordinary' places, unless seen as extensions of the two families by comparative lawyers, must be satisfied by regionalists or anthropologists but not comparative lawyers.

Thus, legal systems together with the legal families in which they sit must be the starting points of macro comparison. A legal system is made up of a set of interrelated parts, each with a specific function to make the system work. The comparative lawyer analyzes the working of these parts; comparative law is the comparison of rules

The farthest limits we can go to in studying legal systems may be to say with Konrad Zweigert and Hein Kötz that we should 'grasp their legal styles'.[29] However, the concept of the 'legal style' does not go beyond history, mode of thought, institutions and legal sources; the last factor ideology is often discarded today as all five factors need not be used cumulatively. The comparative lawyer finds, describes, juxtaposes and identifies the differences and similarities between statutes, judicial decisions and related material but must ignore context when not of a legal nature. This is a technical perspective which is shared with traditional legal doctrine applicable to domestic law.

Most comparative law research is intra-cultural, that is, the subject of comparison remains legal systems or legal rules and institutions in legal systems 'rooted in similar cultural traditions and operating in similar socio-economic conditions'.[30] Attempts to harmonize laws, which is one of the practical purposes for

---

[29] K. Zweigert and H. Kötz, *An Introduction to Comparative Law*, 3rd ed., trans. T. Weir (Oxford, Clarendon Press, 1998), p. 67.

[30] W.J. Kamba, 'Comparative Law: A Theoretical Framework', (1976) 23 *International and Comparative Law Quarterly*, 494 at p. 511.

which comparative research is undertaken, will be successful only if kept 'within the family'.

2. MICRO-COMPARATIVE LEVEL: RULES OR BEYOND?

At the micro-comparative level the most frequently asked question is, 'What is law?'. As Rodolfo Sacco puts it: 'If one asks what students of comparative law compare, the most obvious answer would be, "the rules of different legal systems".'[31] What then is meant by a 'rule'? This question must be addressed at the micro comparative level. The traditional approach is of a positivist and looks at statutory rules, law as created by the State. To these rules may be added case law and pertinent legal documents. However, it is also obvious that there are other strands such as consideration of legal history, the political, economic, cultural and sociological environment in which law lives, legal techniques and the ideological or conceptual backgrounds of the actors of the law. Furthermore, in the context of 'legal pluralism', law goes far beyond the so-called 'official law', and extends to multi-layers of systems.

Today, 'law' spans the range of positive law and then moves to non-state law, rules, custom and tradition. What is a comparative lawyer to look at? Below, Variation I advocates looking beyond 'official law', that is, 'law as rules'; while Variation II only at law created by nation States.

VARIATION I

A broad approach to comparative law moves us away from legal systems as macro-units of inquiry and the 'law as rules' approach. Law cannot be understood or re-presented unless regarded within broad historical, political, socio-economic and psychological contexts. Hence, context is what counts. We have already seen that macro-comparison must be carried out in context and legal systems – at present the hallmark of the nation State - must be approached within their social, cultural, economic and political environment in order to lead to a deep understanding of law as it actually unfolds. The question of 'What is law?' must be approached in the same manner.

At the micro-comparative level comparative law presupposes the existence of rules and legal institutions, and their plurality, but statutory rules alone cannot be the object of comparative inquiry.

The first step is to regard judicial decisions as law. Even a monolithic legal system built on a Kelsenian hierarchy may regard both statutory law and judicial law as part of the legal system and yet not become pluralistic merely by the acceptance of judicial precedents as formal law. Judicial precedents must be considered by the

[31] R. Sacco, 'Legal Formants: A Dynamic Approach to Comparative Law (Installment I of II)' (1991) 39 *American Journal of Comparative Law*, 1-34, at p. 21.

comparative lawyer whatever the inclinations of the legal system. In addition, great value must be attached to the decisions of lower courts and not only of the highest courts in systems under investigation. It is also commonplace today to talk of 'state legal pluralism' a weak version of normative legal pluralism.[32]

That said, it must be added that this is not the whole picture. Rodolfo Sacco for one, first stresses that the two keys to comparative study are 'evolution' and 'diffusion' and then goes on to point out that, 'it is wrong to believe that the first step toward comparison is to identify "the legal rule" of the countries to be compared.'[33] We should be talking of 'rules of constitutions, legislatures, courts, and, indeed, of the scholars who formulate legal doctrine'; although 'within a given legal system, the jurists assume' a unity between all these rules, since the 'main goal is to discover "the legal rule" of their systems'.[34] Rodolfo Sacco is here on a quest to discover the 'formants' of the law and therefore refutes the existence of a 'single rule' and, looking at the 'living law', sees many elements in the search for 'one rule'. Having stated that one needs to recognize the diversity of the 'legal formants', he says that 'within a given legal system with multiple "legal formants" there is no guarantee that they will be in harmony rather than in conflict.'[35] The legal formants cited by him are constitutional and legislative rules, case law, operational rules and scholarly writings, although no list is compiled to include all possible 'legal formants'.

It must be kept in mind here that the number of legal formants and their comparative importance will vary from one system to another. In addition we may ask ourselves, 'What about 'formants' other than the legal'? Rodolfo Sacco goes so far as to say that some 'legal formants' are 'explicitly formulated' and others are not. He calls these 'cryptotypes' representing 'non-verbalized' rules and 'implied patterns'. Once verbalized, 'ctyptotypes are perceived and passed on from one generation of jurists to another'.[36]

However, other 'formants' of the law are also to be taken into account. The comparative lawyer must look at all the elements at work in a given legal system in context.. She must remember that rules, institutions and processes must be studied in context and that 'legal formants' themselves develop under the influence of 'contextual formants'. For instance, Tibor Varady presents ideology as yet another important 'formant'. Any attempt to analyze the formants of private law in Central and East European countries for instance, indicates that strong value judgments or ideological precepts have acted as formants of private law during recent decades there. It is further suggested that the importance such a formants have is not

---

[32] See for a discussion of 'weak' and 'strong' version of legal pluralism, J. Griffith, 'What is Legal Pluralism?', (1986) 24 *Journal of Legal Pluralism*, 1.
[33] Sacco, above note 31, p.21.
[34] *Ibid.*
[35] *Ibid.* p. 23.
[36] R. Sacco, 'Legal Formants: A Dynamic Approach to Comparative Law' (Installment II of II) 39 *American Journal of Comparative Law*, (1991), 343-401, at pp. 384-385.

confined to Central and East European countries, nor is it confined to the past decades.[37]

It must also be noted that a link to statehood has never been a prerequisite for the existence of a legal system.[38] Since this is the case, why should we compare only the 'official rules' created by the State? The State does not have a monopoly on creating law. Whenever possible the 'bottom-up' approach must be resorted to and the comparative lawyer must be prepared to go behind the rules, looking backwards, sideways and forwards at all times. For true comprehension, a feeling for 'law in action' is vital at all times and not only when looking at judicial decisions.

So, in a world of legal pluralism, there is much to consider. 'Official rules' are only one type of rules. Law however, is made at a number of 'layers'. For instance, according to Boaventura de Sousa Santos's broad conception of law, 'modern societies are regulated by a plurality of legal orders, interrelated and socially distributed in the social field in different ways', rather than 'being ordered by a single legal system'.[39] This is the idea of legal pluralism, indicating that 'more than one legal system operates in a single political unit', that is, 'non-state law' has equal place with 'official law'. However, he also observes that 'there is nothing inherently good, progressive, or emancipatory about "legal pluralism"', and therefore, the better choice is to regard this phenomena as given and speak of 'a plurality of legal orders' rather than 'legal pluralism'.[40] He also introduces the concept of 'interlegality' to capture the complex relationships of superimposition, interpenetration and mixing between legal orders and semi-autonomous legal fields. Comparative law studies should attempt to extend to norms of non-state law, folk law and customary law, remembering that the law is global, national and local.[41]

VARIATION II

Only the 'top-down' model of law-making interests comparative law. Law is a creation of the nation State. As we have seen at the macro-level the units of inquiry are the legal systems, and law is what is laid down by formal law-makers and elaborated upon by the appropriate high courts. Comparative lawyers are not interested in a broader approach and such an approach would be dangerous. Normative inquiry is all that is needed. The normative approach is not involved in any way in empirical field studies to find out how things actually are, but confines itself to the study of law in the books. Law is a system of rules. Comparative law is for the comparison of rules. If the primary sources of law include court decisions,

[37] See T. Varady, 'Notes on Ideological Precepts as Formants of Private Law in Central-East European Countries', (2002), Vol: 2, No 2, *Global Jurist Frontier,* pp. 1-18.
[38] See for example, the four definitions given in Chapter 2 above.
[39] B. de Sousa Santos, *Toward a New Legal Common Sense*, 2nd. edn. (London, Butterworths, 2002), p. 89.
[40] *Ibid.*
[41] *Ibid.* See map on p. 371.

these would also be included in the inquiry, thus a degree of 'law in action' is present here too.

Moreover, there is no special way of dealing with foreign law. Whether one is investigating the rules of foreign law or of domestic law makes no difference. Since the comparative process starts with the juxtaposition of the unknown to the known, the rules of the domestic system must be studied first and then functional equivalents sought.

The core of research in micro comparisons is the 'law as rules' approach. Any other approach would side track the comparative lawyer into sociological and anthropological research. She must resist this. It is also wise to remember that comparative law is a practical pursuit and not a theoretical one. Theories often coincide with the theorist's political preferences and comparative lawyers are not political players. They juxtapose, contrast and compare 'official law' for practical purposes exclusively.

If a discussion of 'legal pluralism' is to be entered into, 'legal pluralism' could only be understood to mean 'state legal pluralism'- the so-called 'weak version - and thereby could only imply 'officially recognized rules' such as case law, gentlemen's agreements in contract law or regulations of professional bodies, complementing the rules made by the 'law-maker' and allowed by the State to co-exist.

Chapter 5

HOW TO COMPARE?

> When lawyers, as a sideline, indulge in what they consider scientific work, their method is usually to take up a subject, read and think about it, try to find out as much as possible about it, and hope vaguely that all this will result in conclusions which are in some way interesting, useful, surprising, etc. The choice of a subject is dictated by personal taste (of the author himself, of his editor, his boss, etc.) and there are almost no rules concerning research methods, except the one which says that the more legal provisions, cases and other pertinent material you read, the better the research.[1]

So, which methods can and should be used by comparative lawyers? When and with what expectations? If it is accepted that social science research methods are essential in comparative law, can and do comparative lawyers make full use of social science research methodology?[2] Can there be a standard comparative law methodology? Considering that there has been little systematic inquiry into methods of comparative law, as indeed admitted by many comparative lawyers, it is essential to study answers to the question: 'How should we compare?'.[3]

Apart from regarding comparison itself as a method, the problems of comparative legal methodology are very varied and have been discussed in different ways by many comparative lawyers,[4] and the methodology of comparative law has been referred to in a number of ways. 'Functional equivalence' and the 'problem-

---

[1] F.J.M. Feldbrugge, 'Sociological Research Methods and Comparative Law' in M. Rotondi (ed) *Inchieste di Diritto Comparato*, Vol 2: *Aims and Methods of Comparative Law* (New York, Oceana Publications, 1975), p. 215.

[2] These issues were also discussed by me elsewhere: E. Örücü, *Symbiosis between Comparative Law and Theory of Law – Limitations of Legal Methodology*, (Erasmus Universiteit Rotterdam, Mededelingen van het Juridisch Instituut No: 16, 1982).

[3] The reader may wish to read this sub-theme together with the sub-theme 'Comparability' in Chapter 2.

[4] See G.K. Roberts, *What is Comparative Politics?* (Macmillan, Essex, 1972); and also a number of Chapters in P. Legrand and R. Munday (eds), *Comparative Legal Studies: Traditions and Transitions* (Cambridge, Cambridge University Press, 2003).

oriented' approach,[5] 'model-building' and 'common core' studies – the 'factual' approach,[6] the 'multi-axial method' made up of the historical, functional and dogmatic axes and the law as a system of rules in a national context[7] and 'method in action'[8] are just some approaches to 'How to compare?' put forward in the last century.

'How to compare now' is actually the title of an article by one of the more controversial comparatists of our times.[9] There we find the accusation that comparatists do not carry out comparison proper but just contrast rules of law, which means that they take a very narrow view of 'how to compare', and an analysis of what comparatists must concentrate on.[10]

VARIATION I

The simple answer to the question, 'What is the method to be employed in comparative law research?' is, that 'comparison' is the method. It is clearly a fact that 'comparison' is used in all fields of study, be they social sciences or natural sciences. One can 'encounter the use of comparisons in various fields – governance, economics, linguistics, architecture and so on. Thus it is quite obvious that comparison itself is a method. It is a way of looking, it is a mode of approaching material, a method in the process of cognition.'[11] Thus, used alone, the 'comparative method' can be employed in various fields of discourse. In this sense it is an empirical, descriptive research design using 'comparison' as a technique to cognize. However, when the term 'comparative' is included in the name of a subdivision of a field such as comparative architecture, comparative linguistics or comparative law, it denotes an area of study and in that context, the word 'comparative' in the title no longer depicts a method, but indicates an independent branch of that science, in our case, legal science. This subject then, develops its own methods.

Though law is not cited among the subjects covered in works designed as guides to the social sciences which include subjects such as sociology,

[5] K. Zweigert and H. Kötz, *An Introduction to Comparative Law*, 3rd edn., trans. T. Weir (Oxford, Clarendon Press, 1998), pp. 34-36; and K. Zweigert, 'Methodological Problems in Comparative Law', (1972) 7 *Israel Law Review*, p. 466.

[6] R.B. Schlesinger, (ed), *Formation of Contracts: a Study on the Common Core of Legal Systems* (Dobbs Ferry, Oceana, 1968).

[7] F. Schmidt, 'The need for a multi-axial method in comparative law' in J.C.B. Mohr (ed), *Festschrift für Konrad Zweigert* (Tübingen, Paul Siebeck, 1981), 525-536.

[8] M. Ancel, *Utilité et methodes du droit comparé* (Neuchatel, Editions Ides et Calendes, 1971).

[9] P. Legrand, 'How to compare now' (1996) 16 *Legal Studies* 232, also in P. Legrand, *Fragments of Law-as-Culture* (Deventer, W.E.J. Tjeenk Willink, 1999) as 'A Redemptive Programme', pp. 1-13.

[10] *Ibid.*, p. 234.

[11] A.E. Örücü, 'Method and object of comparative law' in: H.W. Blom & R.J. Folter (eds.), *Methode en Object in de rechtswetenschappen* (Zwolle, W.E.J. Tjeenk Willink, 1986), p. 57.

anthropology, psychology, political science, economics and geography, 'comparative law' is surely one such subject. Comparative law is more closely related to social sciences than to 'pure' normative inquiry which seems to characterize other types of legal research. To indicate its place with social sciences, the first fact to note is that comparative law has borrowed some of its methods from behavioural sciences and from the field of statistics; its methods are adaptations of various methods of cognition. Comparative lawyers have not 'invented' their methods or the 'process' of the methods used. The borrowed methods have been creatively applied to the problems of comparative law research. Nevertheless, there remains much confusion about methodology and methods.

Although comparative law research is open ended, the methodology being dictated by the strategy of the comparative lawyer, and there is no standard methodology, the possibility of comparison is dependent upon the existence and availability of data. Data can best be obtained by employing social science methodology. Direct investigation, understanding and analysis of data recorded for a specific purpose provide an essential and healthy starting point to comparative inquiry. The inquiry stage is also related to concept building where concepts that are neither so broad as to be meaningless nor too narrow to cover more than one instance, have to be devised; umbrella concepts may have to be created.

Later in the process a set of general statements can be used as the premise for explanation. The classical technique of legal methodology of reading texts of all kinds and hoping for insight, has serious limitations for collecting data to serve comparative inquiry adequately. This black-letter-law approach confining law to rules is totally inadequate for comparative law research. Indeed, unless there is collaboration between legal and social science researchers, comparative law falls short of its function, not only as a way of enhancing understanding and knowledge of law in context, but also as a source of models and of empirical information and knowledge. Though scholarly comparative law has philosophical underpinnings, it follows from the above that it is a social science based on positive observation rather than on philosophical speculation. The goal of any science is to develop valid, precise and verifiable general theory, theory supported by empirical generalization, that is, it should be based on comparative data and theoretical distillates as well as informed imagination.

Ferdinand Feldbrugge has shown the limitations of both lawyers and legal methodology, as we have seen above. His observation is pertinent to comparative research. Studying the law in books or reading more and more textbooks and cases would not have enlightened our research team on the specific problems of education and specialization of lawyers in European Law for example. Moreover, it would not have told us anything of value about those lawyers' attitude to European Law.[12]

---

[12] See the research in M. Aitkenhead, N. Burrows, R. Jagtenberg and E. Örücü, *Law and lawyers in European integration: A comparative analysis of the education, attitudes and specialisation of Scottish and Dutch lawyers* (Mededelingen van het Juridisch Instituut van de Erasmus Universiteit Rotterdam, No: 43, 1988).

Inquiry is only the starting point. Thereafter, a comparative lawyer is expected to describe, juxtapose, identify similarities and differences and then venture into the field of explanation. It is here that hypotheses are needed and it is here that real comparison starts. Now this explanation, this discovery of the *raison d'etre* for the differences and similarities, also necessitates moving from the domain of pure legal reasoning to that of social factors. In explanation, hypotheses must be consistent with the facts and verification of the findings needs transformation of an empirical nature. That is, the comparative lawyer must collect and describe data on the basis of carefully constructed classificatory schemes, discover and describe uniformities and differences on the basis of such data, formulate interrelationships between component elements of the process and other social phenomena as tentative hypotheses, subsequently verify the tentative hypotheses by rigorous empirical observation and construct the cumulative 'acceptance' of various basic propositions.[13]

The empirical school may suggest that the appropriate method should begin with the facts rather than hypotheses, and end in description. This is said to be a more realistic approach, since the present day lawyer is well equipped to use this method. Yet this Variation tells us that comparative inquiry should not stop at description, but move on into explanation where the real comparison starts, and then, on into confirmation of findings. Hence the need for hypotheses.

Whether a comparative lawyer starts with hypotheses or with facts, when she goes on to explanation, as she must do if the intention is to use the universal method of science and extract ultimate legal knowledge, she must make sure that the hypotheses are consistent with the facts. According to John Merryman, when instances are comparable and results interpretable, descriptions - sets of empirical observations - should be made, compiled and juxtaposed. Only then should the comparative lawyer launch into an explanation when further empirical observation may also become necessary. This is compatible with explanatory generalizations as the objective, and with legal systems as the matter or object of comparison.[14] Explanation of the differences and similarities identified is an accounting for these findings. However at this stage context becomes indispensable for understanding. Here the help from economists, historians, anthropologists or cognitive psychologists may be needed. Yet the imagination and creativity of the comparative lawyer cannot be replaced by any of those specialists. At this stage more information and therefore the expansion of the research may become necessary. At the end of this activity the comparative lawyer will be in a position to offer tentative hypotheses.

We have noted that it is also possible to start with hypotheses and then conceptualize, describe and so continue. The choice depends on whether the comparative lawyer is a follower of the empirical school or whether she already has

[13] See R.G. Macridis, *The Study of Comparative Government* (New York, Doubleday, 1955).

[14] J.H. Merryman, 'Comparative Law and Scientific Explanation', in J.N. Hazard, W.J. Wagner (eds.), *Law in the United States in Social and Technological Revolution* (Brussels, Bruyland, 1974), p. 95

certain phenomena in mind on which she has a speculative theory, the aim of the comparative research being to prove or disprove it. However, the possession of a purely curious mind is not the only reason why a scholar finds it worthwhile to carry out research. A specific project may rest on a number of middle level hypotheses on which there is prior agreement by the research team, as well as curiosity. It is possible to regard this as scientific research in its simplest form, in the sense that hypotheses are deduced from a set of theoretical propositions and then investigation is carried out to determine whether the outcome predicted by the chosen hypotheses manifests itself empirically.

Comparative analysis can be used to test or suggest propositions that can be applied, and by extension, to explain all cases, if only on a probability basis, at the level of generality of the cases compared. John Merryman says that, 'the explanatory approach represents one attempt to choose error over confusion'.[15] An explanation of findings, of exceptional and typical cases, an accounting for differences and similarities, is thus not just a necessary step in comparative research but is its essence. Some of the hypotheses may also serve as explanations, but for some findings new explanations have to be found.

It has been observed that contemporary comparative law has become very modest, very realist, very pragmatic and that comparative lawyers hesitate to venture into explanations.[16] Perhaps the main reason for this is not modesty but that the methodology to be employed for a fruitful extraction and explanation of legal knowledge is often beyond the realm of law and thus beyond the lawyer's competence, or even her interest. In fact, a comparative lawyer who follows the logic of Variation II below, may not believe that explanations are within the remit of a comparative law researcher. Most of the time explanation necessitates moving away from the domain of 'pure' law to that of social, cultural, religious or economic factors. How is the conventionally trained lawyer to do that?

Let us assume that a comparative lawyer who speaks the language of this Variation is investigating 'adoption' as seen in Turkey and Scotland, two legal systems that do not belong together according to the traditionally accepted classification. In neither system is adoption a part of the indigenous law; it is a historical addendum through historical accident. Her findings would show the comparative lawyer that in Turkey between 1926, when this institution was introduced through the Civil Code adapted from the Swiss Code, and 2002 when the Civil Code was amended, only persons over the age of 35 who had no natural children of their own could adopt, that the age difference between the adopter and the adoptee had to be at least 18 years, that if the adoptee was married the consent of his/her spouse was also required, that the adoptee did not lose his/her relationship with the natural parents and therefore could inherit from them as well as from the adopter who in turn could not inherit from the adoptee.

---

[15] *Ibid.*, p. 100.

[16] C.L.J. Constantinesco, *Traité de Droit Comparé, La Méthode Comparative*, Tome II (Paris, Libraire Générale de Droit et de Jurisprudence, 1974), p. 123-256 where he shows what he thinks comparatists should be doing.

In Scotland things are very different. Through the adoption process, a single person or a couple can adopt if they are over 21, unless one of the two applicants is already the natural parent of the child. An adoption order can only be made for a child who is under 18; the child must be at least 19 weeks old and must have lived with the applicant adoptive parents for the preceding 13 weeks. A married young person cannot be adopted. On adoption the legal relationship between the child and her birth parents is severed and a new relationship between the child and the adoptive parents, now the substitute parents is created. Adoption is still operative after the child reaches 16, whereas parental rights would by then have ceased.

The explanation for the difference lies in a number of tentative hypotheses: In Turkey the aim of adoption, as in Roman law, is to provide care for the elderly and continuation of family name and family business for persons who have no children. As a result, it is not for the interest of the child that adoption is available and therefore the adoption of adults would be the more appropriate for the stated aim. There must be an age difference of 18 to avoid sexual relationships between the two adults. Arising from the underlying aim of adoption as stated, only childless persons can adopt; the ban on adoption for those with children of their own also protects the inheritance rights of the blood relations.[17]

The comparative law researcher must examine these explanations in order to understand why the legal systems have produced the institutions they have, although these explanations are not legal ones As expected, the texts themselves only show the differences but do not offer explanations.

Yet explanation is not the final step in a piece of comparative research. Findings must be verified and confirmed, and only then can the work be called complete. This is the theory testing stage for the tentative hypotheses offered through explanation and for this the research must be extended. When the frame, the methodological grid and the hypotheses which have a probable validity for comparables are available, then the choice of two other appropriate legal systems is easier. In this way both comparability of subject matter and generalizability of the results can be secured. Further research would verify this degree of probability.

Traditional black-letter-law oriented comparative law research, with which Variation II deals, is normative, structural, institutional and positivistic, and would not use any approach other than the reading of statutes, cases, parliamentary debates and sometimes doctrinal works, and would regard description to be the final stage of the inquiry. Even the conceptualization stage might be suspect. The present Variation is concerned with law in action and law in interaction with social and cultural systems. Therefore, rule based research is regarded as useless since it leads to only partial truth and a misleading picture. Creative comparative law research can also be interested in suggesting 'core concepts' and point the way to 'ideal systems', or at least to the 'better law' approach. William Twining has remarked that comparative lawyers are concerned 'with description, analysis and explanation,

[17] See for further discussion of adoption Chapter 10.1 below.

rather than evaluation and prescription.'[18] In relation to the search for 'better law' however, there is scope for evaluation and prescription, but the legitimacy of this activity will always remain questionable.

The Variation I comparative lawyer has to grapple with a number of serious problems as well as the above. These include choice of systems, appreciation of cross-cultural systems, language, terminology, translations, both participant and non-participant observer effect, access to material beyond the legal, absurdity of explanations offered, reliability of secondary sources, the existence of historical accidents and anachronism of predictions. For the black-letter comparative lawyer in Variation II, these are not seen as great concerns.

In his article 'How to compare now?' Pierre Legrand expects the following from comparatists: They must concentrate on translation and the 'foreignness of languages'; bring a 'deep' understanding of rules by tying them to *mentalité* and culture; be committed to theory which must include a commitment to 'interdisciplinarity' special attention being paid to anthropology, linguistics and cognitive psychology; acknowledge differences and cherish them and develop an empathy for 'alterity', and at all times remain critical extending the notion of 'law' beyond that of 'binding law'. Pierre Legrand ends his thoughts on how to compare thus:

> To privilege a commitment to theory, to follow a practice which respects and values difference, to foster a way of acting in the world that is critical, even polemical, will naturally take the comparatist away from the traditional approaches to comparative legal studies which, because such obsolete routines only focus on crude formalistic solutions to raw legocentric problems, do not accept the need for theory and obstinately pursue similarity and consensus as if confined to a groove. In other words, the comparatist is invited to register a dissenting opinion, to mark her disapproval of what continues to be done in the name of comparative legal studies. She is asked to place herself firmly in opposition. She is asked to pursue the 'contrarian challenge'. Indeed, there is no more pressing research and teaching programme for a comparatist to undertake at this historical juncture than actively to promote the merits of the 'contrarian challenge' for comparatists themselves, for comparative legal studies, and for the European legal order.[19]

This Variation would argue that in order to fulfil the requirements of scholarly comparative research both similarities and differences must be considered, keeping in mind however, that the purpose is not to search particularly for similarity or difference but, to observe what is actually there. When there is similarity, this cannot

---

[18] W. Twining, *Globalisation and Legal Theory* (London, Butterworths, 2000), p. 185; and also W. Twining, 'Comparative Law and Legal Theory: the Country and Western Tradition' in I.D. Edge (ed) *Comparative Law in Global Perspective* (New York, Transnational Publishers, 2000), p. 34.

[19] Legrand, above note 9, p. 242.

be ignored just because the researcher is keen to follow the 'contrarian challenge', neither can a difference be glossed over because some other policy consideration such as European integration or globalization dictates that only similarities should be highlighted. The science of law can only be built on truth, though it must be admitted that absolute objectivity is not always attainable. Therefore this Variation would agree with the first half of the above quotation from Pierre Legrand.

In carrying out comparative law research, a decision has to be taken as to what to ignore as accidental rather than essential and what as temporary rather than permanent. Certain factors may be deemed irrelevant for the purposes of a project. However, seemingly irrelevant dimensions may in fact be of great significance. The problems associated with looking at the temporary rather than the permanent can cause instability in the research.

It is understandable that when a comparative lawyer starts with a hypothesis there is a tendency to read meanings into facts when they do not match or support the hypothesis. Rather than accepting that the hypothesis should be restated or corrected, the researcher may tend to misread the facts or ignore them. Although it may be reasonable to ignore accidental and temporary factors, differentiation between the accidental and the essential, the temporary and the permanent must rely on sound and dependable criteria. This in turn necessitates knowledge of the cultures under consideration with their different ethical theories, techniques of social control, and the values and attitudes which bind the system together. Only as a result of an empirical survey can the temporary, irrelevant or accidental be determined and drawn to the attention of those in a position to affect the ultimate outcome, such as the legislature. This is all part of the comparative law venture.

Among the many obstacles on the course of comparative research, the most difficult to overcome is often the 'observer effect'. Others mentioned earlier, such as concept construction and abstraction, languages of comparison, problems of translation, cross-cultural terminology, imprecision of terminology and recognition of similarities and differences are easier to surmount through cross-check control. The 'observer effect', being subjective, is difficult to detect and overcome. It exists in various forms, such as the 'participant observer effect' and the 'non-participant observer effect', which pose separate problems. However, there is always the danger of being over-sensitive to the observer effect.[20] The observer effect may arise while the technique of observation is employed, or when the sample is surveyed, content analyzed, results evaluated and differences and similarities explained. Awareness of the problem is the best precaution.[21]

VARIATION II

Comparison is of legal rules, provisions and institutions. Following on from the premise of 'functionally equivalent' rules, provisions and institutions, the

[20] Roberts, above note 4, p. 53.

[21] I return to the subject of obstacles in Chapter 10 under 'Limits of Comparability'.

comparative lawyer starts with rules whose functions are equivalent and collects relevant data that lead to a succinct description. Thus comparable concepts, rules etc; are first described and then juxtaposed. Contrasting is the first step of comparing. As suggested by the empirical school, the appropriate method begins with the facts, 'the problem', rather than with hypotheses, and ends in description. Similarities and differences brought to light by this contrasting and comparing are then identified. This is a down-to-earth approach, which the present day lawyer is well equipped to handle. The question, 'Should comparative inquiry stop at description without venturing into explanation?', is an unconditional 'Yes'.

If a comparative lawyer were asked, say by the English Law Commission, to look into 'do-it-yourself divorces' in the laws of the Members States of the European Union with a view to facilitating divorce in England, all that she would have to do is to report on the different schemes, describe them and identify the differences and similarities between the different schemes and also between them and the domestic law. She would not be asked to evaluate the findings since this is the task of the Law Commission and would be determined in keeping with the policy decisions made there for the type of desirable law reform. If the comparative law researcher had also been asked to comment on the most efficient rule, she would have indicated that also, though based on conjecture, so not necessarily reliable. But her remit would not take her beyond that. The comparative lawyer is purely a facilitator and not a political player.

It is not for the comparative lawyer to give explanations, build theories, test these in the confirmation phase of her methodology and then offer generalizations. These activities entail going beyond the realm of law. Lawyers can only compare laws. What makes the comparative lawyer a different and special species of the genus lawyer? Offering *a posteriori*, futuristic suggestions is a dangerous and unnecessary activity, so is starting from *a priori* hypotheses. Comparative lawyers should not become policy advisors nor try to create blue-prints for the future. They are not social scientists and have not been trained to be anything other than lawyers. They are simply lawyers looking at laws comparatively. They facilitate the jobs of others, be these historians, economists, politicians or practitioners who may then use the findings exposed by comparative research to build theories or suggest reforms etc;. Comparative research itself must end at the description or the identification phase. The comparative lawyer presents the actual in law. It is for others to build with these bricks. Neither should she enter the arena of prescription of a 'better law' consequent to an evaluation.

Language, terminology, translation, access to material and the reliability of secondary sources will be among the problems faced by comparative lawyers but when working in teams they have others to act as correctives to the research. Most of their research assistants will be from the jurisdictions under review who are fluent in the foreign languages in use.

Let us assume that a comparative lawyer takes on a research project inquiring into the workings of review of constitutionality in the United States of America and Germany. She could end her research by the following observation: The established traditions in judicial review of constitutionality can be studied in two broad types: The first type is the decentralized, diffuse, *incidenter*, *inter partes*, concrete, legitimating and retroactive *ex tunc* as noted in the United States, and the second centralized, concentrated, *principaliter*, *erga omnes*, abstract, invalidating and prospective *ex nunc* as observed in Germany. All others, developed under the influence of these two original models, are intermediary systems.[22] Her job is done. She does not thereafter venture into explaining these striking divergences. It is for political scientists to look into explanations if they so wish. She should not pass judgement.

Some comparative lawyers have suggested blueprints which could be successfully employed for the comparative law method. For example, Peter de Cruz suggests an eight step method, an outline laying down a plan of action which starts with identifying the problem, identifying the foreign jurisdiction and the parent legal family, deciding on primary sources of law that will be relevant, gathering and assembling the relevant material – and here he offers a normative checklist -, organising the material in accordance with headings, tentatively mapping out the possible answers to the problem – here bearing in mind cultural differences –, critically analysing the legal principles according to their intrinsic meaning, and finally, setting out the conclusions within a comparative framework with caveats if necessary.[23] Peter de Cruz does not claim to be a black letter lawyer and therefore his suggestion entails the explanatory stage and a critical conclusion where extra-legal phenomena become important. So for the purposes of this Variation the researcher following Peter de Cruz's blueprint should stop earlier in the research as indicated above. Carrying out comparative law research is not in any way different to carrying out research related to domestic law.

[22] See M. Cappelletti, *Judicial Review in the Contemporary World* (Indianapolis, Bobbs-Merrill, 1971).
[23] P. de Cruz, *Comparative Law in a changing world*, 2nd edn. (London, Cavendish Publishing Limited, 1999), pp. 235-239.

Chapter 6

INTERMEZZO

In this brief interlude we ask ourselves the question: Are we facing a schism here, an unbridgeable split, incompatibility between the two Variations of the above five Chapters? Are the positions mutually exclusive? I do not believe this to be the case.

It is true that there are comparative lawyers who claim that comparative law is a science with its own separate sphere, others who call comparative law merely a method of study and research or even a technique, and some who see it both as a comparative method and a comparative science of law or see in comparative law more than one of these aspect. It is immediately obvious that those who see comparative law as a method only, do not fully discuss what that method is, leaving this issue unanswered or very vaguely covered, and those who think or feel that comparative law must be more than a mere method, do not seem to agree on what this subject matter is. We have seen that the answers to 'What to compare?' and 'How to compare?', for example, can be extremely varied. Are we then to conclude that comparative law will depend entirely on what is to be compared and that the purpose of the comparison, and the purpose for which comparative law is studied or taught will determine the form which the study or instruction should take? Is this a satisfactory position to assume today? Obviously we would not want to put comparative lawyers, who pride themselves in the freedoms they have, into straight jackets, but at the same time, we do not want them to have no jackets at all!

It is not too fanciful to predict that the twenty first century will be 'the age of comparative law', though it seems still open to discussion whether comparative law is indeed an independent discipline and there is some disquiet concerning the methodology to be used. There is decidedly a renewed and growing interest in the subject and the meaning of the term 'comparative law', and varying views on what it is or how we compare, yet the subject seems well rooted. Academic study, law reform, policy development, research and teaching, international practice of law and law courts all avail themselves of it, in various ways. There are practical, sociological, political and pedagogical objectives in the above activities. However, comparative lawyers have been called upon to rethink their subject and it has also been suggested that comparative law would have a better future if it were to penetrate other subjects rather than profess to have an autonomous value. So some confusion can be said to continue. Nevertheless, out of confusion clarity will emerge as essential theoretical insight is developed by comparative lawyers. Cacophony will recede and be replaced by euphony. An unprecedented amount of excellent theoretical work is being carried out in comparative law today.

It can be accepted that our prime objective is the provision of wider access to legal knowledge and universal understanding of the phenomena of law. It can also be accepted that comparative law research has a number of practical purposes and that the entire argument is misplaced and misleading as both positions can in fact happily co-exist under the broad umbrella of comparative legal studies.

Can the Variations on the theme of 'comparative law' so far observed be merged? In the twenty first century, should we remain exposed to one of the streams only or to both streams of Variations and be allowed to develop a contrapuntal taste for this polyphonic texture? Why not utilize all that is being offered by comparative law?

The generalist comparative lawyer with a curious mind and who is fascinated by legal phenomena shaped by extra-legal factors, by movements of the law and the tuning that has to take place to make it successful in its new surroundings, and with an interest in theoretical aspects of the subject may well feel more at home in the first series of Variations. The comparative lawyer working for a specific purpose may be satisfied to seek answers to problems either at the legislative or judicial levels in foreign jurisdictions. However, these two positions may be embodied in the very same comparative lawyer who at times works for the furtherance of knowledge satisfying the social science objective of comparative law as well as for her own interest, and at times, for example, as a General Rapporteur for one of the topics in the four yearly Comparative Law Congresses, setting out lengthy specific questionnaires for the National Rapporteurs to answer and then drawing the threads together in the preparation of her General Rapport in that specific topic.

Every perception can be criticized from the point of view of every other perception. However, this does not mean that one perception is 'better' than the other or that there is one perception which is 'best'. Moreover, one can respect all perceptions without sharing them. I would like to explore this.

Let us take a situation such as that in the *Fairchild* case.[1] F was employed at different times and for different periods by both A and B. Both A and B had the 'duty to take reasonable care' to prevent F from inhaling asbestos dust because of the known risk that asbestos dust, if inhaled, may cause mesothelioma, a form of cancer. Both employers were in breach of this duty. F inhaled excessive quantities of asbestos dust during both employments, developed mesothelioma and later died. It could not be proven, on the balance of probabilities, whether A or B should be liable. The question in law is whether F's widow can recover against either A or B or against both A and B. Can the application of the conventional 'but for' test of tortious (delictual) liability (*causa sine qua non*) give a satisfactory answer here? If the 'but for' test for causation were used, the claim would be dismissed, as was the case at the level of the Court of Appeal. However, the House of Lords, on appeal,

[1] *Fairchild* v *Glenhaven Funeral Services Ltd and others*; *Fox* v *Spousal (Midlands) Ltd*; *Matthews* v *Associated Portland Cement Manufacturer (1978) Ltd and others* [2002] UKHL 22, [2002] 3 All ER, 305.

introduced a modified approach of proof of causation seeing that an insistence on principle would yield unfair results. The House of Lords found that common sense and policy considerations weighed in favour of allowing F (his widow) to recover against both employers.

The facts of this case could be the concern of many professionals. A medical researcher may be interested in seeking proof of the connection between asbestos dust inhalation and mesothelioma, may want to measure the incidence or to discover a cure or find methods of prevention. A social worker may think of the plight of the widow and the children who might need counselling. A sociologist may look into context and the respective status of, and power balance between, employers and employees in society. An economist may assess the costs and benefits involved in order to discover whether the expenses required by 'duty of care' measures would outweigh the damages to be paid if an employee develops the disease. An ecologist may consider the problem of 'asbestos dust' and propose legislation to ban the use of asbestos altogether. A practicing lawyer may deliberate upon whether to apply the law as is or to extend its scope keeping in mind coherence, consistency and certainty as well as justice and fairness. A jurisprudent may theorize on the place of principles, policy considerations, common sense, justice and fairness, how judicial precedents are to be treated in judicial decisions and the role of judges as law-makers. A comparative jurisprudent may discuss how foreign law is to be used by courts.

The *Fairchild* case could also be looked at by comparative law researchers, each following her own perception of what is comparative law, and how comparative law research should be carried out. They would each start by reading the case. In the opinions written by the Law Lords, there are references to domestic and foreign doctrine, cases and legislation from Germany, Austria, the Netherlands, France, Greece, Norway, Scotland, Australia, Canada and the USA, as well as reference to Roman law. The conclusion reached by Lord Bingham is that, 'though the problem underlying cases such as the present is universal, the response is not'.[2] Lord Bingham goes on:

> Developments of the law in this country cannot of course depend on a head-count of decisions and codes adopted in other countries around the world, often against a background of different rules and traditions. The law must be developed coherently, in accordance with principle, so as to serve, even-handedly, the ends of justice. If, however, a decision is given in this country which offends one's basic sense of justice, and if considerations of international sources suggests that a different and more acceptable decision would be given in most other jurisdictions, whatever their legal tradition, this must prompt anxious review of the decision in question. In a shrinking world (in which the employees of asbestos companies may work for those companies in any one or more of several countries) there must be some virtue in

[2] [2002] 3 All ER, 305 at p. 333.

> uniformity of outcome whatever the diversity of approach in reaching that outcome.[3]

Let us suppose that one were a comparative lawyer given the task of analyzing the laws referred to in the opinion cited above with a view of discussing fundamental issues of comparative law. How would one approach one's task? One could approach this task and the cases and codes used in the opinions - both from the common law and the civil law jurisdictions and Roman law - with any one of the methodological options available, depending on one's perception of these methodologies. There is ample scope here for making a case for any one of them: universalism, functionalism, culture, legal history, unity of common law, convergence and the *ius commune novum*, difference and identity, competition of legal rules and transposition. This case could be approached and analyzed by all these means. One could now venture to apply each approach to the analysis of the *Fairchild* case. Each perception would yield a different answer. However, only when one comparative lawyer gathers the whole range of analyses provided by her colleagues of all convictions, would we gain a comprehensive impression.

---

[3] *Ibid.*, p. 334.

Chapter 7

COMPARATIVE LAW AND LEGAL EDUCATION

It is important that law students as well as legal practitioners receive education tailored to meet the challenges of the modern world, but the unknown is intimidating and it may seem unnecessary to spend time on comparative law. In overburdened curricula with space being sought for an ever increasing number of new topics such as e-commerce, law and technology, communications law and law on terrorism, how is comparative law to be accommodated? In law teaching institutions the number of students taking comparative law courses, when on offer, is rather small, especially in undergraduate studies.

However, it is certainly true that legal professionals, including judges, are today more closely involved with foreign law, foreign lawyers and foreign clients. Therefore how foreign law is taught is becoming a more important issue. The way of teaching comparative law reflects the two approaches to comparative law used by comparative lawyers: normative inquiry and contextual or jurisprudential inquiry. This sub-theme of the theme Comparative Law fits very well with the two Variations approach adopted throughout this work.

Although there appears to be a trend in law schools around the world to improve the teaching of law in general, and comparative law in particular, and although academics and practitioners are increasingly aware that solutions to today's transnational problems require the application of international laws and harmonized national legislation, it is not easy to substantiate this.

How is comparative law taught in universities and comparative law institutes and in fact how should it be taught? What is the impact of current world-wide developments, in particular of globalization and multi-culturalism on the teaching of comparative law?[1]

Below, Variation I looks at comparative law teaching as the teaching of a theoretical subject integrated with cultural studies. Variation II emphasizes the practical aspects of the teaching or even suggests that comparative law should not be taught as an autonomous course.

---

[1] I have discussed issues arising from teaching of comparative law and comparative law teaching elsewhere. See E. Örücü, 'Teaching Comparative Law and Comparative Law Teaching in the UK' in J. Bell (ed) *Studies in UK Law 2002*, United Kingdom Comparative Law Series Vol: 21, (London, UKNCCL/BIICL, 2002), pp. 3- 30.

VARIATION I

Comparative law is primarily an academic discipline. Its achievements depend on how it is taught, what is taught, and what is expected of it. Comparative law must be regarded as a distinct category of law. It may be that problems faced today in law teaching institutions related to the status of comparative law courses are due to the crisis in which comparative law finds itself. As we have seen, its working assumptions and methodology are today being challenged, and the need to build a theoretical base is stressed. The importance of this subject increases with the increasing interest in the peculiarities of localisms, in appreciating cultural differences and the particular, and yet, working towards commonality and the universal; comparative lawyers are busy re-thinking their subject.

To provide insight, comparative law must be taught as a theoretical subject, perhaps under the name 'comparative jurisprudence;' 'comparative analysis of law', or 'comparative legal studies'. It should be the autonomous, general, theoretical core course. In the teaching of comparative law the traditional teaching methods, including lecture and seminar methods, backed up by problem-focused examinations and essays, are considered to be the most appropriate, particularly when the legal systems covered are from the same or similar socio-legal traditions. However, when the systems are not from such traditions, area and case study analysis within a theoretical framework provided would be more appropriate.

Comparative law teaching should focus on an exploration of the historical, jurisprudential and cultural backgrounds of studied legal systems or legal institutions. It may be true that many law teachers are sceptical of cultural analysis and prefer normative inquiry, but an increasing number of them, and therefore, institutions, are now trying to focus students' minds on social, historical, cultural and economic contexts.[2]

In the common law world, the historical legacy of largely vocational training persists with little contact between lawyers and social scientists. The reasons for the lack of interest and confidence in theory and the relative lack of methodological debate are partly cultural and partly institutional. In the civilian world, where law is seen as a social science, the constraints of the curricula indicate that comparative

---

[2] See generally, G. Samuel, 'Comparative law as a core subject' (2001) 21 *Legal Studies*, 444; *id.* 'Comparative Law and Jurisprudence' (1998) 47 *International and Comparative Law Quarterly*, 817; J. Gordley, 'Is Comparative Law a Distinct Discipline?' (1998) 46 *American Journal of Comparative Law*, 607; G.P. Fletcher, 'Comparative Law as A Subversive Discipline' (1998) 46 *American Journal of Comparative Law*, 683; R.B. Schlesinger, 'The Past and Future of Comparative Law' (1995) 43 *American Journal of Comparative Law*, 477; V.G. Curran, 'Dealing in Difference: Comparative Law's Potential for Broadening Legal Perspective' (1998) 46 *American Journal of Comparative Law*, 657; N.V. Demleitner, 'Challenge, Opportunity and Risk: An Era of Change in Comparative law' (1998) 46 *American Journal of Comparative Law*, 647; P.G. Kozyris, 'Comparative Law for the Twenty-First Century: New Horizons and New Technologies' (1994) 69 *Tulane Law Review*, 165.

law is increasingly regarded as a practical subject. Comparative law provides the opportunity for developing these interests and skills, but at present comparative law courses often remain either simply descriptive or, at best, functionally oriented. The approach is either an anatomical survey of the rules, or is oriented around legal problems by laying down rules with similar functions side-by-side, and only occasionally expose students to variations on a larger general picture.

In undergraduate programmes, when comparative law is taught, this is on an individualistic and idiosyncratic basis, its flair depending entirely on the teacher, there being no programmed approach to comparative law in the curriculum. Individual academics are left to fend for themselves. For both students and younger members of staff there is a danger of being left in partial ignorance. Unfortunately, rather than being fundamental to the education of the lawyers of tomorrow, comparative law is often envisaged as at best, an 'add-on'.

It must be remembered that there is a place for the comparison of 'decontextualized facts' just as there is a place for the appreciation of the 'big questions' and that one cannot study formal legal texts alone. 'Comparative law loses some of its utility, and most of its charm, if it reduces itself to a level of dry, formalistic, historical introduction to foreign legal systems, and comparison of legal rules and institutions'.[3] 'Comparative law must come to life and help us confront the major choices of the times, ... policy analysis ... must be integrated into comparative law.'[4]

It is in fact possible to combine the two approaches in one comparative law course. The aims of the course and the interests of the lecturer determine this choice. As long as students are aware of the options in comparative law scholarship, there can be nothing wrong with 'the fragmentation of comparative law'. Thinking within the law and thinking upon the law are both fundamental to legal education and it is not possible to do one well without the other.

Visits by students to law schools and comparative law institutes in other countries are valuable. These visits are at present only possible through programmes such as Erasmus, Socrates and Tempus. Such programmes can be beneficial for future practitioners depending on how they are run, and how much is done for purely educational reasons and how much for the prestige of the institutions concerned. If well run, they introduce students to different socio-legal cultures and help in overcoming barriers between peoples of different traditions and creating broader minds.

For teachers of comparative law also, 'teaching tourism' can be a very beneficial experience; however, whether 'teaching tourism' is really of value to teachers and students depends to a large extent on the integrity of the individual researcher and teacher. 'Teaching tourism' can of course be regarded as 'disguised imperialism of legal systems'. To generalize on this point however, is dangerous and makes individuals, institutions and legal systems into stereotypes. When carried out within the European Union for example, the purpose of 'teaching tourism' is more to

[3] Kozyris, above note 2, p. 175.
[4] *Ibid.*

facilitate legal integration than to establish the hegemony of one legal system over another. If however, it is an American or a German scholar on a teaching visit to the Ukraine or Turkmenistan, this could be a step towards facilitating the export of her own legal system.

Law should be taught in context. When taught in context, comparative law teaching contributes to an evaluation of one's own culture and the culture of others. In this way, comparative law teaching can create a synergetic interrelationship between two or more cultures. However, the dominant normative approach may not only inhibit this but lead to self-satisfaction. Instead of widening horizons, it could lead to re-assertion of the superiority of one's own legal culture and ready criticism of others. There is a danger that the teaching of comparative law can be used to expose weaknesses of other legal systems and overemphasize the merits of one's own. Much depends on the teacher and the systems chosen for study.

Comparative law teaching should lead to cultural criticism and become a genuine attempt to understand the thinking of other lawyers. A cross-cultural approach to, and an understanding of, different cultures is the key to successful comparative law teaching. However, most courses on comparative law do not approach the subject in this manner. Comparative law training must create an awareness of both differences between the similar and similarities between the different. '... The value of studying foreign law alongside one's own is even greater when they do differ',[5] as the student is encouraged to think when she sees more than one answer.

Comparative lawyers who put the emphasis on legal theory do indeed include the cultural and contextual approach in their teaching. Theory is vital for developing effective tools for interpreting legal information in on-line studies and for a better understanding of the process by which we acquire, process and transmit legal knowledge. There must be a 'language of comparative law'.[6]

Comparative law should be thought of in connection with Jurisprudence and Legal History, rather than having a mainly practical character and remaining normative in nature. There are universities in which courses dealing with other legal systems such as French law, are explicitly courses on comparative law, and others in which foreign legal systems are taught but in the relevant courses where any comparison is more implicit than explicit. In the latter case, foreign legal systems are taught but not in designated comparative law courses. In such courses there may be incidental comparisons but 'no sustained attempt to draw comparisons between the two systems as comparative lawyers seek to do for the various reasons which

[5] J. Gordley, 'Comparative Law and Legal Education', (2001) 75 *Tulane Law Review*, 1003 at p. 1008.

[6] D.J. Gerber, 'Globalization and Legal Knowledge: Implications for Comparative Law' (2001) 75 *Tulane Law Review*, 949 at p. 972.

draw them into the field of comparative law.'[7] In the past century, the historical approach was found to be the mainstream approach to the teaching of comparative law, followed by the functional approach. Generally comparative law courses deal with private law and only more recently with public law, constitutionalism and human rights. Most courses deal with systems in the western legal tradition, and mainstream comparative law narrowly focuses on national legal systems. This situation needs to be redressed.

Today, most general comparative law courses begin with an introduction to methodology and the aims and purposes of comparative law, and then follow the traditional path of encouraging students to observe rather than to appreciate the major legal families of the world in a century-old fashion. Specific autonomous comparative law courses and integrated courses often expose student to but one or two examples of how a foreign legal system deals with a similar problem. In the United Kingdom for example, the systems chosen are usually the more prominent systems of the Commonwealth or systems in the European Union. It is true that Asian and African legal scholarship is growing, as is literature on the former communist nations, but the discourse is conducted mainly with the traditional tools of the western legal tradition and the teaching is from the point of view of the law of the country in which the course is offered. It must be accepted that moving from the Euro-centric to the global is difficult and there are serious linguistic and cultural obstacles. Moreover, even if these obstacles can be removed for those engaged in comparative law research, how can this be done for students taking comparative law courses? All these points are of concern for the future of comparative law studies.

It could be asked whether comparative law teaching should also have the task of helping students to 'make informed legal decisions with respect to problems arising out of globalization', or 'equip them with academic tools sharp enough to model the future of global societies'.[8] If the answer is yes, then unfortunately, the reality is that courses are too short and remain rather shallow. If the importance of teaching comparative law were to be fully recognized and more time and space allocated to it, there are ways in which this aspect could also be considered. However, this should not be the main aim of autonomous general comparative law courses.

The potential effects and implications of globalization for teaching law have not been fully assessed. Though comparative law is regarded as one of the tools needed to enable students to penetrate the density of information, students have little time, little background knowledge about foreign systems and few resources to invest in this process. How should they be taught the way foreign systems operate? Should not the pedagogical focus be on developing abilities so that students can orient

---

[7] W.M. Gordon, 'The Place of Legal History in the Teaching of Comparative Law and in the Education of Comparative Lawyers', in J.W. Bridge (ed), *UK Law For the Millennium*, United Kingdom Comparative Law SeriesVol: 19, 2nd edn., (London, UKNCCL/BIICL, 2000), 286-297, at p. 287

[8] This question was asked by the General Rapporteur, Professor Gabriel Moens for the topic IC at the XVI Congress of Comparative Law in Brisbane in 2002.

themselves within a foreign institution, interpret information, decide what kinds of questions to ask and where to look for information, rather than on merely transmitting data?[9]

A 'Global Law School' could enhance comparative law teaching in order to deal effectively with changes caused by globalization and trade liberalization, though, especially at the undergraduate level, this is ambitious. At a regional and therefore, more practical level, there are plans to set up European Law Schools in the European Union; and since 1995, Maastricht Law Faculty in the Netherlands is the first such. Another is the Hanse Law School, University of Groningen (in collaboration with the Universities of Bremen and Oldenburg) where Dutch and German degrees are on offer and the whole spirit of the teaching and research is comparative. On a wider note the European Higher Education Area (EHEA) must be mentioned. A project was started in 1999 in Bologna. This is a collective university project involving 38 countries forging new links in order to integrate qualifications both at the undergraduate and the postgraduate level. The countries involved go well beyond the Member States of the European Union with universities from the European University Association (EUA) represented. This project is to complement the European Union's European Research Area project. The European Commission has also launched Erasmus Mundus which aims to spread the Erasmus programme model worldwide. The process of integration in Europe has had a most positive impact on such developments and has enhanced interest in comparative law.

The Global Law School Programme launched in 1995 in New York University is another ambitious project in which 58 foreign professors belonging to various foreign jurisdictions form the Global Law Faculty and teach a variety of courses.[10] However, these courses do not systematically integrate the study of foreign and domestic law. There are no full-time comparative lawyers on the Faculty, and there are no autonomous comparative law courses involved in systematic comparison of the doctrines of different legal systems in specific fields of law.[11] At the postgraduate level and at the level of comparative law research 'Global Law Schools' could be of great value in facilitating the teaching of comparative law. The main question though would be related to what is to be understood from the term 'Global'.

Traditional comparative law works on the horizontal plane, whereas, national and transnational systems work vertically.[12] If, 'comparative law must also provide the students with a map of the legal universe in which they will have to work'[13] then, not presenting law in a comparative and transnational perspective would mislead the student and foster over-simplistic thinking. So, it may be appropriate to ask not only what is the purpose of the autonomous comparative law course, but also whether the

[9] Gerber, above note 6, p. 973.
[10] Gordley above note 5, p. 1004.
[11] *Ibid.*
[12] M. Reimann, 'Beyond National Systems: A Comparative Law for the International Age' (2001) 75 *Tulane Law Review*, 1103 at p. 1113.
[13] *Ibid.*, p. 1116.

autonomous comparative law course indeed serves its purpose, in spite of the numbers teaching and writing in the area of comparative law being probably at an all-time high.[14] It must be accepted that the present picture is not very heartening.

Law schools are changing their curricula at undergraduate and postgraduate levels in order to establish an infrastructure of skills to help students to become more effective lawyers. In this context, comparative law teaching could help to create the 'global lawyer'. Success depends very much on how the subject is taught and what is taught however. Yet, it must also be remembered that 'global lawyers' are not necessarily more effective lawyers nor are they more effective thinkers, and they may well be merely filling convenient niches.

Comparative law should be taught as a distinct subject rather than be integrated into the teaching of domestic law. Comparative law need not move from being 'learned law' to 'practical law'. If this were to happen how could teachers of comparative law combat the risk of the students having superficial knowledge or insufficient understanding of foreign law, a 'legal polyglottism'?[15] The 'pure' academic comparative lawyer may not be in much demand, but increasingly, as interest in foreign law '*secundum comparatum*' mounts and literature of foreign legal systems abounds, experts in foreign law are in constant demand to aid the courts in transnational cases. It is vital that practitioners also master '*secundum comparatum*'. These developments may have positive impact on the numbers of students wishing to take the integrated comparative law courses or courses on particular legal systems such as the French, German or American, if not general autonomous and theoretical comparative law courses. This would be an encouraging start for the development of scholarly comparative law.

The time has come to replace the traditional 'nationally-centred' curriculum by a more 'internationally-centred' curriculum with comparative law as the core subject. The postgraduate level may be more appropriate for this. The internationally-centred curriculum at present falls within the remit of a small number of Centres within law schools, which must also cater for the needs of international lawyers and researchers. The mere introduction of an 'internationally-centred' curriculum is no short cut to the goal of educating 'more effective' lawyers however. The number of students at the undergraduate level interested in comparative law studies is not great. It may be that the real place for comparative law studies is at the postgraduate level. But this could be a 'chicken and egg' situation in that, if students do not come into contact with the 'world elsewhere' in the early part of their education, why should they later find this kind of education and research desirable? In any case, the number of students entering postgraduate studies in law is also rather small. Academics, lawyers and judges have always been aware that there is a 'world elsewhere'.[16]

---

[14] V.V. Palmer, 'Insularity and Leadership in American Comparative Law: The Past One Hundred Years' (2001) 75 *Tulane Law Review*, 1093, at p. 1097.

[15] R. Sacco, 'One Hundred Years of Comparative Law', (2001) 75 *Tulane Law Review*, 1159, at pp. 1169-70.

[16] J. Bingham, 'There is a World Elsewhere: The Changing Perspectives of English Law' (1992) 41 *International and Comparative Law Quarterly*, 527.

However, this 'elsewhere' is limited by the fact that law is first and foremost a parochial and vocational subject.

Comparative law has been heralded as the science of this century. Judges and academics have given impressive papers on its role and importance, and the last few years have witnessed a number of significant seminars and conferences on comparative law and comparative legal studies. Yet, comparative law teaching has remained a marginal activity for far too long, the courses being taken by only a small number of enthusiastic and dedicated students. Full-time teachers of comparative law are few and they remain in the outer circle of academia. They themselves see their work as vital but others often do not. They may be considered 'an élite clique' and there subject 'a cloistered subject'. The value of comparative law research for academics, researchers, law-makers and even courts is more easily understood, but for law students, it is still regarded as being for those who have not yet made up their minds about their future careers. The fact that comparative law is indeed the major tool for 'providing a better understanding of one's own law' and for 'broadening the mind' has not yet been fully appreciated.

The legal education law students now receive through comparative law teaching is not tailored to meet the challenges of the modern world. Topics covered are the same as they were twenty years ago, the methods of teaching and assessing remain on the whole unchanged and comparative law courses are evaluated in exactly the same way as all other law courses. Concepts and aims have changed so little over the past century that it has been said that, 'there is nothing new in 2000.'[17]

There is now a more optimistic outlook. There are glimmers of hope. Innovative approaches are emerging, many substantive law courses do now contain comparative elements and many dissertations show signs of such curiosity. The number of academics and legal professionals aware of the important role of comparative law in enabling the law graduate to live up to the present and future challenges is on the increase. More students are going abroad to study. When and how these glimmers become beacons however, is not easy to predict.

Demands on time and financial resources are growing. Unless comparative law is taught more extensively and is concentrated in centres of excellence, it may remain just an interesting but ornamental addition to a crammed curriculum.

To fully prosper, comparative law should re-think itself in the light of critical legal studies, law and economics, feminism and critical race theory, acknowledge and integrate cultural diversity and avoid Western hegemony. The continued emphasis on the common law/civil law comparison must also change. What of interdisciplinary comparative jurisprudence and a change of emphasis towards cultures other than common law/civil law? But then we may also ask whether in the market of students and lawyers studying and practicing law with its parochial and nationalistic vision, there is enough interest in this direction. The cultivation of a new interest in moving the clash between law as a science and law as a practical tool into a dialogue should be part of the task of comparative lawyers. They should

[17] D.C. Clark, 'Nothing New in 2000: Comparative Law in 1900 and Today' (2001) 75 *Tulane Law Review*, 871, at p. 911.

develop a common agenda to be reflected in their teaching. Today, there is heightened awareness of theory and method in comparative law rather than regarding and teaching it only as an aid to the practicing lawyer.[18]

If we are expected as comparative law teachers and researchers to promote globalized teaching in, and denationalized understanding of law, positivism and localism must be overcome with a 'multinational body of law teachers devoted as much as possible to an interdisciplinary approach to law'.[19] We must devise ways of achieving this.

As pointed out, there has been little change in the teaching of comparative law over the years apart from new general methods of teaching and learning, which affect the whole law curriculum. The introduction of new electronic facilities are among these changes: Lexis-Nexis, Westlaw and other Internet sources are now available to students. Teaching comparative law itself might not have been influenced greatly by these new developments but comparative law teaching has been influenced considerably. With awareness of the importance of comparative law and as a result of instant and easy access to foreign sources such as court decisions on the electronic facilities, electronic comparative law journals, comparative law discussion fora and electronically published draft research papers, more material has become available for research purposes. The academic is now in a better position to be fully informed of foreign law developments without having to go to foreign countries or even as far as a library to access sources. However, the danger is that one may neglect the real world and live in virtual reality. For the student another danger is that this information may remain superficial, be imperfectly selected and might not be transferred into knowledge, especially if autonomous comparative law courses were not offered, but were replaced by integrated courses.

Many comparative lawyers believe that the theory and methodology of comparative law need to be strengthened, and this is the field in which they should concentrate their efforts now. The changes in the globalizing world related to integration and to specific system analysis are also catching up with comparative lawyers as more and more systems in transition seek their help. Comparative law, its role, value and relevance is changing and the hope is that this will impact on the teaching of comparative law and comparative law teaching now and in the coming decades.

The teaching of comparative law has always been attractive for a certain kind of academic. Most of such academics are appreciated by their students and other comparative lawyers. Their teaching and research have benefited from the electronic information age, but the tools for translating this information into usable knowledge, and the using of these tools, is very much dependent on the human factor - the researcher, the teacher, and also the student herself. Creative, imaginative, innovative and enthusiastic academics and students can benefit from this new world

---

[18] But see, B. Markesinis, 'Comparative Law: A Subject in Search of an Audience'(1990) 53 *Modern Law Review*, 1.

[19] F. Werro, 'Notes on the Purpose and Aims of Comparative Law' (2001) 75 *Tulane Law Review*, 1225, at p. 1233.

and themselves bring great benefit to it. The tools are there. We need informed and discerning users and a new vision.

If we want to further legal knowledge, legal education must aim beyond the intending practicing lawyer. The first step is to recognize the present limitations of legal education and legal science methodology. Without such recognition one cannot undertake reform. Reform is necessary at three levels: legal education, the competence of the legal researcher and international team work. At the level of legal education, students must be given the opportunity and encouraged to study general comparative law, sociology, anthropology, politics, economics and foreign languages in greater depth than at present. They should also be encouraged to develop a critical attitude to law and be made aware that they are living in an ever changing world. A broad based legal education, relying heavily on interdisciplinary study will produce law graduates better equipped to go on to advanced comparative studies. For this purpose the present training of the law student is inadequate in many institutions. At the level of the competence of the individual researcher, much rests on specialist teaching at doctorate level in universities and in comparative law centres and institutions. Here, the main emphasis must be on research methodology. Researchers must have an extensive working knowledge of social science methodology and be able to apply it in projects. They must also be trained to use law-related subjects in the explanation phase of their research. The increasing interest in team-work among comparative lawyers, sociologists, anthropologists and economists is an extremely healthy sign.

VARIATION II

Comparative law can only have a place in the undergraduate law curriculum if at all, as part of substantive courses, that is, in integrated courses. General comparative law is on the periphery of the curriculum and there it should stay; it should remain as an interesting but ornamental addition to an already crammed curriculum.

In the teaching of comparative law to students or practitioners, traditional teaching methods such as the lecture and seminar, backed up by problem-focused examinations and essays, are appropriate, since the legal systems covered are from the same or similar socio-legal traditions. Comparative law teaching must concentrate primarily on an examination of statutory regimes adopted in different legal systems.

When comparative law teachers accept the fact that their subject has practical applications, then the picture could change. Interest in comparative law will only increase when law firms see the benefits of employing lawyers who have received some training in comparative law and foreign legal systems. However, if this were to happen, the approach to teaching comparative law and comparative law teaching would also have to change. Comparative law teaching should not presume to enhance cultural understanding or cultural criticism, but serve purely as a source of information. The approach should either be an anatomical survey of the rules, or be oriented towards legal problems by laying down rules with similar functions side-by-side thus exposing students to possible variations. There is a place for the comparison of 'decontextualized facts' but not for the appreciation of the 'big questions'. These could be left to legal theory which itself should remain an elective course.

Comparative lawyers teaching comparative law to undergraduate students cannot regard studying and then teaching the legal thinking of a foreign culture as their primary concern and cannot believe that comparative law should aim at understanding ideas at work behind foreign legal systems. Fortunately, 'theory has seldom been an important part of comparative law scholarship because it has been perceived to have little value for existing objectives'.[20] And so it should remain. Comparative law should not be taught as a distinct subject but be integrated into the teaching of domestic law. It should move from being 'learned law' to 'practical law' if it wants to have a future.

It is generally accepted that law schools have two options for acquainting their students with foreign law. One is to have their students study foreign law under foreign professors in programmes such as summer programmes abroad, Junior Year Abroad, Socrates programmes, or in foreign universities long enough to obtain a foreign law degree along with their own. The other option is to bring professors from abroad to teach students who remain at home. Visits by students to law schools and comparative law institutes in other countries can be valuable. Such visits are on the whole possible only through programmes such as the above. These programmes can be beneficial for future practitioners if they are well run. How much is done for practical reasons, how much is done for purely educational reasons and how much for the prestige of the institutions concerned are the determinants. If well run, they can introduce students to different socio-legal cultures and may help in overcoming barriers between peoples of different traditions. However, the prior decision here must be on whether this is the function of a law degree.

For teachers of comparative law, 'teaching tourism' may be a beneficial experience. However, exchange programmes such as Socrates are really only ornamental and do not involve students in either comparative law or the foreign law concerned. Since the courses offered are mostly in English, the students do not have a real taste of the foreign legal system, do not study primary sources and often do not mix well with the host student body tending to stay within their own groups. At present, these programmes remain at the level of interesting experiences for both teachers and students, although, it must be admitted that participatants in such programmes are reported to be more interested in comparative law upon their return and perform generally better than those who stay at home.

It must also be admitted however that the degree of specialization required in order to offer comparative law courses and sufficient funding for significant comparative law studies do not exist. There are no special funding bodies such as those for socio-legal studies, dedicated to comparative law research. With awareness

[20] Gerber, above note 6, p. 969.

of the growing importance of foreign law and as a result of instant and easy access to foreign sources such as court decisions on the electronic facilities, electronic comparative law journals, comparative law discussion fora and electronically published draft research papers, more material has become available all of which can be used to enhance research. The academic can be fully informed of foreign law developments without having to travel abroad or even go to libraries for access to sources. This is an important development.

'Traditional' law schools are still the norm and not a species on the verge of extinction. Teaching is nationally-centred and should not be transformed into internationally-centred teaching. Law is and should remain a parochial subject, and this must be reflected in comparative law teaching. Although some would regard internationally-centred teaching as interesting, the majority of lawyers, both academics and practitioners, believe in the higher value of nationally-centred teaching of law, with reference to the international or foreign where appropriate. There are few specific transnational courses on offer at the undergraduate level. Problems in practice are more effectively solved through 'networks'.

Comparative law is a method, a way of looking at the law for a number of purposes. It is not a 'supra law' intertwined with other legal disciplines. It could be used to highlight international aspects of any legal subject, but very few institutions undertaking comparative law teaching would use the subject in this way. At this moment its use is fashionable and decorative rather than real and practical, and comparative law teaching has little impact on national jurisdictions

The generalist approach might attempt to 'broaden the minds or help students to better understand their own systems', but what about the needs of multinational companies and multinational law firms? Can law schools help here? What sort of comparative law is needed for those who are 'just interested in doing business abroad'?[21] Is it vital that practitioners become also masters of '*secundum comparatum*'? Globalization may have had an impact on the numbers of students wishing to take integrated comparative law courses or courses on particular legal systems such as the French or German, but not on the numbers taking general autonomous and theoretical comparative law courses.

Teaching comparative law can be regarded as directly related to the import-export market of law, since one of the main functions of comparative law is to provide a pool of models for use in law reform. Legal transpositions are much in evidence today and comparative lawyers are constantly being asked to aid in the smooth import-export of legal institutions. Globalization forces lawyers to become familiar with, and to operate smoothly in, other jurisdictions. This requires a rethink of the basic core curriculum of law schools. If insight into comparative legal traditions, comparative legal reasoning and major legal systems is what should be taught in the belief that comparison lends perspective, then this cannot meet the needs of multinational companies.

---

[21] X Blanc-Jouvan, 'Centennial World Congress on Comparative Law: Closing Remarks' (2001) 75 *Tulane Law Review*, 1235, at p. 1244.

Although it is true that many more courses now contain scattered comparative elements, this does not mean that all academic lawyers are comparative lawyers, if such an academic exists, nor that all courses are replacements for unnecessary general comparative law courses. Comparative lawyers will soon be regarded as redundant and autonomous general comparative law courses will be replaced by integrated courses.

A knowledge of national law, the methods of handling legal documents, texts, and cases, and the construction of logical legal arguments are more important than any other skill a law student may acquire. The additional transferable skills now provided in most universities will stand them proud in their future careers.

Enigma of Comparative Law

Chapter 8

COMPARATIVE LAW AND THE TUNERS OF THE LAW

Does comparative law simply facilitate the incorporation by judges of 'holus bolus from some other system of law'.[1] Is such a view tenable?

The term 'comparative law' is used in this sub-theme in the widest sense, 'not just as a theoretical distillate and an abstraction, the *tertium comparationis*, but covering even passing reference to foreign law by a court' or a practicing lawyer.[2] The use of a foreign solution by a domestic judge either in its entirety or as a guide to interpretation suffices. Although it seems today commonplace to see judicial comparativism as a method of interpretation and as a legal technique, it is difficult to discover patterns as to how far foreign law is referred to by the practicing lawyer and the judiciary, for what purposes, when and how.

It is important to note that judges and counsel go through three phases: first discovering, then endeavouring to understand and finally applying foreign law. Of what is found, what is to be used: the result or the reasoning? How is this foreign material to be used: in gap filling or interpretation of ill-defined terms?

Borrowing from the international to the national, from one national to another or even one international to another, now seems natural in the development of globalizing law. Therefore the debate on the use or non-use of comparative experience remains theoretical when viewed from the ground of what is actually taking place. However, the degree of, and the reasons underlying the borrowing differ. In addition, the attitudes of academics, practicing lawyers and judges to the use of foreign material in deciding domestic cases also differ. The most frequently asked questions are: How far does this activity of borrowing go? Which jurisdictions are chosen for borrowing and why? Why are some judges in some jurisdictions more ready to use comparative law while others are not?[3] How can one tell whether comparativism is successful? What is the measure of success? If a sign of success is

---

[1] Lord Diplock in *McShannon* v *Rockware Glass* Ltd [1978] A.C. 995, 811.

[2] E. Örücü, 'Comparative Law in British Courts', in U. Drobnig and S van Erp (eds) *The Use of Comparative Law by Courts* (The Hague, Kluwer Law International, 1999), p. 253.

[3] For the use of comparative law by courts in general in 17 jurisdictions see the General Report submitted by E. Drobnig, 'The Use of Comparative Law by Courts', in U. Drobnig and S. van Erp (eds), above note 2,.3-21.

uniformity of treatment and values, then, do we also need to create uniform socio-economic and cultural conditions?

Our answers to these questions will determine our place on the spectrum of attitudes to the general question of the use of comparative law by legal practitioners and judges in the twenty first century. As legal standards are not derived from national sources alone, but from comparative and supranational sources, inhibitions related to specific legal and political culture and the power of history and routine recede. Courts appear to be integrating national law with international law. Can it be said that though the past may have been nationally and culturally specific, the future cannot be so?

Can we also claim that though private international law represents the law as a normative phenomenon, comparative law represents the law as a cultural phenomenon? If so, then the role of comparative law in reaching judicial decisions is much more complicated than the choosing of an appropriate answer to a question from a pool of answers provided by comparative lawyers.

Below, Variation I will display a positive attitude to such usage and offer legitimation for it, whereas Variation II will present the negative response and point to the shortcomings in the use of comparative law by the legal profession and the judiciary, the actors and tuners of the law.

VARIATION I

Lawyers and courts need to be aware of a number of answers to practical questions in order to be able to analyze and assess domestic law and to contribute to its development. Foreign law should not be considered only in cases with a foreign element being dealt with by practicing lawyers or judges in courts, but in every case. Extensive use must be made, and is increasingly being made of foreign material. The use of foreign material and comparative analysis is a reality. Ornamental use is becoming a thing of the past. This is true in private law, commercial law and consumer protection, as well as in environmental law, public law and constitutional law; and it is especially important in the area of human rights.

If comparative law is to be the basis of some form of new natural law, then domestic courts must look forward, look sideways, at each other and beyond. Comparativism must be at the heart of all judicial activity if law is to embody principles that are 'universal' rather than purely domestic or even 'European'.

If actors of the law, that is academics, judges and lawyers adopt a pragmatic and progressive approach rather than using negative terminology in the face of foreign law such as 'pollution' and 'contamination', or aligning themselves as 'purists' or 'pollutionists', then comparativism provides the tool for interlocking legal systems.

For example, English and Scottish judges utilize comparativism on a much wider scale than judges in most other jurisdictions. They converse with judges of the Commonwealth, the European Court of Human Rights and the European Court of

Justice through the multi-focus provided by their conversations with Commonwealth and American judges; they interpret law by approaching their own cases through those decided in Canada, Australia, New Zealand, South Africa and the United States, and recently, systems from the civilian tradition. The crucial issue here is whether comparativism is used for inspiration and as an interpretative tool, or for the purpose of seeking the legitimation of a foregone conclusion. It can be said that sometimes there is a real effort at a 'common enterprise' and sometimes a search for justification for a domestic decision. For example, in discussing 'compatibility' with the European Convention on Human Rights as embodied in the 1998 Human Rights Act in the UK, judges are rapidly becoming conversant with human rights issues and in this area comparativism is gaining weight.[4]

The use of comparative law can now be seen as a 'common enterprise' as judges and practicing lawyers try to enlarge the scope of the protection of many rights. For example, South Africa has the first Constitution in the world setting out an explicit mandate for the courts to use comparative and international law in their human rights reasoning. The 1996 Constitution in the interpretation Section 39(1)(b)&(c) provides that a court, tribunal or forum, in interpreting the Bill of Rights, 'must consider International law' and 'may consider foreign law'. This is a tacit invitation to the judiciary to apply comparative law. So we see here that in South Africa, there is strong academic comparative law groundwork on which higher courts rely. In this context, extensive use is made of American, Australian. Canadian, Indian and German cases. There is a lack of African perspective however.[5] The basic question is whether European and North American models are appropriate here. In certain areas of law where the aim is to correct past failures and respond to specific or unique home truths, cultural exceptionalism is preferred over comparativism in human rights cases. The South African example points to the importance of the contribution of academic comparative lawyers to the development of the system by aiding the tuners of the law, the judiciary.

David Carey-Miller has classified the use of comparative law in human rights cases by South African courts as 'illustrative', 'supplementary', 'elucidatory' or 'going to core substance', rightly stressing the fact that transplants in human rights cases need careful management. However, this warning does not detract from the value of such an enterprise.

There could of course be 'bad comparativism' when comparative law is used solely for the furtherance of a cause, or its use is solely ornamental. But more often judicial comparativism comes from an 'awareness of a common enterprise', the confronting of common problems and the balancing of conflicting rights and interests. Today, comparativism is becoming second nature to judges and providing

---

[4] See P. Kearns, 'United Kingdom Judges and Human Rights Cases', in Örücü (ed), above note 4, 63-83.

[5] See D.L. Carey-Miller, 'The Great Trek to Human Rights: The Role of Comparative Law in the Development of Human Rights in Post-reform South Africa, in Örücü (ed),above note 4 , 201-228.

a significant interpretative tool.[6] Obviously we have to assess this 'transjudicial communication'.[7] The starting point of this assessment however, should be a positive welcoming approach.

It is important to look first into why is comparativism needed. As well as being tied to cultural and historical influences, current role models and knowledge of the specific language of the models among domestic lawyers, further explanations can be given, such as prestige or the quality of the legal rules to be exported and imported; efficiency, the role of the national elite; chance; practical utility; cultural forces; and imposition. We see examples that support all of these when we look at legal systems.[8] Reference to other jurisdictions usually gives broader legitimacy to judicial decisions.

When we review cases - especially those from the common law jurisdictions - we see clauses used by judges when referring to foreign cases such as 'ample support', 'particularly useful', 'helpful', 'compatible with values of democratic societies', 'instructive', 'persuasive but not binding', 'of assistance', 'of interest' and 'gives comfort'.[9] In developing the law, in cases when the existing law is inadequate, or in extending the law, judges often turn to foreign jurisdictions to achieve some uniformity within the 'civilised' world. This may also be done in order to soften the impact of a domestic rule. Judges may be confronted with novel issues. They may wish to depart from domestic understandings. Concepts of equality, morality and justice may demand new approaches. There may be insufficient domestic guidance on a matter. In such cases, comparative law is a most valuable tool of interpretation.

Judges are 'tuners' of the law. While they adapt the law to the evolution of society and create bridges between the law and the values of the society in which they live, they also build bridges between that society and other societies and universal values by means of comparativism. The basic values used are those of the judge's own society but as integrated into a wider universe. This also provides a certain anchorage for domestic decisions. Obviously there is also the added assumption in the western world, that the basic values underpinning democratic societies are shared values. Comparisons reveal these shared values and therefore it is seen as appropriate to use comparativism as the interpretative tool. However, it is not the technical aspects of the foreign solution that should be studied, but the legal,

---

[6] Although it is said that in the US courts rarely cite foreign law (See D.S. Clark, 'The Use of Comparative Law by American Courts', (Supp. 1994) 42 *American Journal of Comparative Law*, 23), it has also been shown that in hard cases in the area of constitutional law, the US Supreme Court does consider Canadian and ECJ and ECHR cases (See D. Fontana, 'Refined Comparativism in Constitutional Law' (2001) 49 *UCLA Law Review*, 539, who calls this type of reference 'refined comparativism' which he says is 'a contingent strategy of interpretation'.)

[7] See A.M. Slaughter, 'A Typology of Transjudicial Communication' (1994) *University of Richmond Law Review*, 99.

[8] See Drobnig, above note 3.

[9] See Örücü, above note 2.

economic and cultural contexts within which similar cases are decided by judges of foreign jurisdictions. Here integration can be created by comparative analysis since looking at things comparatively brings an incremental common perspective. This gives rise to a gradual 'internalization of common values' by the courts of national legal systems. Practicing lawyer should take part in this process.

It is true that accepting commonality may be seen as ignoring cultural differences, but it may also be seen as a means of transcending those differences. However, it could be questioned whether a claim of universalism gives a court authority to interpret and apply specific rights, for example. Comparativism does not in itself lead to integration or the creation of a '*ius commune*', it can only be a tool for selecting appropriate approaches to solving common problems.

Cross-fertilization and transposition are the most promising ways of establishing such a '*ius commune*'. Comparativism feeds cross-fertilization and cross-fertilization encourages instrumentalization and transposition of the received. Thus commonality is developed, though be it at a more abstract and higher level of principle than at the level of rules. Comparativism certainly broadens the spectrum of choice and provides inspiration to an activist judge. Balances can always be struck by using the tool of 'evolutive interpretation' and looking for current meanings of inconclusive terms in texts, and 'margin of appreciation', whereby nation States can use democratic discretion to regulate the way of life of their citizens in areas where there is a legitimate range of opinion. If this were happening voluntarily rather than out of necessity and comparativism were used as the legitimate or preferred tool of interpretation, then genuine interlocking of legal systems could occur more smoothly.

Comparative law is often treated today by courts and practitioners as 'an auxiliary source of law', 'a subsidiary method of interpretation.' Though comparisons are made mostly within 'the circle of systems culturally linked by common ethical standards',[10] this is not a necessary condition for comparisons being used by the judiciary and practicing lawyers. We observe how the courts of developing countries and newly emerging democracies look to other legal systems considered 'western' or 'developed'.[11] In the future, localisms will gain in importance alongside the growing interest in universalism.

VARIATION II

[10] B. Grossfeld, *The Strength and Weakness of Comparative Law*, trans. T. Weir (Oxford, Clarendon Press, 1990), p. 33.

[11] See for example C. Dupré, *Importing the Law in Post-Communist Transitions: The Hungarian Constitutional Court and the Right to Human Dignity* (Oxford, Hart Publishing, 2003); and also I.C. Kaminski, 'The Power of Aspiration: The Impact of European Law on a non-EU Country', in M. van Hoecke and F. Ost (eds), *The Harmonisation of European Private Law* (Oxford, Hart Publishing, 2000), 239-252.

The 1856 General Code of the Canton of Aargau stated in Article 14: 'No court may, by way of interpretation or amplification of the Code, base its judgment on any foreign law'.[12] Not much has changed today.

This Variation starts by looking at a survey on the subject of the use of comparative law by courts by Ulrich Drobnig, the General Rapporteur of the fifteen National Rapports submitted to the XVIth International Congress of Comparative Law in 1997. Ulrich Drobnig, having considered the submissions, reported that practical experience shows that most courts when referring to foreign law do not undertake comparisons or use the methods used by academics. Neither do they indicate why a particular country is selected. However, this usage indicates that they are at least aware of other solutions and are willing to look abroad. He also pointed out that in certain countries there are general limits of a procedural kind that prevent certain courts from considering foreign law. It is only when the court expressly refers to the corresponding part of the Attorney-General's opinion that we can detect such usage by the courts. Ulrich Drobnig also questions whether one can refer to a law as 'foreign' when that law has been already assimilated into the law of the forum State by an academic comparative lawyer and therefore the foreign law is presented to the court in an already 'translated' form.[13] He differentiates between necessary and voluntary recourse to foreign law, citing among the necessary recourse, general principles of law and conflict of laws; then come legal rules with an international element such as uniform international rules, European Community Law, rules shared with other countries, maritime and air law, conflict of laws and extradition. In all these areas, there are foreign law references.

The problematic and most important area of concern is related to legal rules of a purely domestic character. Here, references to foreign solutions are few and even exceptional, and their use difficult to justify. However when comparative law is used in these cases, it is used 'either to abrogate existing national rules or to fill gaps, although sometimes also for merely decorative purposes.'[14] This last use is not to resort to foreign law as a necessary element of the judge's reasoning but to show the judge's learning to the target audience! This type of reference is regarded by Ulrich Drobnig as, 'a superfluous ornament at best and may even do a disservice to the serious study of comparative law.'[15] It is also reported that with few exceptions courts, look only at the contents of the foreign rules rather than their context or effects, that the weight of foreign solutions is always limited with no court basing its decision solely on foreign law, such references being also rather short with attention paid only to results and rarely to reasoning and that courts proceed pragmatically. The selection of countries also seems random, sometimes certain groupings are used and problems of language and documentary access are the main obstacles. Comparative literature presented in the court's language is a helpful source of information though some courts do have research services. References are over-

[12] Borrowed from Grossfeld, above note 11, footnote 16 at p. 4.
[13] Drobnig, above note 3, pp. 4-5.
[14] *Ibid.*, p. 16
[15] *Ibid.*, p. 17.

simplistic. Ulrich Drobnig is of the opinion that, 'A general postulate, such as Zweigert's characterization of comparative law as a "universal method of interpretation" appears to be too undifferentiated.'[16]

For this Variation, comparative law is only important as knowledge of foreign law when cases arise involving such law. For lawyers, it is only necessary to bring foreign law to the attention of the courts, and for the courts to have sufficient knowledge to ask the foreign law expert the pertinent questions. Foreign law could only concern a lawyer if his client had a traffic accident in a foreign country, or the company he represents established a new branch in a foreign jurisdiction for example. Then, he could use the services of pertinent foreign lawyers in his international network. As no comparative lawyer, let alone a practicing lawyer, can fully understand foreign law, it would be dangerous if she were to get involved in the finding and appreciation of foreign law directly. All she can do is to give the foreign expert the right instructions and ask the right questions.

It is also important to note that in the common law world for example, the practicing lawyer is in essence looking out for foreign cases in order to ask the court for a departure from an established precedent and therefore is searching for solutions that are different from the domestic to further her cause. However, in many cases, a court uses foreign decisions to strengthen its hand in reaching what is in fact a foregone conclusion. So the practicing lawyer and the judge will not always be working towards the same end and the stressing of the similarity or the difference will not agree.

Global players and/or multinational law firms do not necessarily have much impact on comparative law teaching. It is possible that the needs of multinational companies are better met by the expertise of multinational law firms promoting harmonization of legal systems and globalization of law. This they can do much more successfully than law schools ever could. It must be stressed here that necessity as perceived by multi-national law firms is not the same as that perceived by academics. In addition, the knowledge gained through multinational companies and law firms offering such training to their staff is on the whole practical but superficial; just enough to cope with the specific problems of the companies and firms. The in-house training is always purposive and narrow and should be undertaken in a practical environment - for example, in law firms - rather than exclusively in law schools

A factor to be considered is language skills. Whether the importance of this is stressed in legal education or not, not all practicing lawyers and judges are in a position to be conversant with decisions of foreign courts, in spite of the fact that many jurisdictions today have Internet sites and decisions of higher courts are translated into the languages of the major jurisdictions. Within the common law world the concept of the 'unity of common law' is more than a rhetoric. It is easy to detect the growth of a 'common law of human rights' for example, utilizing

[16] *Ibid.*, p. 19.

extensive comparative activity in this legal culture. Obviously this is closely tied to shared language, culture and appreciation of mental constructs.

Another factor is the need for awareness and use of foreign cases by counsel as well as the judge, especially in jurisdictions where proof of foreign law is a question of fact such as in England, Scotland and South Africa.

However, if there are domestic answers there is no need to look elsewhere unless, as pointed out above, this need arises in the particular type of case being dealt with. 'Why bother with foreign cases when we have so much material of our own?'[17] is a valid question. Thus, pride, over-confidence and the self-reliant spirit of the judiciary are obstacles additional to language deficiency, nationalism, the importance attached to domestic socio-political needs and belief in cultural exceptionalism rather than universalism that could all make the legal profession and the judiciary shy of foreign law.

Is this what is happening? It might appear to be so when a number of jurisdictions are reviewed. What use there is of foreign law and foreign cases is selective and there is no logical approach to the choice. Neither is a specific methodology applied. In addition, the decision to use foreign judicial judgments remains largely in the realm of judicial discretion, and the exercise of this discretion may be due to many factors. We should also ask whether courts are properly equipped to carry out detailed comparative law surveys as a matter of course in every suitable case. Courts may make decisions on the basis of superficial or even misleading comparisons; or the contemporary 'standards of justice' presented by comparativism may do no more than confirm an interpretation already arrived at by a court on the basis of other considerations. Picking and choosing is a grave danger. One may also wonder whether we can indeed talk of increased reciprocal influence or only of one way trajectories.

In any event, very often, the exact nature of foreign law influence may not be obvious from reading the case. This is so especially in the civilian tradition where it is the advocate-general who writes the advisory opinion, carries out comparisons and makes a thorough analysis of foreign laws. Courts would rarely discuss or refer to such material. A court may be willing to use comparative law but may be overworked and therefore need the advisory opinion, decisions being then based on the conclusions of the advocate-general. Of course a court may be under a duty to investigate foreign law such as in 'conflict of laws' cases and under Conventions. Or a court may rely on comparative material in order to find a solution to a particular problem, or, refer to foreign law to justify a solution already arrived at. There may be no obvious reference but it is clear to the comparative lawyer that comparisons have been carried out; the judgment is silent but the advisory opinion discusses aspects of foreign law, usually when new problems have to be solved; or more rarely, the court itself refers to foreign law. In many cases, comparative work may have had an effect on the preliminary investigation but does not find an explicit place in the decision, though it may have inspired that decision and can only be

[17] B Markesinis, 'Comparative Law – A Subject in Search of an Audience' (1990) 53 *Modern Law Review*, p. 4.

traced by inductive reasoning by the researcher. It is natural that courts want to claim full decisional autonomy.

It is true that in the Commonwealth, there is an intra-family comparativism, the Privy Council having acted over the years as the anchor point. There has always been cross-fertilization between the members of the Commonwealth, and the courts of common law jurisdictions are increasingly influenced by each others' case law. Commonwealth judges take an activist position. In addition, the Privy Council's acceptance of the fact that fundamental rights provisions require a broader, more liberal interpretative approach than ordinary statutory provisions, has led to a degree of freedom in interpretation among the Commonwealth judges. Moreover, the Privy Council has had far more comparative experience than any other court in the world. However this does not mean that all courts at all levels would be in a position to do the same.

Domestic legal science is on the whole nationalistic, the classical view being that the legal system has nothing to learn from elsewhere. So when comparative law is made use of, its role remains largely decorative. We could ask the question: Is the role of comparative law today moving away from being 'decorative' to being a 'source of universal reason'? Can it be said that as the professional training of legal actors is directed more towards European and comparative law this movement is inevitable? The answers are negative for the time being, considering the present state of comparative law teaching and practice.[18]

The position at present is that comparative law is employed only when there is a gap in national law, when there is good reason for looking abroad or when there is something interesting to look at. On the whole, liberal democracies with different cultural backgrounds are not considered. For example, Luc Heuschling indicates four functions for comparative law in France: 'decorative', 'cognitive', 'legitimation' and 'inspiration'.[19]

In the presentation of a unified picture, the use of comparative material may not be visible but concealed as in the case of the European Court of Justice. Citizens who claim equal treatment wherever they happen to be do not expect the distinctiveness that they find in the laws of individual nation States to be applied to them.

When a choice is made between a number of solutions, and a 'better law' approach is preferred, the legitimacy of making this choice points to value-oriented comparativism. Is comparativism used here for ideological reasons? In particular, radical departures from previous bases necessitate new and clear criteria. So here, one is not talking of norm or concept borrowing, but the transplanting of moral positions. Is this acceptable? This Variation would say 'No'.

Cross-breeding comes through the direct and indirect influence of the European Union, through the 'better law' filter applied by Community judges and the judges of the European Court of Human Rights; through the spreading of knowledge by

[18] There is a further discussion of this in Chapter 7, Variation II.

[19] See L. Heuschling, 'Comparative Law and the European Convention on Human Rights in French Human Rights Cases' in Örücü (ed) above note 4, pp. 23-48.

academic writers; or following a transplant deriving from an autonomous action by the courts. The cultural gap in the training of judges and lawyers and their use of foreign law remains, but a corpus of fundamental principles common to European orders is identifiable. This may be seen as an irreversible phenomenon, especially apparent at the level of legislative activity. However from the point of view of 'localism' it may not be regarded as desirable.

It must be admitted that comparativism may be used solely to further a particular cause. This use is 'ornamental', with the aim of having a particular 'effect' on a target audience. Judges would have reached the same conclusion without comparativism. This may be called 'bad comparativism' by a comparative lawyer following Variation I, however, it is the only legitimate use of foreign law. Sometimes comparative research is undertaken to show that while a particular problem is universal, there can be in fact different solutions; here, the danger is eclecticism since judges can choose whichever solutions they like. Thus again, comparative law can be merely a means to an end. The choices made can also be tied to cultural and historical influences, a current role model, knowledge of a specific language by a group of lawyers. There may also be misunderstandings, errors, or even deliberate choices. On the whole, it would appear that references to foreign decisions are made either because of historical ties, because a legal system is fashionable at that particular time and there is imitation and mimicry, because of the influence of European Union law or the European Convention on Human Rights, because there are similar circumstances to the case at hand and there is no domestic law, or because the changing culture of judges through education and new technical developments makes access to foreign judgements easier. Using the comparative approach might also be seen, as a 'distancing device'.[20]Here, comparative material is used as the authority judges rely on for such a purpose. Would this use also be called 'bad comparativism' by comparative lawyers? It must be remembered that these explanations all remain at the level of conjecture, since a judge may not reveal the sources of his reasoning nor expressly quote them and he may not tell us why he preferred one case rather than another even when the reference is overt.

As comparisons made are analyzed, we do sometimes see a 'functional use' of comparative law, yet, as pointed out, usually the use is 'ornamental' or 'decorative'. Sometimes 'integrationalism' and 'internationalism' is evident. However, 'cultural exceptionalism' seems to prevail for a variety of reasons. The influence of foreign cases must go through the sieve of domestic values and be mediated. Obviously no legal tradition can be totally self-referential and impermeable to outside perspectives. Comparisons provide multiple viewpoints and interpretative options. However, only the technical aspects of the foreign solution should be studied, as the legal, economic and cultural contexts within which similar cases are decided by judges of foreign jurisdictions cannot be identical. The intention is to solve particular problems, not to lead to integration by comparative analysis or to give rise

[20] J. Raz, 'On the Authority and Interpretation of Constitutions: Some Preliminaries', in I. Alexander (ed), *Constitutionalism: Philosophical Foundations* (Cambridge, Cambridge University Press, 1998), 152 at p. 190.

to a gradual 'internalization of common values' by the courts of each national legal system.

By surveying the terms used in resorting to foreign cases, it becomes obvious that foreign law is used 'transnationally as an interpretative source' rather than as a source of direct application. The degrees of influence also differ. In addition, as already noted, sometimes the reference is explicit, sometimes not. For example, Christopher McCrudden[21] classifies jurisdictions into those whose courts do not use foreign human rights law at all, such as the United States Supreme Court, those whose courts use this law but not explicitly such as Japan, and those whose courts use foreign judgments explicitly such as Canada, South African and the UK. It is also worth noting that it is the judiciaries of liberal democratic regimes that cite each other. They have both common fundamental assumptions and also common goals. Democracies with 'supplementary visions' such as Turkey, where ideas of the nation State and legal positivism are strong and law is seen as a national response to national problems, find this type of reference difficult even though they have a well developed capacity to assimilate foreign material. Nevertheless in such democracies too there may be a desire to convince the relevant audience, such as the European Union or the liberal democratic world at large, of a universalist approach.[22] Isolationism may be one of the reasons for not citing from other jurisdictions but isolationism itself can in turn be the result of not doing so. Seeking closer integration, on the other hand, brings an added impetus to such activity. Comparativism may even be 'explicitly built into the fabric of judicial decision-making' as in the European context.

It is interesting to note that the European Court of Human Rights also makes comparative reference to national laws, that is, there is 'reverse reference back to national laws'. This type of reference is the expression of a coherent doctrine, part of an interpretative process and is not piecemeal, the European Convention on Human Rights having established a bridge with two-way traffic between international law and national law. The contracting states are under an international obligation to make their national legal orders compatible with specific common standards. The European Convention on Human Rights, as the inspiration and continuing source of those standards, derives from principles already recognised under the domestic law of all democratic countries.[23]

---

[21] See C. McCrudden, 'Human Rights and Judicial Use of Comparative Law', in Örücü (ed), above note 4, pp. 1-22.

[22] See E. Örücü, ' The Turkish Experience with Judicial Comparativism in Human Rights Cases' in E. Örücü (ed), above note 4, pp. 131-158.

[23] P Mahoney, 'The Comparative Method in Judgments of the European Court of Human Rights: Reference back to National Law', paper delivered at the BIICL Conference 'Comparative law Before National and International Courts' on 21 February 2003 (unpublished) which is an updated version of an article P Mahoney, 'The Role of Comparative Law in the Emergence of European Law, 2000 (a publication of the Swiss Institute of Comparative Law)

Yet is it legitimate to refer back to national legislation when the aim is to create international judicial control? Can the European Court of Human Rights be led by what it is to govern? According to Paul Mahoney,[24] such reference is first an 'evidentiary indication' and second, a means of seeking to identify the present day contours of the shared European legal principles that originally inspired the European Convention on Human Rights standards. The European legal community shares 'a common heritage of legal traditions, ideals, freedom and the rule of law.' 'The European Convention on Human Rights can be taken as creating a more or less homogenous European legal community with a common ethos in human rights matters.'[25] Also the anchoring of an evolved meaning to empirical evidence counters the argument that activist judges are trespassing on the treaty amendment domain or simply relying on their own personal sense of justice to make new law. They are trying to discern a common will. However, it must again be remembered that the same comparative law material may lead different judges to different conclusions.

Judges give such concepts an 'autonomous' meaning, the same for all countries, in order to avoid inequality of treatment and to secure an international standard, since national definitions may differ. National legislation provides one source for deciding the common core of the concept. This is the 'common European ground'. Thus the Strasbourg approach for example, includes 'autonomous concepts', 'evolutive interpretation' and 'margin of appreciation', thereby deriving legitimacy for a particular meaning on the basis of a comparison of national legislation.[26]

In the area of human rights, for instance, can comparativism in human rights cases create the basis for an a-historical development not specific to any one nation State's own history but universal history? When established understandings are challenged in the name of this universalism, what should judges do? It has been said that 'courts are talking to one another all over the world'[27] and that judges are carrying out a 'brisk international traffic in ideas about rights'.[28] Research shows that courts of some jurisdictions in constant conversation, while others are insular. So, apart from the matter of why this is the case, an additional matter arises as to what are the frontiers of judicial comparison. How far can courts go? It is possible to say that human rights case law is more likely to flourish if it is supported by the legitimacy of virtual unanimity amongst the judges. However, if selective cases are to be followed, what does the 'selection of suitable cases' mean? Are they simply the cases that support foregone conclusions?

---

[24] *Ibid.*
[25] *Ibid.*
[26] *Ibid.*
[27] Slaughter above note 8, at 99.
[28] M.A. Glendon, *Rights talk: The Impoverishment of Political Discourse* (New York, Free Press, 1991), at p. 158.

When the law is well established and satisfactory, judges may feel no need to look abroad.[29] Where there is a legislative framework in an area under consideration, judges may feel bound to follow the direction laid down for them by the legislature, even though they may feel that there are other, and possible better, answers elsewhere. Many laws deal with problems of a national past and therefore, the correspondence between these and universal rules and standards may not fully accord. In such cases, when the issue is regarded as purely domestic or related to the solution of a specific domestic problem, judges again allow 'particularism' to prevail.[30]

The issues of whether the judiciary is in fact competent to play such an active role and whether the judge is interpreting the law or making a political judgement, seem to be ignored in the analysis of judicial comparativism empirically.

Christopher McCrudden considers judicial comparativism through three related questions. The first is an empirical one: How far is comparativism used? The second is a jurisprudential question: What are the criteria for explaining why it is used? The final question posed is a normative one: Is this use legitimate?[31]

But the crucial question always remains: Should judges be autonomous actors; the 'tuners' of the law working together towards some universal truth? This leads us to the concept of 'the common enterprise'. However, is such a development necessary, feasible or desirable? What about peculiar socio-cultural needs of a country that might bar comparative activity? What of the question of elitism? What about legitimacy? This Variation would err on the side of caution.

[29] See N. Weiss, 'The Impact of the European Convention on Human Rights on German Jurisprudence' in Örücü (ed), above note 4, pp. 49-62..
[30] See Örücü, above note 23.
[31] See McCrudden, above note 22.

Enigma of Comparative Law

Chapter 9

COMPARATIVE LAW AND LAW REFORM BY 'TRANSPOSITION'

What is the role of comparative law and the comparative lawyer in law reform? That comparative law provides a pool of models to choose from when law reform is planned is shown to be one of the most important practical functions of comparative law. As legislatures look forward they also look sideways. The same is true of the courts. Is this a use of comparative law? Is this a proper role for comparative law? Comparative lawyers do not all agree on the answers.

If pools of models are used for choosing appropriate solutions. should legal systems only look at systems similar to their own or can systems different to their own be also of use?[1]

Borrowing, transposition and reciprocal influence is in the essence of law reform. Yet, there is a significant division of belief among comparative lawyers as to whether such borrowings work, whether movements are only one way rather than reciprocal and, most important, whether law reform should indeed be based on foreign models.

By giving examples of successful transplants, in which the recipient has used import, even of the different, for its own benefit through its own creative efforts without unduly disturbing the domestic socio-culture, comparative law can show legal transplanting or transposition as the best road towards law reform. Here we see that diversities can interlock and 'transpositions' do work for law reform. Paradoxically, by showing examples of unsuccessful transplants, notably from the colonial period, comparative law can also reveal the frequent failures and weaknesses of transplants in the past where it was used as a method of law reform and modernization. Here we see that diversities cannot interlock and 'transpositions' do not work for law reform.

There is a wide divide between comparative lawyers and the two Variations below inquire into this divide.

---

[1] Related to this is the question of whether, as a result of cross-border import/export of legal ideas, legal systems are converging. This is another area where a strong divide of belief exists. This will be dealt with in Chapter 11.

VARIATION I

Very little in law is original. What is original, is the selectivity in borrowing, the ensuing mix and the homogenization process in the courts, that is, successful 'tuning'. According to Rodolfo Sacco, 'Borrowing and imitation is... of central importance to understanding the course of legal change', and '... the birth of a rule or institution is a rarer phenomenon than its imitation'.[2] This observation accords with Alan Watson's view who says, 'the moving of a rule or a system of law from one country to another has now been shown to be the most fertile source of legal development since most changes in most systems are the result of borrowing'.[3] This view ties in with the 'family trees' approach developed in Chapter 10 below. Pier Guiseppe Monateri goes even further and says that almost every system has grown out of 'contamination' and the legal world itself is a world of 'contamination' rather than a world split into different families.[4]

Many issues of law reform are related to transfrontier mobility of law and the reality of reciprocal influence and cross-fertilization - issues such as European integration, the reconciliation of common law and civil law and of socialist and civil law, the future of developing legal systems in transition and the problems of the recipient of legal export. Influences are not just between legal systems but also between socio-cultures and legal systems, and legal culture and legal systems.

One of the richest areas of study for comparative law is reciprocal influence and transposition of law. Transposition tells us much about how law develops and allows us to understand cultural and legal navigation as well as the role of 'tuning' in legal development.

Most 'reciprocal influence' in Europe today is within the European Union, but transpositions from the Western legal traditions to the Central and East European legal systems may be of greater importance. The primary task for comparative law in Europe itself is in the area of 'new *ius commune*' studies in order to facilitate integration and make a case for the success of legal transpositions as the basis for convergence. Europe also seeks the support of comparative law studies in exporting legal ideas and institutions and aiding the law reform of others by providing a convincing display of competing models from a pool representing Western European legal systems. Elsewhere, other cross-fertilization is occurring, such as that between China and Hong Kong. The overall consequences are the birth of a 'new genre of *mixité*', the blurring of the demarcation lines between the generally accepted classifications of legal families, and the emergence of new clashes between legal cultures themselves, and legal cultures and socio-cultures.

---

[2] R. Sacco, 'Legal Formants: A Dynamic Approach to Comparative Law (Installment II of II)' (1991) 39 *American Journal of Comparative Law*, p. 394.

[3] A. Watson, 'Legal Transplants and Law Reform', (1976) 92 *Law Quarterly Review*, p. 94.

[4] P.G. Monateri, 'The "Weak" Law: Contaminations and Legal Culture', in *Italian National Reports to the XVI International Congress of Comparative Law*, Bristol 1998 (Milano, Giuffre editore, 1998), p. 107.

While States in transition, poised for law reform and modernization, look for models from other States, progress – assumed in our day to be in the direction of democracy, rule of law and a free market economy - surely demands that these models should be imported from systems which are socio-culturally and/or legal culturally diverse from their own. However, such models will only really help if properly transposed, and if in that transposition, local tuning takes place. Since even systems from the same legal tradition have problems when borrowing from each other, obviously, there are more serious problems when legal systems from diverse traditions such as the socialist, religious or traditional look towards civilian or common law systems. This must be of great concern for legal systems that have never been fully part of a single legal tradition. However these are not insurmountable obstacles. In addition, these issues are general problems of comparative law though they are of particular interest for legal and social systems at the receiving end of movements from the civilian and the common law models as they endeavour to re-shape their societies and their law.

Alan Watson's view is that one need not know much about the background of either the donor or the recipient, one just has to find an 'idea' suitable for importation, and similarity is not vital for successful tranplantability or fruitful cross-fertilization. Differences between national rules do not restrict the importation of them, though, legal cultural difference is the most frequent cause of mismatch. Alan Watson claims that even the misunderstood can be transplanted. Is it then the 'tuning' that is the vital spark? As the history of law is largely the history of legal transpositions, often from a number of sources - law being a constructive synthesis - harmony can only come through carefully tuned transpositions. Though divergence is fruitful and the differences between the similars are interesting, there is now a move towards 'bridging' and harmony.

The most common means of transposition is now by voluntary reception rather than by colonization and imposition as in the past, though, as stated above, imposed receptions are more prominent in some instances. It must be remembered that often, transnational spread of law does not happen owing to the force and the intrinsic or instrumental value of the ideas or institutions themselves, but depends on extrinsic factors such as the political, and the symbolic. The political reputation of the donor, the desire to belong to or harmonize with a particular group, or ease of access are all causal factors that may determine the pattern of transmigration of legal ideas, institutions and structures.[5]

Catherine Dupré ably demonstrates how the Hungarian Constitutional Court imported the concept of 'right to human dignity' from the German Constitutional Court to aid post-communist transition in Hungary, and 'tuned' it and 'fitted' it to its new environment, so demonstrating how a creative court acting as a 'prolific

[5] F. Schauer, 'The Politics and Incentives of Legal Transplantations' *Law and Development Paper* No: 2. CID Working Paper No: 44, April 2000, Center for International Development at Harvard University, http://www.cid.harvard.edu/cidwp/044.htm , p.2, 18.

importer of foreign law' can successfully anchor law reform to 'law importation'.[6] Catherine Dupré's choice is to analyze the developments from the 'importer's perspective', a very strong position for understanding the role of the 'tuners' and 'transposition' in law reform. The concept of human dignity was imported into Hungary from German Constitutional case law, and in spite of the developing differences of interpretation due to context, the new understanding is now reconciled with the still 'lingering' communist understanding of rights and enhances protection of the human right to dignity. Catherine Dupré argues that law importation for law reform 'can be likened to a modern form of natural law and that it overlaps with a justification drawn from the globalisation of law.'[7]

To those who object to the foreignness of importations, Rudolf Jhering gave the conclusive answer when he said: 'The reception of foreign legal institutions is not a matter of nationality, but of usefulness and need. No one bothers to fetch a thing from afar when he has one as good or better at home, but only a fool would refuse quinine just because it didn't grow in his back garden.'[8] The crucial question must be about how one takes the quinine. For example, within Europe, since there is no room for negotiation on the acceptance of a rule or solution, such as in putting into practice a European Union directive, the obstacle of *mentalité* must be as to the structure of what is accepted and the technique of how it is accepted, rather than as to what is accepted - that is the quinine.

It is important to assess the consequences of encounters within the European Union today as instances of 'reciprocal influence' or 'cross-fertilization', rather than only consider the contamination of common law by civilian input into European Community law.

'Law and economics' scholars opposed to top-down models of integration propose competition of legal systems in a free legal market as opposed to both codification, which is in effect unification, and direct harmonization. The main criteria here are the elements of choice and efficiency. Stressing the need for re-systematization of the law and the development of a European legal doctrine, some advocates of the 'new *ius commune*', also claim that this could be done without a final synthesis and unification,[9] this perhaps to appease the proponents of the following Variation.

It is a fact that law reform can most fruitfully take place by choices from a pool of models, a pool of competing legal solutions provided by comparative law research. With the aid of local and other comparative lawyers, a model can be transposed to fit the home soil. The fine 'tuning' and navigation is undertaken by the actors of the law of the recipient system

---

[6] See C. Dupré, *Importing the Law in Post-Communist Transitions* (Oxford, Hart Publishing, 2003).

[7] *Ibid.*, p. 12.

[8] Quoted by K. Zweigert and H. Kötz, *An Introduction to Comparative Law*, 3rd edn., trans. T. Weir, (Oxford, Clarendon Press, 1998), at p 17.

[9] M. Van Hoecke and F. Ost, 'Legal doctrine in crisis: towards a European legal science', (1998) 18 *Legal Studies*, 197, at pp. 211-215.

Terminology used in classical statements of such legal movements were transplant, imposition and reception. Today these have been supplemented by a colourful vocabulary highlighting nuances in individual instances of this mobility such as 'grafting', 'implantation', 're-potting' and 'cross-fertilization'. New notions and bases for analysis are being developed such as 'collective colonization', 'contaminants', 'legal irritants', 'layered-law', 'hyphenated-law' and 'competition of legal systems'. Images such as 'contamination', 'inoculation', 'irritation' and 'infiltration' may all be appropriate in describing present day encounters, and the terms 'reception', 'imposed reception' and 'concerted parallel development', the activities.

Although the term 'legal transplant' has been the usual one applied to all these import and export activities, I believe the term 'transposition', as used in music, is more appropriate. The term 'transposition' is more apt in instances of massive change based on competing models, in that the pitch is changed. In musical transposition, each note takes the same relative place in the scale of the new key as in the old, the 'transposition' being made to suit the particular instrument or the voice-range of the singer. So, this principle when adapted to law means that each legal institution or rule introduced is used in the system of the recipient, the transposition occurring to suit the particular socio-legal culture and needs of the recipient. In fact, there may be a number of 'transpositions', since no single model is necessarily used by any one recipient to reform its laws.[10] Even what is called 'reciprocal influence', a more acceptable term today among comparative lawyers, is actually a number of two-way transpositions.[11]

Thus, many developments of our day can be seen as instances of transposition, and the 'tuning' that takes place after transposition by the appropriate actors of the recipient is the key to success. If old models are abandoned with 'optimistic normativism' while new legal models are looked for,[12] a transplanted legal system not compatible with the culture in the receiving country, without the appropriate transposition and tuning, will create only 'virtual reality'.

In answer to the question, 'How do legal ideas, institutions and structures find their way from one location to another?', it has been aptly put that 'laws do not have wings'.[13] This alone highlights the importance of those who move the law and those who help in its internalization, and hence, the 'tuning'. The importance of the tuners in turn is strengthened by the fact that countries which adapt transplanted law have more effective legality, that is, they further develop their formal sources and in this

---

[10] A perfect example is the Turkish receptions of Swiss, German, Italian and French laws.

[11] E. Örücü, 'Law as Transposition', (2002) 51 *International and Comparative Law Quarterly*, 205-223.

[12] G. Ajani, La circulation de modèles juridiques dans le droit Post-Socialiste' *Revue internationalle de droit comparé* –4 (1994), 1087-1105 at p. 1087.

[13] Schauer, above note 5.

way build effective legal systems, and have effective economic development.[14] A 'voluntary transplant increases its own receptivity by making a significant adaptation of the foreign formal legal order to initial conditions, in particular to the pre-existing formal and informal legal order.'[15] Therefore 'the way in which the law is transplanted is a more important determinant ... than the supply of a particular family'.[16]

In historical terms, most 'tuning' was carried out by imposers or exporters of law. Such was the case when the British codified the common law for its introduction into the Indian Continent. This is not a very sensitive kind of tuning, since, it cannot consider the new pitch in its entirety, the tuner not being an active player of the new instrument. It is internal tuning that is required and the fine tuners should ordinarily be the domestic judges. However, for successful transposition, tuning is necessary at all levels, including legal education. Even old instruments have to be tuned to new problems. Such is the case in electronic commerce or Internet fraud. One could go further and say that every time a court distinguishes a case from a prior case, it is undertaking tuning and may be transposing a rule or principle from another area of law to solve the problem at hand.

When Nicholas Grief says that Community Law is exerting a passive influence on common law and is re-shaping the English legal order, for example, he suggests that one should assess this influence critically to determine whether it is a corrective or a 'contaminant'.[17] Nicholas Grief sees it rather as a 'habit forming factor' whereby a practice enters into judicial consciousness, judges appreciate its value as they employ it and then find other uses for it. This could be a 'healthy infusion'. The term 'infusion' indicates a more subtle, positive and penetrating infiltration than the term 'contaminant'. One could of course, regard common law itself as the 'contaminant' of Continental civil law, since some English common law concepts and institutions have already infiltrated the laws of the Member States of the European Union and European Community law itself. How one assesses the process is entirely related to one's stance in these matters, sending us back to the image of half a glass of water as either 'half-full' or 'half-empty'. In addition, in the plethora of activities and examples one can always choose illustrations to support one's own stance.

If one considers the term 'legal irritant' through the example of the concept of 'good faith' one can glean some useful indications for the phenomenon of 'transposition'. Gunther Tuebner says, 'Legal irritants cannot be domesticated. ...

---

[14] D. Berkowitz, K. Pistor and J-F. Richard, 'Economic Development, Legality, and the Transplant Effect', *Law and Development Paper* No 1, CID Working Paper No 39, March 2000, Center for International Development at Harvard University at http://www.cid.harvard.educidwp/039.pdf p.5.

[15] *Ibid.*, p. 11.

[16] *Ibid.*, p. 19.

[17] N. Grief, 'The Pervasive Influence of European Community Law in the United Kingdom', in T.G. Watkin (ed), *The Europeanisation of Law*, United Kingdom Comparative Law Series Vol: 18 (London, UKNCCL, 1998), p. 110.

Rather they will unleash an evolutionary dynamic in which the external rule's meaning will be reconstructed and the internal context will undergo fundamental change.'[18] Thus, 'good faith' will be reconstructed anew under British law, and its meaning will be transformed. Even if the transfer is formal and direct rather than through infiltration or seepage, according to Gunther Teubner, the rule 'may look the same but actually it has changed with its assimilation into the new network of legal distinctions.'[19] He also puts forward the argument that new divergences will appear as unintended consequences of the Europeanization of national legal orders. Going back to 'good faith', it follows that it will not be transplanted as it is, but irritate British law and create markedly different understandings.

The development of a concept, even in a specific historical and cultural 'constellation', determines its final shape. So even if the starting point is the same, divergences will occur. Gunther Teubner's guess is that in Britain, 'good faith', together with 'legitimate expectations', 'proportionality' and other 'continental noise', 'will trigger deep, long-term changes from highly formal rule focused decision making in contract law toward a more discretionary principle-based judicial reasoning'.[20] It is not a question of whether the British contract doctrine will reject or integrate good faith. Rather, the question is, once reconstructed anew under British law, 'what kind of transformation of meaning will the term undergo, how will its role differ?'[21] Accordingly, a transfer will always be 'confronted with the idiosyncrasies of the new legal culture' and face resistance external to the law, that is, a variety of social expectations of highly diverse social environments. In this Variation, this would be a desirable outcome and therefore Gunther Teubner's view supports the claim that law is a process of transposition.

'Irritant' can also accord with Alan Watson's beliefs in the power of reception on the imagination and the fact that, 'borrowing is often creative'.[22] A 'healthy infusion' is a more positive and penetrating infiltration. Is it correct then to say that the implantation into British soil of a 'living law', fed and fertilized by the specific nutrients and conditions of a foreign soil, cannot take root or grow new roots? In fact, imports into Britain have survived even with their roots cut, thanks to the 'rooting powder' provided by British 'gardeners'. Neither is it true to say that the British soil is infertile and continental concepts and institutions cannot grow and blossom in it. Why expect 'repulsion' and not 'interaction'? The metaphor 'irritant', taken in a positive sense, could actually bring about the desired result. This is what is needed for successful transposition. This is harmony rather than harmonization. To converge does not mean to attempt to create sameness, but to accept diversity. Only when diversity is accepted can there be 'healthy infusion'. Only then can the

[18] G. Teubner, 'Legal Irritants: Good Faith in British Law or How Unifying Law Ends Up in New Divergencies', (1998) 61 *Modern Law Review*, 11, at p. 17.
[19] *Ibid.*, p. 19.
[20] *Ibid.*, p. 21.
[21] *Ibid.*, p. 12.
[22] A. Watson, 'Aspects of reception of law' (1996) 44 *American Journal of Comparative Law*, p. 345.

transferred norms become 'internalized' and work. Interlocking diversities lead to convergence. If legal relationships are seen within a framework of 'reciprocal influences', that is, as a series of cross currents rather than as one way flows of 'contaminants' or 'irritants', then on the 'reverse seepage' the legal world at large may benefit and be enhanced by divergences created in different soils. Such movements, especially when they take place under some type of 'imposed reception', as is the case under European Directives, cannot be rejected outright. The already existing plants can blossom under this 'irritation' and so produce workable new sub-categories that intermingle - as for example between the Member States of the European Union – and interlock to enrich the market of legal systems. The fact that the identity is fundamentally altered is of no matter if the new species is expertly and creatively handled.[23] Good fruit does indeed grow on grafted plants! It is the 'rooting powder' provided by the gardeners that often makes the difference!

Harmony is, after all, the possibility of communication and conversation. In value-neutral terms both 'contaminant' and 'irritant' can be used to explain what is taking place between the legal systems and the social systems of the Member States of the European Union, be they common law, civil law or 'mixed' jurisdictions. Contamination can give rise to an irritation. An 'irritant' can also serve as a 'corrective' by inspiring a new development to correct for example, a 'historical accident'. Seen in this light, all 'reciprocal influences' can be 'healthy infusions'. This infusion may comprise the most efficient solutions presented by the competing legal systems. If all legal systems engaged in this enterprise were to serve as contaminants and produce irritants for each other, law would only be enriched and social cultures benefit. This needs proactive systems and 'good faith'!

As already stated, borrowing and imitation are of central importance in understanding the course of legal change since innovation in law is very little.[24] However, in order to be useful in 'law reform' projects, the present transplant theory does need some conceptual refinement. Yet, this theory can be challenged without going down the path followed by Pierre Legrand that 'legal transplants are impossible'.[25] For example, though Gunther Teubner does not support Alan Watson, he claims that the conceptual refinement needed would 'allow us to analyse institutional transfer in terms different from the simple alternative of context versus autonomy', as law's contemporary ties to society change.[26] Concluding that transplantation is hazardous, John Allison points to the need for considering 'both

---

[23] Transplant theorists should not mind 'distortions' and 'irritants'. In fact they should welcome them, since, if these did not happen, the transplanted institutions would not be 'transposed' and therefore not 'fit'. Borrowing is and should remain a 'selective activity'.

[24] Sacco, above note 2, p. 395.

[25] P. Legrand, 'The Impossibility of Legal Transplants' (1998) 4 *Maastricht Journal of European and Comparative Law*, p. 111.

[26] Teubner, above note 18, p. 17.

the present and proposed contexts of a transplant'.[27] I have developed the concepts of 'transposition' and 'tuning'.[28]

Though ill-considered transplants are dangerous, the use of transplants is inevitable, especially in 'extraordinary' places looking for law reform.[29] We have already noted that a colourful vocabulary highlighting nuances such as 'grafting', 'implantation', 're-potting' and 'cross-fertilization' have supplemented the terminology used in classical statements of transfrontier mobility of legal institutions. 'Collective colonization', 'multi-culturalism', 'legal pluralism', 'contaminants', 'legal irritants', 'layered-law', 'hyphenated-law' and 'competing legal systems' are concepts being developed as the new bases for analysis. It is generally recognized that influences are not only between legal systems but also between socio-cultures and legal systems; and legal culture and legal systems are the contemporary bases for analysis. The more 'extraordinary' the place the more important comparative law research becomes.

Many systems are in transition and are considering, and are inspired by, systems socio-culturally or legal culturally different from their own. Legal rules seem to be able to settle in various places. As systems in transition search the pool of competing models available in Western Europe and America with the purpose of re-designing and modernizing their legal, economic and social systems, a whole new world of research possibilities is opening up. In order to put their feet in the doors of these new markets, the models are competing hard to sell their legal products to those striving to reform their legal systems. Comparative lawyers will be system-watching and studying the success or failure of this new world of *mixité*. And, most important, they will be called upon to provide an understanding of this major law reform tool by supplying models and will be pressed to create blue prints for the importer of models. In this way, comparative lawyers can assist systems in transition in structured change. As comparative lawyers examine the way in which legal institutions are connected, disconnected, and transposed, they will extend their subject beyond the traditional areas, both geographic and substantive. Depending on the metaphors employed, 'good tuners' with 'good instruments', 'good gardeners' with 'good fertilizers and soil', and 'good cooks' with 'good ingredients' are needed.

Transposition is a reality. Legal change and social change are reciprocally linked. Modernization and law reform can fruitfully take place through transposition and systems can converge even though differences remain since harmony is the intended outcome rather than sameness which is neither desirable nor feasible.

---

27 J.W.F. Allison, *A Continental Distinction in the Common Law: A Historical and Comparative Perspective on English Public Law* (Oxford, Clarendon Press, 1996), p. 236.

28 Örücü, above note 11.

29 See Chapter 10, Section 3.

VARIATION II

Comparative law should ignore the usefulness of the so-called 'transposition'. Legal cultures are specific to individual general cultures and therefore such study is fruitless, misleading and even dangerous. Comparative law is of no use in law reform or modernization of domestic law since law can only develop from within itself and modernization must be achieved internally. Some might call this insular modernization. However, it accords with views such as the 'spirit of the people', it has a nationalist bent and is the product of the view that only differences matter.

If legal systems must look at each other for law reform purposes, then the best systems likely to benefit from each others' experience are those closely related historically, legally, politically, socio-culturally and economically. Even legal systems in transition should not look for models which are socio-culturally and/or legal culturally diverse from their own. History tells us that when the encounter is between legal systems of diverse socio- and/or legal-cultures, the diverse elements co-exist separately in the resultant legal system. They may intermingle if, for example, there is no socio-cultural diversity but only a legal-cultural diversity, so that in time the diverse elements blend, or one becomes the dominant element owing to political factors. Or again, from the beginning one of the elements may be systematically erased by the use of power in its various forms. The outcome however, is often not a matter of choice but a matter of chance, or necessity. For example, the East European systems poised to join the European Union must somehow prepare themselves for change in 'the desired direction', this desire being not necessarily that of the bottom but of the top, an elite or of outside forces. These systems have little choice in the matter since the relationships are negotiated between parties of unequal power and influence.

Although ours is not a period of imposition and we no longer see colonial relationships, it is also not a time of voluntary reception. Ours is a time of imposed reception, a seemingly voluntary activity of import but under circumstances in which exporters hold all the cards. In the market, the exporter packages his model as the most efficient; the one to be preferred over others. True, it is a buyers' market in the sense that there is a large number of models to choose from, but it is in fact a sellers' market since, for the importers, there is no real freedom to go down any particular route, as market forces tie them to certain of the models only. Most Western academics do try to avoid the failures of the 'law and development movement' of the 1960s and 1970s, yet transplantation remains a dangerous task. Of course, today, imposed reception is not taking place only on the Central and East European States. The Continental civilian systems also are trying to impose civilian type Codes on English common law within the context of European integration. The understanding of codification as top-down centralist legalism has led 'law and economics' scholars to propose the competition of legal systems in a free legal market rather than codification, which is in effect unification, and direct harmonization. The elements of choice and efficiency remain the principal criteria. Some advocates of the 'new *ius commune*', stress the need for re-systematization of the law and the development of a European legal doctrine, and claim that this can be done without necessarily final synthesis and unification.[30]

Past receptions from Civil law and Roman law into English law have been called 'sporadic receptions' or 'injections', with 'civil law based reasoning filtering into common law'[31] so enriching English law. However, any rules based on Roman law or the later *ius commune* 'were immediately cut off from their roots', and 'assimilated into the specifically English framework, and given life outside their original context'. The resultant new law 'did not remain in dialogue with the old law from which it derived'; and 'once the borrowings are cut off from their roots they cease to be part of the same culture'.[32] Therefore, the influences were not systematic and the solutions did not remain the same upon import. 'Once the continental ideas were imported into England, the umbilical cord was cut.'[33] Today, European Law is also regarded by many as an 'irritant', or a 'contaminant' of the common law.[34]

Gunther Teubner uses the concept of 'legal irritants' in relation to the transplanting of the continental principle of bona fide (good faith) directly into the body of British contract law by the European Consumer Protection Directive 1994. A 'legal irritant' is defined by that author as an alternative to 'legal transplant', in that 'when a foreign rule is imposed on a domestic culture ... something else is happening. It is not transplanted into another organism, rather it works as a fundamental irritation which triggers a whole series of new and unexpected events ... it irritates law's "binding arrangements".'[35] Documents such as the Principles of European Contract Law, and the UNIDROIT Principles of International Commercial Contracts extend good faith into other fields. 'The infecting virus had already found inroads into the common law of contracts, especially in the United States ...'.[36] Gunther Teubner also claims that this phenomenon should not be assessed in terms of legal transplantation and not as a matter of repulsion and rejection or interaction and integration - that is, the question of whether 'good faith' once transplanted will 'be rejected by an immune reaction of the *corpus iuris britannium'* or will take and interact productively 'with other elements in the legal organism'.[37] Many scholars are concerned with this development.

Although Variation I may regard the terms 'contaminant', 'seepage' and 'irritant' as very welcome additions to the vocabulary for analysis of transposition and reciprocal influence, surely in their everyday usage these are not neutral words.

---

[30] Van Hoecke and Ost, above note 9, pp. 211-215.

[31] D.J. Ibbetson, 'A Reply to Professor Zimmermann', in T.G. Watkin (ed) *The Europeanisation of Law*, United Kingdom Comparative Law Series No: 18 (London, UKNCCL, 1998), 224 at p. 228.

[32] *Ibid.*, p. 229.

[33] X. Lewis, Europeanisationof the common law', in R. Jagtenberg, E. Örücü and A. de Roo (eds.) *Tranfrontier Mobility of Law* (The Hague, Kluwer Law International, 1995), 47 at p. 50.

[34] Grief, above note 17.

[35] Teubner, above note 18, p. 12.

[36] *Ibid.*, p. 11.

[37] *Ibid.*, p. 12.

For example, anyone hearing the word 'contaminant' in this context does not regard it as good that transpositions occur and foreign concepts and structures seep into domestic legal soil. They irritate. They contaminate. They do not purify or correct. One would surely be advised to stand clear of any source of contamination. 'Contaminant' has the connotation of spoiling the thing it touches, be it only by leaving a mark. The word 'seepage' is not neutral either. Neither is the word 'irritant' neutral. 'Legal irritant' implies the 'production of new and unexpected reactions' -side effects of the first 'contamination'.

In most transmigrations of law the process is in one direction. Therefore the argument that 'transplants' should be avoided but 'cross-fertilization' is desirable is not convincing, as even in what is called 'cross-fertilization' there is at least one, if not a number of transpositions. Moreover, 'pollenization' may be a better word to use, since 'fertilization' services only the soil, but 'pollenization' the product. Soil cannot be cross-fertilized, only products may be effected by such processes. It may be that structure can be transposed with less difficulty than content and values, these being on the whole untransferable. The difficulty lies not in the transposition of techniques and forms but of values and substance. Here, as transposition takes place distortion will inevitably occur in order to adjust to the existing traditions. These in turn will seriously effect how the structure and substance work. How the transposed become 'irritants', what these irritants produce as 'anti-bodies', and the health of the systems in transition of today, will be assessed in this new century.

There are even stronger reasons why we should reject the use of foreign institutions and concepts in law reform, which in effect, aim to transform mental constructs. This point can be demonstrated with an example; an example borrowed from Brian Tamanaha where he illustrates the futility of such efforts by looking at Micronesia:

> Micronesian law was transplanted in its entirety from the United States; even the majority of the legal actors, like myself, were American expatriates. Their customs and values could hardly have been more different from the legal system and its norms. ... they has a thriving caste system, yet the law prohibited discrimination; their culture was consensual in orientation, but the law was based upon the adversary model; their understanding of criminal offences required a response by the community itself (literally), but the state insisted that it has a monopoly on the application of force, and any direct community reaction is illegal vigilantism; property and ownership was a complex mixture of possession rights, use rights, consultation over use and possession, and community ownership simultaneous with chief ownership, whereas the property and mortgage laws were based upon common law notions of fee simple, life estate, and remainders; their political system was democratic, but for most elections candidates stood unopposed because the approval of traditional leaders was de facto required of anyone who wished to win; the law was written in English legal language, while many people had a rudimentary command of English, and others could not speak it at all ...; courts

decisions were filled with legal arguments based upon U.S. common law and constitutional analysis which simply had no parallel or grounding in Micronesian society; many people were ignorant of the law, and feared or avoided it; state law was a marginal force in the maintenance of social order. The law in Micronesia was like an alien presence in their midst, mostly irrelevant, taking care of tasks related primarily to the operation of the government, occasionally intruding on their lives in various unwelcome ways.[38]

[38] B. Tamanaha, *A General Jurisprudence of Law and Society* (New York, Oxford University Press, 2001), pp. xi-xii. William Twining reviews this book and cites this example in this recent review article, 'A Post-Westphalian Conception of Law' 37 *Law and Society Review* (2003), 199-258.

Enigma of Comparative Law

Chapter 10

CADENZA AND EXTEMPORIZATION

In this Cadenza I seize the possibility to improvise or extemporize, that is 'play without fixed notation'! This indeterminancy gives me the freedom to go into a number of unrelated topics with no Variations; to provide and consider some issues I regard as important and bring my personal concerns into this work. I deal with five such issues: those arising out of complex cases for comparative lawyers, those arising when law meets culture and culture meets law, those related to the deconstruction of classifications of legal systems, those to do with the fact that all systems are continually mixing and finally those related to the limits of comparativism.

1. COMPLEX CASES FOR COMPARATIVE LAWYERS

Regardless of whether the reader is following the first or the second Variations, she will in the course of her work come across complex cases the understanding, interpretation and the re-presentation of which will rely on factors that are not at all obvious from the reading of the material alone. She will have to go away and re-think how she can develop insight and adopt a 'deep level comparative law' approach.[1] She must be able to grasp the underlying assumptions, conceptions and values as well as the economic, social or cultural contexts surrounding the facts and the handling of the law. She must grapple with the cultural matrix into which law is embedded. She must develop an awareness and understanding of the multiple layers of systems and the significance of what is observed. Having comprehended, she must then re-present it for her audience with an explanation and provide an insightful comparison.

The following examples[2] are from a legal system which I call 'hyphenated' and regard as a legal system of an 'extraordinary' place.[3] This legal system is that of

---

[1] I borrow this phrase from Mark Van Hoecke. See M. Van Hoecke, 'Deep Level Comparative law' in M. Van Hoecke (ed), *Epistemology and Methodology of Comparative Law* (Oxford, Hart Publishing, 2004) and M. van Hoecke and M. Warrington, 'Legal Cultures and Legal Paradigms: Towards a New Model for Comparative Law', (1998) 47 *International and Comparative Law Quarterly*, 495.

[2] Unless otherwise noted, translations from Turkish are mine.

Turkey, apparently totally civilian, most of her laws being derivatives of Swiss, Italian, German and French laws. The State is secular. 98% of her people are Moslem and of complex ethnicity. It has been said that Turks have not only been European for 600 years, but that they are Asian, Caucasian and Middle Eastern and European all at the same time.[4] A candidate to the European Union since 1999, Turkey is an 80 year old Republic based on a particular vision. This vision, partly entrenched in the Turkish Constitution itself and now often called 'westernization and contemporanization', refers to nationalism, secularism, republicanism, populism, statism and reformation – the six arrows of Kemalism, Kemal Atatürk being the founder of the Turkish Republic. This bundle is tied to the historical and political baggage carried by Turkey. Turkish courts first and foremost consider the legal framework and then, acting as the tuners of the law, the political and social realities in Turkey.

What kind of comparative lawyer do we need to understand, interpret and re-present the following complex cases? [5]

Before we consider these cases however, one thing must be kept in mind and that is, that all Turkish legislation in use in these cases is based on civilian legislation; the Civil Code on the Swiss, the Commercial Code on the German, the Penal Code on the Italian and the uncodified administrative law on the French. Therefore, a comparative lawyer may be inclined to make comparisons with legal systems which provided the 'source-laws' before attempting to look beyond. However, would this strategy be as straightforward as it appears? The first challenge may be that of 'true comprehension'. The second challenge may be in deciding on which approach to take. Her predisposition may be to regard 'law as rules', 'law as fact', 'law as function', 'law as interpretation' or 'law as culture'. Would any one of these approaches first help her comprehension and then any comparative study she wishes to pursue?

1.1 My first example is divorce for irretrievable breakdown and divorce by mutual consent. This will be looked at in comparative perspective. The institution of divorce, under whatever name, and these grounds for divorce, are to be found in most Western legal systems today. Therefore comparability issues may not arise.

---

[3] For a number of meanings attributed to the terminology, see E. Örücü, 'Comparatists and extraordinary places' Chapter 13 in P. Legrand and R. Munday (eds), *Comparative Legal Studies: Traditions and Transitions* (Cambridge, Cambridge University Press, 2003, pp. 467-489.

[4] See E. Örücü, 'Turkey Facing the European Union – Old and New Harmonies' (2000) 25 *European Law Review*, 57-71.

[5] In fact, two further cases, one dealing with the removal of the name of a trainee lawyer from the bar list because she refused to appear without her head cover, and another, related to 'honour killing' or 'customary murder', considered below under Section 2 on 'Law meets culture and culture meets law', could be read in conjunction with the cases dealt with here. I have used most of the cases covered in this Section as examples in a number of my published work elsewhere.

Yet how these grounds are understood is totally different in different legal systems. Comparative research into this legal institution shows us that similar institutions interpreted in different ways because of social differences can only make sense if compared in a deep local context. Let us look at Sweden and Denmark for example, where the fact that one spouse applies for divorce is sufficient proof of breakdown of marriage and no further judicial discretion is involved in granting divorce. In such societies the fundamental assumption is that if the marriage had not broken down a spouse would not have applied to court for a divorce. The context behind this assumption must be analyzed. In Scotland, the only ground for divorce is 'irretrievable breakdown', but in order to prove that the marriage has irretrievably broken down, the traditional grounds have to be shown to have caused this breakdown. These include adultery, behaviour, desertion and two year's separation, that is non-cohabitation, where both consent to divorce, or five year's separation where there is no mutual consent. This picture reflects a gradual development over the years from the time of the Reformation when divorce could be obtained only for adultery. The ground of desertion was introduced in 1573 and these two remained the only grounds until 1938. Then the grounds of cruelty, incurable insanity, sodomy and bestiality were added to the list. Only in 1976 did it become possible to obtain a divorce without proof of matrimonial fault on the part of one of the spouses. Nevertheless this objective ground of irretrievable breakdown still has to be established on the basis of one of the five fact situations mentioned above. Most divorces are obtained today by mutual consent after a period of non-cohabitation. This current position can be assessed as the product of continuing reform over the years and reflects the slowly changing social climate. A deeper understanding is again called for to appreciate the difference between Sweden, Denmark and Scotland.

Looking at Turkey, where Section 134 of the Civil Code, amended in 1988 to introduce divorce by mutual consent, and where divorce is obtainable for irretrievable breakdown,[6] we see certain conditions that must be fulfilled: the marriage must have lasted for at least a year, the judge must hear both parties himself, be convinced that they are expressing their wills freely, and endorse as acceptable the arrangements made by the parties for the financial consequences of the divorce and the children. The only objective fact is the duration of marriage. The rest is left to the discretion of the judge. So, the most interesting aspect for a comparative lawyer is the interpretation of these conditions by Turkish judges.

When divorce by mutual consent was first introduced, it was in an attempt to limit the discretion of the judge, in that the court no longer had to weigh the circumstances and decide whether life in common had become intolerable. Yet, the High Court of Appeal (*Yargıtay*) is extremely cautious and holds a narrow view in the application of Section 134 (now 166). Thus, though the Court finds presumption of irretrievable breakdown when the spouses petition together or when one has accepted the lawsuit of the other, and though the judge has no discretion and need

[6] Since 2002, the new number of this Section is 166.

not gather evidence as to the breakdown, the Court believes that divorces apparently based upon mutual consent may not be so, and that women who are often the weaker partners in Turkish marriages, may be forced by their husbands to accept divorce under threat of, for example, their children being taken away from them. Therefore, the *Yargıtay* judges try to ensure that the conditions of Section 134 are strictly met. There are important reasons for this. Most Turkish women from rural areas wear scarves which obscure their faces and hide their identity. There has been anecdotal evidence that husbands, who have in their possession all the documents for the family such as birth certificates and passports, have taken their mistresses to court to pose as their wives. The mistresses have declared that they consent to divorce, while the wives at home had no idea that there was a divorce suit in progress in court! Thus the judge feels that he must hear the two parties 'separately and independently' when he can ask the woman in question to uncover her hair, and then form his conviction on the issues of identity and free consent.

The Second Section of the High Court observed in one case that, 'divorce by mutual consent is a new possibility. It is not part of established tradition and therefore great care must be taken to see that justice is done.' The Court went on to say that the judge must take an active part in this, since the 'parties in their haste to end their relationship may be rash and "one spouse may give up all her rights" or "be under pressure or be deceived".' According to this judgement, the judge is not bound by the facts as presented by the parties, but must directly investigate and determine the truth.[7] This is the general trend in interpretation and indicates an attempt on the part of the courts to ensure that women are not adversely affected. So although the policy behind this ground for divorce is to make divorce easier to obtain and reduce the pre-eminence of fault, in operation all is not what it seems.

These conditions are regarded as so important that in divorces obtained abroad, the High Court refrains from recognizing a foreign divorce decree if the foreign judge has not ensured the existence of these conditions and not adhered to the conditions the Turkish judge expects him to. Usually this arises upon an appeal by the *Yargıtay* Public Prosecutor of the Republic to the High Court after a lower court has recognized such a foreign judgement. Foreign judges, mostly Dutch, French, German or Swiss, would refuse to include in their judgement a statement such as: 'I have met both parties, seen them separately and am convinced that they are expressing their consent freely and approve of their financial and other arrangements', even if this requirement were brought to their attention by a comparative lawyer, since their own law has no such requirements. The Turkish Public Prosecutor is particularly sensitive in this area and raises such issues using his power of *ex officio* objection. One of the unfortunate results of this approach is that it leads to 'limping marriages': divorced abroad, married at home! Nevertheless, here we see the High Court acting as the protector of women and children. This also is an indication that the *Yargıtay* takes into consideration the realities of Turkish

[7] 6979/8890; November 2, 1989.

society rather than European comity or the religious feelings of Moslems which expect that divorce should be easy for men.

A comparative lawyer following the first Variations of the sub-themes in this work would regard the Turkish practice as normal and discuss the issue in the explanation of the differences she has to interpret in order to gain a deep understanding. A comparative lawyer following the second set of Variations however, would regard it as absurd that the Turkish judge cannot see that Dutch or German grounds of mutual consent and irretrievable breakdown are functionally equivalent to the Turkish grounds of mutual consent and irretrievable breakdown. For her, there would be no need even to seek for functional equivalence since all these systems rely on the same ground. Her main concern would be to secure a recognizable pattern and if she could not, she would conclude that only comparables should be compared and that Turkish law in action is 'beyond compare'.

1.2 To illustrate how the same name of an institution can indicate different content and different function, it might be worthwhile to observe another example where common semantic reference undermines the delicate balances struck for social reasons, and where concepts and conceptions may differ. Let us look at 'adoption' as seen in Turkey and Scotland, two legal systems that do not belong together according to traditionally accepted classification. In neither system is adoption a part of the indigenous law; it is a historical addendum through historical accident. Her findings would show the comparative lawyer that in Turkey between 1926, when this institution was introduced through the Civil Code adapted from the Swiss Code, and 2002 when the Civil Code was amended, only persons over the age of 35 with no natural children of their own could adopt, that the age difference between the adopter and the adoptee should be at least 18 years, that if the adoptee was married the consent of his/her spouse was also required, that the adoptee did not lose his/her relationship with the natural family and therefore could inherit from them as well as from the adopter who in turn could not inherit from the adoptee. Statistics would show the comparative lawyer that the adopters were normally around 50 years of age and the adoptees, 30.

Whereas, in Scotland, the subject is regulated quite differently. In the 1930's when adoption legislation was first introduced, adoption may have been seen as a remedy for childless couples but also as a way of making provision for a child whose parents had died or as a means of legitimation. Through the adoption process, the legal relationship between that child and her birth parents is severed and a new relationship between the child and the adoptive parents, now the substitute parents, is created. Adoption is still operative after the child reaches 16, whereas parental rights would have ceased by then. Either a single person or a couple can adopt if they are over 21, unless one applicant is already the natural parent of the child. An adoption order can only be made for a child under 18; the child must be at least 19 weeks old and must have lived with the applicant adoptive parents for the preceding 13 weeks. A married young person cannot be adopted. Statistics show the comparative lawyer that most adoptions are by step-parents.

The explanation for the difference between the two systems lies in a number of tentative hypotheses: In Turkey the aim of adoption, as in Roman law, is to provide care for the elderly and continuation of family name and family business for those who have no children. As a result, it is not for the interest of the child that adoption is available and therefore the adoption of adults is more appropriate for the stated aim. There must be an age difference of 18 to avoid sexual relationship between the two adults. Arising from the underlying aim of adoption as stated, only childless persons can adopt; the ban on adoption by those with children of their own is also to protect the inheritance rights of the blood relations.

The comparative law researcher must examine such explanations in order to understand why the legal systems have produced the institutions they have, although these explanations are not legal ones. The texts show the differences but do not offer explanations.

This area was thoroughly reconsidered in Turkey in the amended Civil Code of 2002. The adoption of minors has now been introduced into Turkish law, and spouses with children can now adopt. The conditions for such adoptions are: the care for and education of the minor for one year and the interest of the minor, while not adversely effecting the rights of other children of the adopter. An unmarried person can now adopt if 30 years of age or over. This is also new. With some exceptions, spouses can only adopt jointly. The conditions for spouses are, to have been married for at least five years, and to be at least 30 years of age. If married for two years or more, with the condition of being 30 years old or more, one spouse can adopt the child of the other - another new development. The adoptee must be 18 years younger than the adopter. Adoption can take place from six weeks after birth. A discerning minor must consent to the adoption and, in addition, the natural parents of the minor must give their consent.

These amendments to Turkish law also can be understood and explained. Three explanations can be offered: They are made to bring Turkish family law into line with the laws of the Member States of the European Union in keeping with Turkey's desire to join the Union; to give additional protection to children, Turkey having ratified the Convention on the Rights of the Child. And maybe the most important reason is the force of the facts of life, that is, the desire to legalize a widespread phenomenon: as in fact aunts and uncles usually treat the orphans of their siblings as their own children to give them economic security and in keeping with traditional family solidarity, a highly valued commodity in Turkish society.

Turkish family law derives from the Swiss where the institution of adoption was also directly influenced by Roman Law. The Swiss law has been amended with the times. The fact that the Turkish law was not amended until now however, indicates that the needs of Turkish society coincided with the needs of Roman society, and the modern approach which regards the institution of adoption from the point of view of the 'best interest of the child' was not regarded as a social value to be legislated on until 2002 when other forces came into play.

A comparative lawyer looking at adoption can only develop deep understanding and genuine interpretation by appreciating the moral, social and cultural contexts which shape the legal institutions. The comparative lawyer following the first Variations may very well be interested in delving deeper into this subject, whereas the one following the second Variations could come to the conclusion that Turkish law lagged behind until 2002 and the situation before that date should not be compared with that in Scotland.

1.3. The following example may be used to show how a legal system accommodates culture and religion, and how answers to social needs are produced within the framework of the over arching legal system of the nation State in a legally monolithic but culturally pluralistic society.

In Turkey, neither the legal framework nor the *Yargıtay* accepts that couples living out of wedlock can be regarded as having a relationship to be protected by law. This approach is taken seriously and is vigorously pursued, as Turkey is a secular State with a predominantly Moslem population. The vision on which the Republic was founded in 1924 regarded Islam as a hindrance to progress and the official framework reflects this vision. Therefore decisions of courts in this area are of the utmost importance for couples living together without an official secular marriage.

A marriage is concluded upon the oral response of the two parties in the presence of a marriage registrar whereupon a marriage certificate is given. A religious ceremony cannot take place without this certificate and such a ceremony has no legal consequence for the validity of the marriage. This well-established principle has been restated in the Civil Code of 2002 to emphasize the importance of the secular nature of marriage in Turkey.

To underline the secular nature of Turkish family law, a recently published decision of the Turkish Constitutional Court (*Anayasa Mahkemesi*), giving an authoritative answer to any question related to the acceptability of religious union as an alternative to civil marriage, must be mentioned here.[8] In a case, Section 237/4 of the Penal Code, criminalizing religious unions entered into without prior civil marriage and imposing a prison sentence of from two to six months on both the man and the woman,[9] was challenged as violating several Articles of the Constitution: Article 2 (the principle of secularism), Article 10 (equality), Article 12 (the character and the scope of fundamental rights and freedoms) and Article 24 (freedom to conduct religious services and ceremonies). The Constitutional Court, referring to Article 13 of the Constitution on the limitation of rights and freedoms, stated that Section 237 had been inserted into the Penal Code in 1936 to give support to civil marriage, that without this Section, polygamous marriages would become possible and that, though such marriages have no legal consequence, they pose a threat to the concept of family, such unions being detrimental to the social order. The Court stated that if couples enter illegal unions, women cannot use rights arising from marriage, any children are illegitimate and lose their inheritance rights; civil

[8] 1999/27; 1999/42; 24.11.1999; *Resmi Gazete* (Official Gazette) No: 24743; May 2, 2002.

[9] Persons performing such religious ceremonies without seeing the official certificate of marriage are subject to the same sanction.

marriage must be strengthened to protect the family and the rights of women and children.

The Court went on to say that there is no violation of the principle of equality here between couples living together with no marriage of any kind and couples in a religious union alone, since the first group do not wish their relationships to be regarded as marriage. Equality before the law does not mean that everyone must be treated alike, differentiation based on Article 13 is not unconstitutional. The Court saw the Civil Code as a fundamental building block in the bridge to a contemporary and secular legal system for the Turkish Republic, and said that civil marriage, being in the essence of that block, is specifically protected by Article 174 of the Constitution. The most important function of secularism is to keep law and religion separate. As a religious ceremony subsequent to the civil marriage is not banned, there is no violation of secularism or any fundamental right. The Court decided unanimously that Section 237/4 did not violate the Constitution. So we see that the secular nature of the Turkish family law has been firmly underlined.

However, in a different area, that of compensation for death in work-related accidents, the *Yargıtay* has extended the right to compensation to the unmarried cohabiting woman (*nikahsız eş*) though on a different basis from the married woman. In one case[10] the childless surviving partner of an *imam nikahı* union[11] asked for material and moral compensation arising from the death of her partner in a work-related accident. The lower court agreed but the insurance company objected. The *Yargıtay*, regarding her chance of getting re-married to be much higher than that of a married woman, decided on a percentage of compensation lower to that which would be the due of the legally married wife. Again, in a later case[12] the insured died in a work-related accident. His partner, who was this time referred to by the *Yargıtay* as the 'cohabiting partner', was 18 and had a child, and according to the *Yargıtay* had more than a 35% chance of getting re-married, 35% being the judicially accepted percentage for an official widow. The Court was of the opinion that her age, social status, position and family ties meant that she was not in the same position as a married woman who could expect to live in the family home for an indefinite period and be supported throughout her life. The Court therefore decided that the compensation arising out of Section 43 of the Code of Obligations should be reduced in keeping with fairness and equity. This time there was a telling dissenting opinion to this decision by a female judge, critical of the differentiation drawn between the two women. The dissenting judge stated that:

> here "cohabiting couple" (*nikahsız eş*) refers to a traditional Anatolian relationship where couples have the intention of living together as husband and wife, with close family ties and children. Therefore, the presence or absence of official wedlock should not be the criterion for treating the two women differently. The Social Security Council only gives a pension to the officially

[10] 96/1606; 96/1661; 21.3.1996, 22 *Yargıtay Kararları Dergisi* 1996, 1291.

[11] This is a consentual religious marriage performed by the *imam*.

[12] 97/3331; 97/4819; 8.7.1997 23 *Yargıtay Kararları Dergisi* 1997, 1785.

married wife, and this for life. This should be the only extra gain for the married woman. The Anatolian woman is already oppressed and faces the risk of remaining officially unmarried owing to tradition, and therefore her position should not be even further weakened when facing the law. This situation would only lead to mistrust of justice. The present circumstance is the outcome of the social structure, and social order cannot be changed by making a weak person even weaker. She also should be given equal compensation.[13]

A comparative lawyer looking at 'cohabiting couples' and into the payment of compensation for death in work-related accidents may have problems in appreciating both the position of the Constitutional Court, the High Court and the dissenting opinion above, unless she can read the normative story in its deep cultural context. If she were following the second Variations she might have to re-think her position if she wanted to embark on a comparative project having now discovered the Turkish position.

1.4. A recent decision of the Turkish Constitutional Court (*Anayasa Mahkemesi*) illustrates the general attitude to equality between the spouses as balanced against the importance attached to the traditional conception of family and the place of women in it. This case was published fully four years after it was delivered and shows how the Constitutional Court finds it somewhat difficult to write reasoned opinions in the field of equality of the sexes. In this case a claim of unconstitutionality was brought to the attention of the Court related to the then Section 153 (now 187) of the Civil Code. The case arose when a married woman wanted to use her maiden surname only, rather then together with her husband's surname as allowed by the challenged Section since its amendment in 1997.[14] This Section, and its new version, Section 187 applicable today, states that a woman acquires the surname of her husband upon marriage, but can add her maiden surname before that of her husband's either upon her written request to the marriage registrar at the time of marriage or subsequently to the administration for personal status. The challenge was that Section 153 violated Articles 10, 12 and 17 of the Constitution related to equality, fundamental rights and freedoms, personality rights and rights to development of personality.

The Constitutional Court saw no such violation and, referring to long established traditions, talked about the family and the place of women in it. First of all, the Court stated that 'soyadı'[15] - a concept that entered Turkish society by legislation in 1934 - is sometimes referred to as 'family name', to differentiate one family from another. It is the common element of the family members and is passed down from one generation to the next. The second observation of the Court was that when a husband changes his surname by judicial decision, the wife's surname

[13] *Ibid.*, at p. 1786.
[14] 15 November 2002, *Resmi Gazete* (Official Gazette): 24937; 1997/61; 1998/59; 29/9/1998.
[15] The word 'soyadı', used for 'surname', is made up of two words, 'soy' and 'ad'. The word 'soy' means race and lineage, and 'ad', name.

changes automatically, but that a married woman has no such personal right to change her surname. The Court also observed that the provision that the wife carries her husband's surname arises from 'necessity born out of social realty' and from 'legislative institutionalization of long rooted tradition'. The Court referred to 'Family Law doctrine' which points to differences between the sexes and to the necessity of the protection of women, of strengthening family ties, of ensuring harmony in the marriage union and of the necessity of avoiding a two-headed family structure. According to the Court, by the passage of the family name acquired at birth from generation to generation, family union is preserved, and public policy, public interest and other necessities demand that this name should be the name of the husband. This cannot be seen as discrimination based on sex. In conclusion the Court opined that these were legitimate reasons for the preference of the husband's surname as the 'family name' and that there was no violation of the principle of equality.

Three judges wrote the dissenting opinion. They saw a violation of all the three Articles of the Constitution and the Convention on the Elimination of All Forms of Discrimination Against Women, which Turkey ratified in 1985. They claimed that the Constitution should be read in the light of International Conventions and contemporary developments. This is rarely done, the Constitutional Court preferring to solve Turkish domestic problems in the light of the official framework provided by the Turkish Constitution and Turkish mores. The dissenting judges made reference to the German family law amendments of 1976 and a 1991 decision of the German Constitutional Court both of which indicated that spouses should be able to choose either of their surnames. Stating that to carry the surname acquired at birth might be extremely important for the development of a spouse's personality and identity, the three judges advocated annulment, but to no avail.

The fact that the amended Civil Code - which specifically reiterates in all of its Sections the equality of the sexes - has retained the same approach in its new Section 187 as in the old Section 153, indicates that neither the legislator nor the courts see a strong social demand to justify approaching the problem in a different way. It might even be conjectured that were there such a demand it would have been ignored by the legislator in the name of the conservative family values prevailing in society. Traditional values of family and lineage for men override claims to modernity. Considering that the possibility afforded by Section 153 has hardly ever been used, a departure from the principle of equality of the sexes, specifically introduced into the Constitution in 2001 by a phrase in Article 41 in addition to the existing 'equality before the law' principle in Article 10, seems justified. Now, added to the phrase, 'The family is the foundation of Turkish society', is the phrase 'and is based on the equality between the spouses'.

Conversely, Turkish public policy considerations prohibit a man from taking his wife's family name. Thus a husband is not allowed to use the right acknowledged to a wife of having her name added to that of the husband's. This prohibition effects even Turkish husbands of foreign wives in cases where the spouses live abroad and the law of that country allows the spouses to choose which family name they wish to be known by. This principle was pronounced in a case concerning a Turkish man who married a Swiss woman in Switzerland and acquired her surname, a possibility under Swiss law where, as in Germany, spouses can choose either of the surnames. He requested his family name to be changed in his Turkish personal status register. The lower court was of the opinion that such a correction was admissible since it had a 'foreign connecting factor'. The High Court (*Yargıtay*) was quick to point out that the lower court's qualification was erroneous as there was no possibility in this case to resort to conflict of laws rules, and declared the Swiss rule to be totally repugnant to Turkish public policy.[16] It can be speculated that this creates another problem of equality of the sexes which could have been corrected in the amended version of Section 153, but was not considered, since in male dominated Turkish society few men would want to choose their wife's surname.

It is apparent that the comparative lawyer must consider many complex issues related to visions and traditions, traditions and transitions, interpretation, human rights and margins of appreciation, interaction of law and culture, modernity and traditionality and the relationship between transposed law and 'source-law'. But for these considerations, a comparison of Turkish law to, say, German law – or even the Swiss 'source-law' - would be problematic.

1.5. When we approach law as the outcome of complex competitive relationships between different layers of law, or between different layers of systems, legal, sociological, cultural or religious, what do we see in Turkey? We know that legal evolution has come about through a succession of imports from abroad. We also know that the Turkish legislature is intent on keeping the legal and the social fabric under centralised control. So, are the various systems successfully interlocking? 'Law and other such systems exist in a world where they are each the background or environment of each other'.[17] Is this so for Turkey, or have the law and other systems 'become increasingly isolated from each other as they become more and more self-referential'?[18] Although the Turkish legal system is self-referential in the sense that it is only concerned with the law as envisaged by the formal legal system and does not enrich itself beyond necessity by discourse with other systems in society, it is at the same time not self-referential, in the sense that it still consults the 'source-laws', thus taking advantage of and strengthening its 'hyphenated' nature.

Some examples of interlocking between the social and the legal culture have already been observed above. Below, two very different and remarkable cases will serve to illustrate the 'hyphenated' nature of the experience.

---

16 *Yargıtay*, 18.HD; 1997/288;1997/1496;25/2/1997; 23 *Yargıtay Kararları Dergisi*, 1997, 1118.

17 Z. Bankowski, E. Christodoulidis, 'The European Union as an Essentially Contested Project', (1998) 4 *European Law Journal*, 341 at p. 348.

18 *Ibid.*

1.5.1. Here is such a case worthy of deeper analysis. Section 475 of the Turkish Penal Code, adapted from the Italian, creates and punishes the offence of the abandonment of a child or persons incapable of taking care of themselves. However it accepts as a mitigating circumstance the abandonment of an illegitimate child less than five days old in order to protect the '*namus*' (honour and good name) - a most significant concept in Turkey - of the perpetrator, the wife, the mother, the daughter, the grand-daughter or the sister. The sentence to be administered can be reduced by up to one third. In the course of one case, there was a challenge of unconstitutionality to this Section, the claim being that the reasons for reduction of length of sentence violated feelings of justice and equity, threatened the life of an illegitimate child, and encouraged the commission of a crime with less stigma. To treat the abandonment and even abandonment to death of an illegitimate child could not be regarded as less onerous than of the abandonment of a legitimate child.

The Constitutional Court held that, in the case of a child born out of wedlock abandoned within five days of birth, the reason for the reduction in the sentence is the negative effect this birth has on the mother and the family and consequently the saving of the honour. The Court went on to say that in contemporary criminal law the personality of the perpetrator is considered to be of importance, not the act but the actor is given priority and that in reality, considering an act as an offence is related to the pressure of society, and that today a person's fright, astonishment, anger, excitement, sadness, aggressiveness and such psychological states must be regarded as important factors. The Court decided that Section 475 should be assessed in this light. According to the Court, the purpose here is not to create inequality between legitimate and illegitimate children but to create justice in sentencing, to give the most appropriate sentence to the perpetrators of the act. The Court held that, although Section 138 of the Penal Code states that judges decide eventually according to their conscience, this is within the framework of legislation and the Constitution; Article 17 of the Constitution guarantees everyone the right to life, the protection and development of their personality and is not applicable to Section 475. Thus there was no unconstitutionality.[19]

There were two dissenting opinions, both of interest. One said that people live in society; its pressure is always felt; and crime is committed related to the effect of society on the individual and these effects are the societal causes of crime. It went on to say that the responsibility of the individual may be lessened by this and responsibility should be shared between the individual and society. It said that it is true that in Turkish society to 'save honour and good name', accepted as a traditional and social value, is very important and it is this that had been taken into consideration in Section 475; the same mitigating circumstances were to be found in Section 592 of the 1930 Italian Penal Code, the 'source-law'; however, that Section was abrogated in 1981. The dissenting opinion went on to say that the draft Turkish Code covered this matter in Section 146 but only as regards the mother, by allowing the reduction of the sentence by one sixth, and the reasoning of the draft stated that

[19] 1997/60; 1998/53; 22.9.1998 (*Resmi Gazete.*: 23770; 29/9/1999). Challenge of Section 475 of the Penal Code as violating Articles 10, 17, 41 and 138 of the Constitution.

sanctity of life was one of the most important values of our times and that only the mother could be given such leniency considering the biological and psychological condition in which she finds herself in such cases. In addition, Section 453, which related to the murder of such a child and also allowed mitigating circumstances, was amended in 1991 and the reduction of sentence was now only applicable to the mother. Therefore, Section 475 should also be regarded in this light. This dissenting opinion supported the majority decision only so far as related to the mother but regarded the extension of this leniency to others as 'unreasonable, unjust and incomprehensible' and suggested annulment of the Section for those other than the mother as being a violation of Articles 2 (rule of law), 38 (crime and punishment) and 41 (protection of the family) of the Constitution.

The second dissenting opinion approached the subject from the point of view of equality in the right to life between the legitimate and the illegitimate child. It said that Section 474 covered abandonment of a legitimate child and considered abandonment of one's own child as an aggravating circumstance, and that the legitimate and the illegitimate child should be protected equally by law. Otherwise this was a violation of Article 10 of the Constitution on equality. The opinion stated that whatever the reason, this difference meant that the right to life of an illegitimate child is less worthy of protection than that of a legitimate one, which understanding violated also Article 17 of the Constitution, since the right to life is inviolable and no other value or tradition can justify its violation. The dissenting opinion went on to say that if Turkey wanted to reach the contemporary levels of civilization, as expressed both in the Preface and Article 174 of the Constitution, then there was no place for such a provision in Turkish law.

How is the comparative lawyer to explain why these received values are so inherent to the receiving system and so cut off from their roots over the past number of years that though changes may have taken place in the 'source-law', in the domestic law they are regarded as an integral part of indigenous societal values and local culture? What kind of a 'fit' was there between the foreign institution and the local culture that the law could not be changed in Turkey, though the 'source-law' changed? Could it be that the values of the Catholic Italy of that time 'fitted' the religious and traditional attitudes of the Moslem society in Turkey? Can the comparative lawyer resolve this paradox by using the traditional tools? How is she to assess this transplant here and what can she as a comparative lawyer say on this issue?

1.5.2. The second illustration is a decision of the *Yargitay* reached in 1979.[20] The case revolved around the sexual involvement of an under-age village boy with a neighbour's cow. The owner of the cow, rather than suing for bestiality under the Penal Code, sued for damages from the father of the boy. He claimed that his cow could not be sold or its meat and milk consumed, since, according to religious sources that he cited, it had become untouchable. The case was dismissed by the

---

[20] 79/1644; 79/14383; 21.12.1979.

lower court for lack of legal grounds as religious law is not a recognized source of Turkish law. The owner appealed. The *Yargıtay* rendered its decision making use of Section 1 of the Civil Code[21] - a saviour in cases where there is no solution to be found in the Code - and overturned the decision of the lower court saying that although religious rules or sentiments could not of course form the basis of any claim, if the complainant could prove by expert evidence that there were local religious or moral beliefs or customs from time immemorial to the effect that the meat and the milk of such an animal could not be consumed, then the animal would be considered to have lost its market value, in which case, by the application of the '*noxal*' rule of Roman law, the cow should be given to the father of the boy and the claimant should be given the market value of the cow by the father. The High Court regarded this case as a case of economic loss.[22]

The formula is a fine example of how the *Yargıtay* avoids openly facing religious issues and yet resolves disputes within the formal legal system, and also how the 'layers' of systems form 'hyphenated' interlocking.

The same issue was dealt with in a more recent case where the lower court decided that the pursuer had no case as there was no 'medical objection' to the utilization of the meat and the milk of such an animal. The *Yargıtay*, overturning the decision of the lower court, declared that when there is no codal provision applicable to a matter then, according to Section 1 of the Civil Code, tradition and custom are to be resorted to. The Court opined that since the facts were not in dispute in this case, tradition and custom were to be investigated in line with the claim, and if custom, tradition, religious and moral beliefs and conceptions were in line with the claim, then the existence of damages could not be questioned, in which case the pursuer should be asked whether he wished to surrender the animal to the defendant in return for the market price, and if not, then reasonable compensation would be decided upon.[23]

What is a comparative lawyer to do facing these cases? Can she compare them with other economic loss cases from other jurisdictions? Where is the functionally equivalent institution to be found? What should her target audience be told and what would they appreciate?

1.6. Here is yet another case[24] which shows how the *Yargıtay* protects custom and still stays within the framework of the formal law, accepting, though be it with distaste, the power of the legislature but not of the executive, to interfere with

[21] This is a most important Section, replicating the Swiss one, which provides the scope for developing of the law to meet the needs of the society and reads thus: 'The law must be applied in all cases which come within the letter and the spirit of its provisions. If no relevant provision can be found in the statute, the judge must decide in accordance with the customary law and , in its absence, in accordance with the rule which he would lay down, were he the legislator. In so doing, he must be guided by accepted legal doctrine and case law'.
[22] *Ibid.*, at p. 103.
[23] 98/2632; 98/3249; 24/3/1998; 24 *Yargıtay Kararları Dergisi,* 1998 at p. 834.
[24] 86/2-584; 86/299; 26.5.1986.

custom. A local administration banned the payment of a dowry. The Court defined dowry as 'an amount of money paid by the family of the groom to the family of the bride to cover necessary expenses, a tradition and custom established over the centuries; it is a fact to be accepted, whether good or bad'. The Court then held that a person refusing to conform to such an administrative act cannot be regarded as an offender and be punished. The *Yargıtay* regards the question to be whether a local administration could erase a tradition and issue such an order and thereby convert a tradition into an offence. The Court said that if the giving and receiving of dowry is against public policy or is seen as being conducive to committing the offence of abduction, only the legislature can ban it. Further, the Court was also of the opinion that these, being matters of education not of law, should not be regulated even by the legislature.

Here, in assessing such a case either as interpreter or even as raconteur, the comparative lawyer must re-think her conception of law in appraising the relationship between law and custom in a monolithic legal system where the formal legal system is trying to erase localism. What should she consider? How can she truly understand the position of the High Court and then re-present it?

1.7. The last type of case is related to economic analysis. Turkish private law is frequently referred to in courts as Swiss-Turkish Law (*İsviçre-Türk Hukuku*), especially when the courts want to refer back to developments in Switzerland from whence the Civil Code comes. One of the areas in which reference to Swiss-Turkish law is often made today is in developing the principle of 'adapting contractual terms to changing circumstances' in private law contracts. Faced with extreme inflation and economic difficulties, the *Yargıtay* has developed and has now adopted the view that judges should have the power to interfere in contractual relationships and apply *clausula rebus sic standibus* or the '*imprévision*' theory - normally used in administrative contracts - to private law contracts also. There have been many such cases since 1988. The Court typically pronounces that if the balance between the parties is disrupted owing to extraordinary circumstances and this becomes unbearable for one of the parties, then to bind them to the contractual obligations is not in keeping with notions of fairness, justice and objective good faith. Burdens brought about by unforeseeable circumstances must be shared by all, even though borne in different proportions. This view is especially applicable to long-term contracts.

One of the most interesting of these cases deals with the concepts of '*force majeure*', 'the collapse of the foundation of contract', 'the intervention of the judge into the contract', and 'adaptation of the contract to changing circumstances' in 'real property sales contracts by instalments' with payments to be made in DM. In this case[25] the *Yargıtay* discussed the above concepts extensively, reiterated the basis of contract law, that is, *pacta sund servanda* and the freedom of contract, and then

[25] 95/145;95/3339; 6.4.1995; 21 *Yargıtay Kararları Dergisi* 1995, 911.

pointed to the necessity of equality between the parties. The defendant claimed that the sales contract had been signed by free will, that the principle of *pacta sund servanda* should apply, that the adaptation of the contract is only possible for continuous and long term contracts, that sales contracts come to an end upon performance, and that, since the title was registered, this contract had come to an end. The Court indicated that *pacta sund servanda* is limited by other principles of private law and that the most important of these applies when the equilibrium of interests is distorted by supervening events, whereupon the courts have to resort to *clausula rebus sic standibus* and adapt the contract to the changed circumstances, even when there is an 'adaptation clause' in the contract itself indicating a different path of action that may lead to an extreme imbalance between the obligations. To justify its position the Court referred to legal writers and views on the doctrine of 'contractual adaptation'.

The *Yargıtay* stated that an insistence on performance may lead to a violation of Section 2/2 of the Code, and be regarded as bad faith. When gaps appear in the contract as a result of the change, these must be filled by the courts through interpretation in keeping with the aim of the contract and the intention of the parties. To fill these gaps, the judge can use powers arising from Section 1/1, thus creating rules for the facts before him; although this possibility is rarely used. The *Yargıtay* in this case referred to a Swiss Federal Court decision, pointing out that this principle could also apply to contracts which would have future results and contracts which do not terminate on performance. So in this case the instalments could be regarded as links in a chain covering a period of 72 months, so that the contract does not terminate by a single performance. Using expert evidence, the *Yargıtay* then declared that the courts must determine the normal value the foreign currency would have reached, taking into consideration the country's economic conditions, accept this value in the interest of the seller, then determine the 'shock' increase in the value of foreign currency as a result of extraordinary levels of inflation, calculate the difference between the two values and measure this against the gain in value of the real property in the same period. Here justification was sought from the 'source-law' and the Federal Court of that source when Sections 1, 2 and 4 of the Turkish Civil Code were put into action and developments in the principle of adaptation were suggested.[26]

In a more recent case,[27] the rules of 'contractual adaptation' and thereby the '*imprévision*' theory were applied to bank credits indexed to foreign currency. The *Yargıtay* again reiterated that freedom of contract and *pacta sund servanda* are the bases of Turkish contract law. However, it went on to say that, as the State has the Constitutional duty to protect the consumer and ensure the orderly and sound functioning of the money, credit, capital, goods and services market and that, in cases where bank credits indexed to foreign currency are obtained, if the price of the goods bought with foreign currency does not change in the foreign market, the bank must adapt the debt taking economic conditions into consideration. Again, Section 4

[26] The Federal Court accepted the doctrine of 'adaptation' on 4.5.1952, at p. 916.

[27] 1996/11-762; 97/77; 12.2.1997; 23 *Yargıtay Kararları Dergisi* 1997, 679.

of the Civil Code was called in to help, and the *Yargıtay*, after referring to works by eight Turkish scholars and three previous *Yargıtay* decisions of 1988, 1992 and 1995, said that in order to alleviate injustice Section 2/2 is normally used in Swiss-Turkish law and that here, Sections 1, 2 and 4 should be employed as supported by doctrine and judicial practice. The Court stated that when the foundation of the contract collapses, the 'source-law' allows the judge to intervene; however, 'adaptation' is a supplementary aid and expert evidence must be used.

A comparative lawyer here must be aware of the economic and social circumstances and implications, the market conditions surrounding these cases, the specific time period and the Turkish and world economic cycles existing when the decisions were delivered. Without an understanding of these contexts it would be difficult to deal with these cases properly.

2. LAW MEETS CULTURE AND CULTURE MEETS LAW

The existence of cultural pluralism and multiple cultural normative orders, the thickening of globalization, the convergence of legal cultures within the context of the western tradition, and the importance of emerging 'universal human rights' cannot be ignored. However, some related questions do not have easy answers. Should cultural pluralism be translated into legal pluralism, and, if so, how? What is the importance of localism, and the relationship of localized globalism to globalized localism? Is there a value to 'diversity in harmony', and, if so, what is it? Should universal standards always trump local exceptions, and if so, with what justification?[28]

We in the west still live in the era of the nation State. The nation State is the source of law and the legitimizer of sources of law. This monolithic, centralized, territorial and top-down model of law may or may not allow competing sources of law to exist. When it does not, the State is regarded as intolerant, undemocratic, even despotic and self-referential. When it does however, this can only be a weak version of legal pluralism where the top-down source of law is receptive to other sources, and therefore is regarded as tolerant, democratic, multi-cultural and as reflecting an open society. In the western tradition, the stronger version of legal pluralism, in which levels of law of equal value co-exist in the same territorial or social space as overlapping orders, is not favoured. The centralist forces of the unitary State do not live comfortably with so many rivals.

Cultural pluralism becomes a serious issue when it appears to be a threat to the territorial integrity of the State and when the nationalism inherent in culture groups is perceived to clash with the dominant values or culture of the unitary State. If cultural pluralism were to be accepted as the rule and reflected as strong legal pluralism, then the modern unitary nation State would be an exception to the rule. If,

[28] I have dealt with some of these issues elsewhere. See E. Örücü, 'Waar wet en cultuur elkaar ontmoeten: Cultureel pluralisme, juridisch pluralisme en pragmatisme, in 5 02 *Culturele diversiteit*, Justitiele verkenningen, Ministerie van Justitie WODC (Deventer, Kluwer, 2002).

however, the unitary State were to be the rule, then cultural pluralism could not be reflected in the legal system as legal pluralism, and legal pluralism would become the exception to the rule. Yet as William Twining says: 'Processes of globalisation stir up old nationalisms, exacerbate cultural conflict, and encourage post-modern scepticism about the universality of values and ideas.'[29]

Normative pluralism, of which legal pluralism is a species, refers to a social fact - the co-existence of different bodies of norms within the same social space. State legal pluralism indicates a single national legal system but plural laws, the State recognising different rules for specific categories of people such as was the case in colonial times. However, the equating of legal pluralism with State law is challenged today as being a narrow and weak version of legal pluralism in which State centralism prevails.[30] It has been suggested that the idea of 'semi-autonomous social fields'[31] should be accepted and substituted for 'closed societies', paving the way for the recognition of local, national, transnational, regional and global orders all applying to the same situation. But, at this point we encounter the complex problem of 'interlegality'. Lawyers in the western world will have to face up to the dilemma of interlegality as multi-culturalism, regional orders, and the laws of indigenous peoples, displaced peoples and refugees challenge even the weak version of legal pluralism let alone 'state centralism' and the monist approach. The move suggests a progression from monism to relativism and finally to pluralism.[32] How can mainstream comparative law cope with this?

The prior and crucial question must be whether the unitary nation State can cope with this progression. Can it accept the fact that all societies have diversity of legal orders - of which 'official' state law is but one – which overlap, interact and often conflict? If not, can official State law legislate for diversity, and if so, how? Can it opt for prohibition or assimilation, or for integration by protection of diversity as part of respect for cultural pluralism? Or, should it opt for the preservation and support of diversity and pluralization by enacting legislation to promote, maintain and develop diverse cultures and localisms in compliance with Conventions such as those for Minority Rights and the Protection of the Rights of all Migrant Workers and Members of their Families? Should value pluralism be dealt with through monistic, relativistic or pluralistic approaches?

---

[29] W. Twining, 'Comparative Law and Legal Theory: The Country and Western Tradition' in I.D. Edge (ed) *Comparative Law in Global Perspective* (New York, Transnational Publishers, 2000), p. 21.

[30] W. Twining, *Globalisation and Legal Theory* (London, Butterworths, 2000), p. 83 and *ibid.*

[31] S. Moore, *Law as Process* (London, Routledge, 1978) and S. Moore, *Social Facts and Fabrications* (Cambridge, Cambridge University Press, 1986)

[32] Isaiah Berlin defines monism as 'only one set of values is true, all others are false', relativism as 'my values are mine, yours are yours, and if we clash, too bad, neither of us can claim to be right' and sees pluralism as bringing respect, toleration and liberal consequences. See Isaiah Berlin on Pluralism, <http://www.cs.utexas.edu.users/vt/notes/berlin.html>. Also in (1998) XLV *New York Review of Books*

The pragmatic option would be to let cultural rules apply to personal or societal relationships alone, with an overarching general system of law reflecting the values of the dominant group, since in a modern unitary nation State there is limited scope for normative pluralism. Yet how is the paradox of cultural pluralism and State law to be resolved? Should 'cultural and localized exceptionalism' and 'cultural relativism' trump 'globalizing uniformity' and universal standards, or can 'globalizing uniformity' always trump 'cultural exceptionalism'? Will a social system based on pluralistic values but guided by a monolithic centralist official law inevitably sink towards crisis? Would this outcome be because a monolithic legal system guides and restricts? What about the impact of universal forces operating inside that society which are reflected in the overarching formal legal system? Is it possible to talk of 'global ethics' as a panacea, or, is it possible that a second legal system enjoying the support of the people or even an 'infrastructure of mutually interdependent interests',[33] would begin to operate parallel to the normatively designed formal legal system? In such situations what is the comparative lawyer to compare and how is she to carry out her comparisons alone?

Though there is a close connection between law and the society in which it operates, many believe that law is social engineering and instrumental in finding practical adjustments, and reconciling conflicting and overlapping interests. It has often been asked whether a legal system can and should be used to change society, or whether the law is 'merely' a codification of social practices. As always, both questions can be answered in the positive or the negative depending on ideological pre-dispositions and choice of illustrations.

It is true that legal development is a rational or natural response to existing social, economic, political, geographical and religious circumstances. Yet, often legal rules are made to produce desired affects, law being regarded as a creative tool, a harmonizing agent with economic, social and cultural implications. Among the wider issues involved and the pertinent philosophical underpinnings are the interaction theory, social engineering, socio-political factors, the relationship between law and morality, universal standards versus local exceptionalism and globalization versus localization.

We know that law can indeed 'lead' and so change society, rather than adjust a legal system to social change, it can 'follow' social change and reflect multi-cultures, or, it can 'tinker' and seek to keep an existing system operating while making adjustments to improve efficiency. Thus, law can be a reactor to social change or its initiator. These two approaches to law have important consequences for the dilemma surrounding the relationship of legal change to social change; law versus culture.

In works looking at the legal cultures of Europe, or considering the European Union as a multi-level system of governance, or talking of Europe's legal pluralism, the nation States are the units of inquiry. However, sub-cultural differences which

[33] See A. Podgorecki, 'Social Systems and Legal Systems – Criteria for Classification', in A. Podgorecki, C.J.Whelan and D. Khosla (eds), *Legal Systems and Social Systems* (London, Croom Helm, 1985), p. 6.

rely on social class, level of education, gender, age, religion, ideology or ethnicity are more difficult to determine. For example, the effects of the level of education on legal values seem to indicate that the more educated support the rule of law, favour individual liberty and believe in the neutrality of law.[34] The fact that differences in legal values are rooted primarily in social class is even more indicative of this: 'It is those who profit from the existing socio-economic structuring of society who tend to view law as a beneficent institution'.[35]

Is it true that only trans-cultural and morally neutral rules can work successfully in a multi-cultural society? Can a modern legal system be independent of social and cultural systems? If transplanted or transposed law can create change in a different socio-culture, can domestic law not do the same? Maybe when problems arise stemming from the interruption of habitual behaviour, the natural fear of unfamiliar institutions would diminish and disappear over time with sensitive handling of the cultural layers, rather than by changing the law to meet the demands of those layers. Convergence in Europe is the acceptance of shared values. In an atmosphere of building a 'common legal culture' and unity in Europe and facing cultural pluralism, should the emphasis be on the demand side of the bottom or the supply side of the top?

Portraying the concept of legal pluralism as an 'effective attack on the common sense of orthodox jurisprudence' by rejecting the 'oneness of state law as law or universality of western law',[36] Masaji Chiba offers a model of official law as one always interacting with unofficial law and legal postulates, and never existing in isolation. The State and its laws, society and its normative orders, and religion and world views, are expected to work together to achieve a balanced and sustainable legal order. Yet, legal centralism reflects the ambition of the modern nation State for total legal control which, by definition, rejects polycentric law. However, John Griffith says, 'legal pluralism is the fact, legal centralism is a myth, an ideal, a claim, an illusion.'[37] But, in the western world, the plural arrangement in a centralist legal system - that is the weaker version of legal pluralism - is the best on offer today. Catering for normative multiplicity - including normative dualism - without an overarching unitary normative framework is not possible in a unitary nation State.

Moral pluralism, value pluralism, ethnic pluralism and cultural pluralism are part of social reality and have to be not only tolerated but preserved. Yet the translation of these into legal pluralism carries with it fundamental problems and may not be in the best interests of progress towards the target of achieving a

---

[34] J.L. Gibbon and G.A. Caldeira 'The Legal Cultures of Europe', (1996) 30 *Law and Society Review*, 1996), 55

[35] *Ibid.*, pp. 70-73

[36] M. Chiba, (ed.), *Asian indigenous law in interaction with received law*, (London, KPI, 1986), M. Chiba, *Legal Pluralism: Towards a general theory through Japanese legal culture* (Tokyo, Tokai University Press, 1989).

[37] J. Griffiths, 'What is legal pluralism?' (1986) 24 *Journal of Legal Pluralism and Unofficial Law*, pp. 1-56

universal, comprehensive, internally reconcilable moral or political monism. The fit will not always be comfortable or trouble free.

Sociology may see pluralism as society being constructed of multiple interacting groups, and anthropology as ethnic units co-existing in dynamic relation to one another, but, how does law regard it? Volkmar Gessner says, 'The nation state originally was built on the idea of an identifiable culture and – in spite of the growing importance of sub-cultural influence – it can in most cases still be treated as a cultural unit'.[38] So what happens when law meets diverse cultures?[39] How can the modern unitary nation State recognize diversity and cultural and religious norms developing independently of officially endorsed rules? Can the state control the entirety of the law? Can cultural and social aspects of legal principles accept outside control?

We know that even in monolithic legal systems, aspects of culture can be dealt with by navigating between the rules of the formal system. However, some aspects of culture do clash with established 'visions' upheld by the formal legal system and the norms of so-called 'modernity'. To what extent should a national legal system accept cultural and religious norms which have developed outside the official rules? Are there choices? Let us look at a few examples from Turkey, Britain and Canada.

In Turkey, an example of a centralist monolithic system in which the cultures and customs met by the law are indigenous, but where by choice, desire and design, the legal system was created by borrowing from the Swiss, French, German and Italian legal systems, the legal system is secular and yet 98% of the people are Moslem. While the legal system aspires to erase certain cultures and create a new culture, thereby assimilating people into a chosen image,[40] when law meets cultures which it does not cater for, the judges, that is, the 'tuners' of the law, either try to eradicate or ignore them in keeping with the vision of the legislator, or accommodate them within the official framework.[41] We have already seen some relevant examples of this in the above Section under 'Complex Cases'.

My first case concerns the issue of a claim based on an Islamic source unacceptable to the official law. In 1993 the name of a female trainee lawyer was removed from the Bar list because she came to court wearing a head cover and refused to remove it. According to the lower administrative court, as she was only a trainee and not a fully qualified lawyer, and the matter solely a moral question, there

---

[38] V. Gessner. 'Global Legal Integration and Legal Cultures', (1994) 7 *Ratio Juris,* p. 132

[39] There is no one definition of what is culture. Culture can be defined as a composite of desires. Culture refers not only to literary, musical and artistic traditions but also to the social code of a minority group, which extends to religion, ethics, traditions and even matters such as dress and food. See L. Prott, 'Cultural Rights as People's Rights' in J. Crawford (ed) *The Rights of Peoples* (Oxford, Clarendon Press, 1988), 91-101, at p. 94.

[40] Western, secular, contemporary, following Ataturk nationalism, democratic state, human rights, the rule of law and the social state.

[41] See for analysis and examples, E. Örücü, 'Turkey: Change Under Pressure', in E. Örücü, E. Atwooll and S. Coyle (eds.) *Studies in Legal Systems: Mixed and Mixing,* (London, Kluwer Law International, 1996).

was no violation of the respect due to the legal profession, though the regulations of the profession do impose certain conditions including a dress code. The Turkish *Conseil d'Etat* (*Danıştay*) however, saw no difference between a lawyer and a trainee lawyer and regarded the issue as not being one of 'the right to religious freedom', saying: 'The behaviour of the trainee is contrary to the principles of a laic State governed by the rule of law, is incompatible with the profession of a lawyer and is an obstacle to her becoming and acting as a lawyer.'[42] The *Danıştay* also found the assessment of the lower court in regarding the matter solely as 'a moral question in a narrow sense', to be an incorrect understanding of the law.

The second case, already looked at in the previous Section, is one in which the High Court (*Yargıtay*) pronounced the banning by a local administration of the payment of dowry, to be illegal, saying that an administration could not ban a tradition or convert it into an offence. The court opined that this centuries old tradition is a fact which can only be banned by the legislator if regarded as being against public policy, and not by a local authority, and moreover, this should be a matter of education and not of law.[43]

My third Turkish case shows how when courts find it difficult to disregard localism and apply universalism, they use their discretion to appease that localism. This often happens when courts have to deal with cases of 'honour killing' or 'customary murder' among people from the Eastern provinces where the honour of a woman is in the control of the male members of her family. The courts always consider this problem within the framework of the Penal Code as received from the Italian legal system, but use the Code's facilities to reduce the penalty. Thus in a typical case, the killing - usually committed by the youngest brother - is regarded as murder. The standard sentence is 24 years imprisonment. Yet as illustrated by the twenty-four court decisions examined between 1988 and 1999, the accused benefits from Section 52 of the Penal Code, which says that if a crime is committed under aggravating circumstances and provocation, this can be taken into account in sentencing as also can the demeanour of the accused. 'This coupled with the age of the boy or young man charged with the crime, often serves to decrease the sentence to virtually nothing',[44] usually a reduction to five years imprisonment. Also there are frequent amnesties in Turkey! Academic debate in Turkey however, regards such killings as the ultimate violation of women's human rights.[45]

Britain is another example of a centralist monolithic system. Here the cultures and customs met by the law are not indigenous but mainly the result of colonial heritage. In Britain, where in the past the legal system reflected the values of a

---

[42] 92/3342, 93/2611, 5 July 1993.

[43] 86/2-564, 299; 26.5.1986

[44] C. Arın, 'Femicide in the Name of Honor in Turkey', (2001) 7 *Violence Against Women*, p. 824.

[45] An additional question arises when these people move to countries such as the Netherlands, Germany or Britain where we also witness differences in the handling of the problem.

largely homogeneous society,[46] the courts regard diverse culture as custom, even when Islamic, and therefore law for those who adhere to Islam. The legal system reacts to these new challenges in a basically defensive manner.[47] The official legal system is assimilationist and therefore 'other' culturally-rooted values are ignored, dismissed or even penalized rather than being officially recognized. However, in the courts, some groups such as the Sikhs get more favourable treatment than others. The legal treatment of diverse cultures in Britain seems to be inconsistent. Case law shows that there are certain unacceptable customs such as forced and child marriage (regarded as violating rights), female circumcision (described as cruel, inhuman or degrading treatment), polygamy (violating sexual equality in the formation of marriage), the religious manner (*halal*) of slaughtering animals publicly (public policy), *talaq* (no judicial hearing and fair trial) and the wearing of beards and turbans (violating certain requirements of employment law).[48]

One area of continued concern both in England and Scotland, is that of forced and child marriage. The issue is seen as one of 'flawed' or 'not true or free' consent, and in British law bilateral consent is central to the validity of marriage. When a person marries out of deference to parents' wishes, the marriage is not void, but any indication of pressure or threat is regarded as beyond the limits of parental influence and can constitute duress, and the courts see this as a cause of nullity. Thus a marriage, even if consummated, can be declared null and void if it can be shown that consent was obtained as a result of force or fear.[49] The disapproval of the parents or the community is not regarded as relevant.[50] The pursuer may be a young man or a girl.[51] A recent Scottish case, in which a girl of nineteen succeeded in having her arranged marriage annulled at the Court of Session in April 2002, highlights the view that to be meaningful, freedoms and human rights must apply equally to all citizens. The underlying reasoning is: In a democracy, tolerance does not mean turning a blind eye to intolerable practices, nor is promoting diversity about accommodating unacceptable behaviour.[52]

Canada however, is an example of a federal system where many cultures came together and blended into a new identity, but where the indigenous culture was ignored. The legal system now allows the idea of pluralism to impinge marginally upon the dominant understanding of law, and increasingly the system is normatively pluralistic thus atoning for problems at its inception. The courts in many cases

[46] People of common European stock, white, Christian with English as their common language, born in particular territories, with allegiance to the Union and loyal to the Monarch.
[47] See, W.F. Menski, 'Muslim Law in Britain' (2001) *Journal of Asian and African Studies,* pp. 127-163.
[48] R. Jones and W. Gnanapala, *Ethnic Minorities in English Law* (Stoke-on-Trent, Trentham Books, 2000) For family law see pp. 106-137 and employment law, pp. 219-231.
[49] In *Mahmud* v *Mahmud,* 1994 SLT 599 the marriage was never consummated, but in *Mahmood* v *Mahmoud* 1993 SLT 589 it was.
[50] *Mahmood, ibid.*
[51] For example, *Mahmud,* above note 49.
[52] Editorial in the Newspaper *The Herald* (24 April, 2002) where the case was reported.

'recognise the semi-autonomous nature of a form of social ordering grounded in culture'.[53] Instead of 'applying the legal rules that would be applied to any other party' in similar disputes, the courts apply norms specific to a particular minority, unless 'the norms of the minority community seem clearly wrong or have unwelcome implications for the well-being of outsiders.'[54] Thus the legal system is implicitly pluralistic. It is said that in Canada the dominant mindset regarded any deviation from uniformity in order to take account of cultural differences with suspicion and 'hence the common objections raised to Aboriginal self-government or recognition of "distinct society" status for Quebec as these measures would constitute "special treatment" and violate equality.'[55]

Three areas were looked at by Denise Réaume to illustrate the judicial attitudes to minority group autonomy in Canada: the expulsion of disobedient members from the Hutterian Brethren and from their agricultural colony (the court upholding natural justice in interpreting communal practices); the dismissal of teachers at religious schools for breach of a tenet of the religion which could have been construed otherwise as wrongful dismissal (the court upholding the denominational decision to dismiss as a 'just case' but subject to an objective standard of reasonableness); and, a Salish community's efforts to force a person into a traditional aboriginal practice (the court, holding that the tradition was only oral, this amounted to battery and false imprisonment).[56]

Analyzing the interpretive techniques used to achieve pluralism in these three cases, Denise Réaume distinguished two such: 'the use of relatively content-neutral legal tools onto which minority group practices can be mapped, and the use of interpretive discretion to interpret abstract legal concepts in a culture-sensitive way.'[57] The first technique is a way of putting a group's practices in a 'form recognisable to the legal system', and the second manoeuvres 'within the vague concepts often employed in legal doctrine.'[58]

All the above examples can be viewed within a divide: a divide between the universal and the particular, homogeneity and heterogeneity, the global and the local, that can be discussed in the context of theories of modernization, world-systems, and the homogenizing and converging force of the global.[59] It has been said that 'the task for social science is to make sense of these new kinds of global-local relations'[60] to accommodate the local dimension.[61] It is also claimed that there is

---

[53] D.G. Réaume, 'The Legal Enforcement of Social Norms: Techniques and Principles' (unpublished paper)
[54] *Ibid.*
[55] *Ibid.*
[56] *Ibid.*
[57] *Ibid.*
[58] *Ibid.*
[59] See R. Robertson, *Globalization: Social Theory and Global Culture* (London, Sage, 1992) and M. Featherstone, *Undoing Culture: Globalization, Postmodernism and Identity* (London, Sage, 1995). Also see for a comprehensive discussion, W.F. Menski, *Comparative law in a global context: The legal systems of Asia and Africa* (London, Platinum, 2000).
[60] S. Lask and J. Urry, *Economics of Signs and Space* (London, Sage, 1994) , p. 312.

now 'interpenetration of the universalisation of particularism and the particularisation of universalism'.[62]

Paradoxically, globalization and efforts to create universal standards have increased the interest in localization and localized exception, and ethnic exclusionism versus universalism occupy much of today's discourse. The trend to integrate and converge moves the focus towards the different. Is the 'global' a collection of diverse 'locals'? Does globalization as cosmopolitanism require us 'to recognise "the other" and, in doing so, to accommodate the "diversity" and "co-existence of cultures"?'[63]

The global is 'deterritorialized' and is not tied to particular locations, whereas the local is fixed. But, globalization need not see the world as one large homogeneous place;[64] the universal can be seen to be constituted in the perspective of each culture.[65] The global is dynamic and effective, the local receptive and affected.[66] Cultural absolutism can only confer identity on societies in their distinct particularity; it is fixed and exclusive. The ideals of universal human rights, for example, seen as integral to liberalism, democracy, individualism and progressive change, are often presented set against the pervasive dominance of the community or the State, and claim inclusiveness.[67]

Though cultures, languages, traditions and religions create and foster diversity, does this diversity require reconsideration of the principle of universality? If universality is considered to be 'globalized localism', then it points towards the values of the dominant culture, language, tradition or even religion being globalized and, for the protagonists of cultural pluralism in Europe, this means western culture. But how can the interconnected categories of law, social structure and culture be easily distinguished? Can cultures be identified with individual countries, societies or regions? What about cultural differences within countries – between areas, age groups, classes and genders, and what about social, economic, political, legal or other cultural features which transcend the boundaries of single countries?

If normative pluralism were to be embraced and law seen as supple and pliable in regulating the multi-cultural dimension of society – and this may be a matter of political will rather than a technical problem – then some fundamental questions

---

[61] R. Robertson, 'Globalization: time-space and homogeneity-heterogeneity' in M. Featherstone et al. (eds.) *Global Modernities* (London, Sage, 1995), pp. 38, 41.

[62] Robertson (1992), above note 59, p.100. See for a good discussion P. Fitzpatrick, 'Globalisation and the Humanity of Rights' (2000) (1) *Law, Social Justice and Global Development*, http://elj.warwick.ac.uk/global/issue/2000-1/fittzpatrick.html. pp. 1-18

[63] U. Hannerz, 'Cosmopolitans and Locals in World Culture', in M. Featherstrone (ed.) *Global Culture: Nationalism, Globalization and Moderity* (London, Sage, 1990), p. 239

[64] See A. Appadurai, 'Disjuncture and Difference in the Global Cultural Economy', (1990) 2 *Public Culture*, p. 7.

[65] B de Sousa Santos, *Toward a New Common Sense: Law, Globalization, and Emancipation*, 2nd edn., (London, Butterworths, 2002), p. 269.

[66] Fitzpatrick, above note 62, p. 9.

[67] R.E. Howard, 'Cultural Absolutism and the Nostalgia for the Community', (1993) 15 *Human Rights Quarterly*, pp. 315-338.

would have to be resolved, such as: What is a minority?[68] How do we recognise cultural practices and how is culture to be measured? What should be the criteria of proof and who should carry the burden of proof? Who represents culture? Do diverse communities have internal governance structures to pronounce authoritatively upon internal rules? Ultimately, should internal 'conflict of laws' rules be developed and applied? What kind of a role does the comparative lawyer have here?

In a modern European unitary nation State, the accommodation of cultural diversity and multiple normative orders can only be brought about by the judge - the tuner of the law - using discretion, and not by the legislators, whose main demarcation lines are clearly drawn within the European Union by the demands of 'ever closer integration'. It must be remembered that European harmonization of rules may override even certain legal exceptions earlier introduced by the Member States in response to the needs of the diverse cultures therein.

The question is then, when a legal system meets cultures different to the dominant value system it represents, what should it do? A comparative lawyer with a cosmopolitan and pragmatic approach would say that in the globalizing world, there is advantage as well as inevitability in convergence, that the fundamental values represented by universal standards of human rights should trump all other claims to 'exceptionalism', that cultural diversity, the spice of life, should remain cultural and not move into the legal world, and that there should be overarching legal systems striving towards transnational, regional and inter-communal levels to bring uniformity of modernity to the legal world and to accommodate multi-culturalism. At no stage should multi-culturalism impede the progress of the law towards this. The object of the pursuit is the attainment of ideals of rationality, harmony and reform using a selection of the legal rules and materials best suited to the task.[69] The acceptance of pluralism must be qualified 'with the proviso that internal group norms that are repugnant to some overarching sense of natural justice and morality will not be enforced.'[70]

One important function of the overarching official legal framework is that it prevents the potential chaos of meaning inherent in the symbolic construction of a culturally pluralist world by cutting through pluriform and pluralistic demands; it establishes a reasonable measure of security and justice. Cultural pluralism cannot be fully reflected in legal pluralism unless the nation State loses its status as the central entity regulating legal affairs or until legal pluralism becomes universally accepted by the forces of a globalized world whereby all nation State laws assume the status of being 'one' of many layers of law. 'Unity in diversity' can only be

---

[68] See for instance, J. Packer, 'On the Definition of Minorities', in J. Packer and K Myntti (eds) *The Protection of Ethnic and Linguistic Minorities in Europe* (Turku, Abo Akademi University Press, 1993), 23.

[69] M. Bussani, '"Integrative" Comparative Law Enterprises and the Inner Stratification of Legal Systems', (2000) *European Review of Private Law,* p.89

[70] Réaume, above note 53.

achieved and remain healthy, where diversity does not threaten 'unity of purpose'. There can be room for only 'qualified legal pluralism'.

3. DECONSTRUCTION OF CLASSIFICATIONS, INTERRELATIONSHIPS AND THE GROWTH OF FAMILY TREES

There must be a fresh approach to the classification of legal systems - a new 'family trees' approach within which legal systems can be classified according to their parentage, their constituent elements and the resulting blend, and then be re-grouped on the principle of predominance.[71]

Comparative lawyers must first take stock of the conventional handling of legal systems by comparative lawyers, and then go back to observe the ground, the seeds of the trees, the emerging roots, the growing of the shoots and the trees, and the spreading and intertwining of the branches. In fact, this is first a deconstruction process with reconstruction to follow. Parts of the new landscape may resemble the old, but parts, and the whole will look different.

Traditionally, legal systems have been grouped into legal families mainly for taxonomic purposes, ease of handling and explanation. Grouping has been one of the conventional tasks of comparative law. It has been said that, 'The idea of a "legal family" does not correspond to a biological reality; it is no more than a didactic device.'[72] The legal families approach serves as an organizing basis. Yet the practice has been to study legal systems that best represent large groupings and then make generalizations. During this process, concepts such as originality, derivation and common elements surfaced,[73] and similarities and relationships were the bases of such endeavours at classification. External criteria and context were generally ignored by comparative lawyers, their attention being focused rather on substance, sources and structure.[74] Until recently, context remained in the domain of sociologists, anthropologists and economists.

Classifications relied only on private law, were Eurocentric and therefore weighted towards the civil law and the common law families. This makes the existing classifications relative to subject matter, that is, the area of law in mind

---

[71] This Section draws on my 'Family Trees for Legal Systems: Towards a Contemporary Approach' Chapter 18 in M. Van Hoecke (ed), *Epistemology and Methodology of Comparative Law* (Oxford, Hart Publishing, 2004), 359-375.

[72] R. David and J.E.C. Brierley, *Major Legal Systems in the World Today, An Introduction to the Comparative Study of Law,* 3rd ed. (London, Stevens and Sons, 1985), p. 21.

[73] For a summary of some past efforts at classification see K. Zweigert and H. Kötz, *An Introduction to Comparative Law*, 3rd edn., trans. T. Weir (Oxford, Clarendon Press, 1998), pp. 63-67. Also see M. Bogdan, *Comparative Law* (Göteborg, Kluwer Tano, 1994), pp. 82-91.

[74] See, for a critical discussion of the theoretical assumptions and points of departure for existing classifications, T.P. van Reenen, 'Major theoretical problems of modern comparative legal methodology (3): The criteria employed for the classification of legal systems' (1996) XXIX *Comparative and International Law Journal of Southern Africa*, pp. 71-99.

when comparisons are made.[75] Moreover, fixed classifications can only have a limited life span as legal systems may shift from one cluster towards another, so that the positioning of legal systems in the legal families framework may have to be re-thought from time to time.[76] In addition, new families may emerge. For example, it has been suggested that an 'African legal family' is emerging.[77]; and interest in mixed jurisdictions is now increasing, such jurisdictions being regarded as members of a so-called 'Third Family'.[78]

It is true that the task of dealing with individual legal systems is simplified by containing the diversity within a limited number of categories. It might be the case that 'legal genealogy' appeals 'to the comparative legal scholar's sense for order and classification, just as a botanist receives satisfaction from classifying plants and discovering the relationship between them.'[79] Thus, biological and linguistic taxonomies have been used in classification schemes as organizing devices. Obviously in this process some elements are regarded as important and some others not. However, the interest in classifications is confined to general characteristics, and the essence does not lie in diversity of rules in a given topic, only the affinities being considered. Yet, classification must look beyond legal rules to factors linked to legal tradition and legal culture emanating from the diverse sources that make up the legal soil and to the seeds that grow into these family trees.

Historically, comparative lawyers used criteria such as language group, race, culture, source of law, structure, substance and ideology as the bases of their classifications.[80] René David talked of 'constant elements'[81] and Konrad Zweigert and Hein Kötz proposed using 'legal styles' to discover shared distinctive elements between legal systems.[82] However, they also pointed out that:

> In any case, as the example of 'hybrid' systems shows, any division of the legal world into families, or groups is a rough and ready device. It can be quite useful for the novice, by putting the confusing variety of legal systems into some kind of loose order, but the experienced comparatist will have developed a 'nose' for the distinctive style of national legal systems and will either not use the device of legal families at all, or will use it with all the circumspection called for by any attempt to force into a schematic order social phenomena as highly complex as living legal systems.[83]

[75] See for problems, Zweigert and Kötz, above note 73, pp. 66-68.
[76] *Ibid.*, p. 66.
[77] *Ibid.*, p. 66.
[78] Mark the recent launching of the World Society of Mixed Jurisdiction Jurists in New Orleans (November 2002), and see V.V. Palmer, *Mixed Jurisdictions Worldwide: The Third Legal Family*, (Cambridge, Cambridge University Press, 2001).
[79] Bogdan, above note 73, p. 82.
[80] See for the history of classifications S. Krislov, 'The Concept of Families of Law' in Podgorecki, Whelan & Khosla (eds.), above note 33, pp. 25-34.
[81] David and Brierley, above note 72 , pp. 17-20.
[82] See Zwiegert and Kötz, above note 73, pp. 67-68 in defence of 'style'.
[83] *Ibid.*, p. 72.

René David also warned us: 'The suitability of any classification will depend upon whether the perspective is world-wide or regional, or whether attention is given to public, private or criminal law. Each approach can undoubtedly be justified from the point of view of the person proposing it and none can, in the end, be recognised as exclusive.'[84]

Yet in the Europe of today in search of a 'new *ius commune*', it is commonplace not only to talk of civil law and common law families, but to treat them as if they are the only two monolithic entities. Such an approach is useful for teaching purposes within Europe, but is inadequate for comparative research. Neither is it any longer satisfactory in our 'globalizing age' to group localisms under the broad headings of civil law tradition, common law tradition and, begrudgingly, socialist laws, others being regarded as derivatives of the civil or the common law traditions, and with others again, pooled as the 'fourth tradition' usually under the name 'traditional and religious legal orders'.[85]

To summarize: traditional classifications mostly based on the 'law as rules' approach, differ as to whether they simplify or multiply the number of legal families and how they place various legal families in their schemes, but they all consider exclusively official law and the 'top-down' models. It might therefore be said that the groups are all 'legally structured', are 'structure-specific' and inconclusive. An approach which is entirely culture-specific may not be conclusive either, but the relationship between legal and social systems must be given due weight. However, a comparative lawyer working alone might not be able to analyze the relationship between legal systems and the corresponding social and cultural systems. This indicates the importance of sociology of law for comparative lawyers as well as the multi-disciplinary approach..

It is apparent that the whole 'legal families' division based on the 'law as rules' approach is now collapsing. Other approaches are being suggested. One such suggestion, presented as being less biased, is the 'Cultural Families' division based on the 'law as culture' approach. On this basis four broad cultures have been distinguished by Mark van Hoecke and Mark Warrington: the African, the Asian, the Islamic and the cultures with European roots, that is, Europe, America and Oceania, which can be called generally 'Western culture', 'certain countries

[84] David and Brierley, above note 72, p. 21. Also see Bogdan, above note 73, p. 85.

[85] However, note that Zweigert and Kötz suggest eight such families. See for a criticism of present day classifications and an attempt to 'trim' and take account of globalization in classifications, de Sousa Santos, above note 65, pp. 191-193. Santos uses a multi-layered comparative strategy, draws on a three-fold analytical framework to survey seven specific types of legal globalization, and combines three positions in the world system with four trajectories into modernity and with eight world legal cultures based on the classification of Zweigert and Kötz.

bridging two of these cultures such as Russia, or having a distinct position within one of these such as India'.[86]

Adam Podgorecki proposes categorizing legal systems into ten groups: based on official and intuitive law; based on different types of legitimacy; adequate, guiding and restrictive; monolithic and pluralist; oppressive (including punitive) and tolerant (including liberal); based on state and less formal types of conflict resolutions; self-generated and imposed; accessible and inaccessible; based on religious attitudes of the population; and rooted in capitalist and communist social reality.[87]

Samuel Krislov puts forward a paradigm which relies on language groups. His object is to trace origins and basic elements derived from each other, 'mapping influence and not "convergence" or "structural resemblance".' Thus he classifies systems as: rule-oriented systems – principally occidental; theocratically-oriented systems – principally Middle Eastern and some Asian; mutual-obligation contract systems (Japan and other Asian Countries, medieval Europe, etc:,); and character-development systems.[88]

Another approach, giving prominence to yet another context, is the 'law and economics' approach. Here we see how Ugo Mattei tries to draw the taxonomy away from the so-called Eurocentric axis to present a new map for the world's legal systems. This classification is based on the rule of professional law, the rule of political law and the rule of traditional law, these three forming a triangle on the apices of which all legal systems can be placed.[89]

Andrew Harding, whose interest is in South East Asia, categorically tells us that all Eurocentric comparatists fall into the 'legal families trap'. According to him, 'Legal families tell us nothing about legal systems except as to their general style and method, and the idea makes no sense whatsoever amid the nomic din of South East Asia.'[90]

All the above indicates that scholars fail to agree on whether the notion of families is basic and scientific, or theoretically and descriptively useless; and that those who use the concept do not even agree on the criteria for classification and groupings.

As already noted, recently there has been increasing interest in mixed, or hybrid systems. Vernon Palmer calls 'mixed jurisdictions' the 'Third Family'[91] - the

---

[86] M. van Hoecke and M. Warrington, 'Legal Cultures and Legal Paradigms: Towards a New Model for Comparative Law', (1998) *International and Comparative Law Quarterly*, 495 at p. 502.

[87] A. Podgorecki, 'Social Systems and Legal Systems – Criteria for Classification', in Podgorecki, Whelan & Khosla (eds.), above note 33, p.3-19.

[88] Krislov, above note 80, p. 335-37.

[89] U. Mattei, 'Three Patterns of Law: Taxonomy and Change in the World's Legal Systems', (1997) XLV *American Journal of Comparative Law*, 1.

[90] A. Harding, 'Global Doctrine and Local Knowledge: Law in South East Asia', (2002) 51 *International and Comparative Law Quarterly*, 36, at p. 49.

[91] Palmer, above note 78.

first and the second being for him, the civil law and the common law. Jan Smits has published a monograph entitled '*The Making of European Private Law: Towards a Ius Commune Europaeum as a Mixed Legal System*'.[92] These are indications that the current classification of legal systems into legal families is no longer satisfactory and I suggest here that it must be abandoned in its present shape.

The discussion might centre on whether there is an emerging 'European legal family', but this would be yet another monolithic approach, a new creation ignoring developments both within and outside Europe. From time to time, there has been talk of a 'Western legal family',[93] but those legal systems allocated to this overarching family covering both the so-called common law and all versions of civil law do not sit comfortable within it. In any case, this new family would only cater for a region with constantly changing borders, and only for a limited period of time. This approach would also restrict the capacities of comparative lawyers. Their work would remain 'within the family', rather than addressing the wider vista made possible by comparison.

To talk of a new family with the name 'Mixed Jurisdictions' would not be satisfactory either, as clearly, not all 'mixes' can be pooled together and not all the existing members of such a family would have the same or similar ingredients. It would be extremely difficult to place for example Quebec and Algeria, both mixed systems, into one family. The simple mixes, the complex mixes, as well as the dual systems and systems adhering to legal pluralism cannot be lumped together.[94]

One might ask, why talk of legal families at all when their only advantage seems to be at the level of pedagogy and convenience? Instead, it could be suggested that one should look only at areas of law and determine in which group the present legal systems sit for the purposes of these areas alone. But areas too may change their borders and new subjects be added as law develops in fields hitherto outside the domain of law. Although it is perfectly acceptable for the purposes of individual research projects to devise classifications according to the area of law in question, if any generalizations were to be attempted, the result would be totally out of joint.

---

[92] J.M. Smits, *The Making of European Private Law: Towards a Ius Commune Europaeum as a Mixed Legal System*, (Maastricht, Metro 2002). Also see J.M. Smits, 'A European Private Law as a Mixed Legal System, (1998), 5 *Maastricht Journal of European and Comparative Law*, pp. 328-340; and J.M. Smits (ed) *The Contribution of Mixed Legal Systems to European Private Law* (Groningen, Intersentia, 2001).

[93] See A. Malmström, 'The System of Legal Systems, Notes on the Classification in Comparative Law', (1969) 13 *Scandinavian Studies in. Law*, 127; G. Eörsi, 'Convergence in Civil law?', in Szabo and Péteri (eds) *A Socialist Approach to Comparative Law* (Leyden, Budapest, 1977) pp. 45-94; G. Eörsi, 'On the Problem of the Division of Legal Systems', in M. Rotondi (ed) *Inchieste di diritto comparato 2. Buts et methodes du droit compare* (Padova, New York, 1973), pp. 179-210. Also note David's prediction that there will be a merge into a common family of Western law, above note 72, pp. 22-31. In this context, also consider, L.M. Friedman, 'Is There a Modern Legal Culture?' (1994), 7 *Ratio Juris*, 117.

[94] See E. Örücü , 'Mixed and Mixing Systems: A Conceptual Search', in E. Örücü, E. Attwooll and S. Coyle (eds) *Studies in Legal Systems: Mixed and Mixing* (London, Kluwer Law International, 1996), p. 344.

Moreover, even when a distinct area of law is under scrutiny, a comparative lawyer can detect further cross-pollination and 'horizontal transfers' between systems sitting on adjacent branches of the proposed family trees.

'Contamination' has been suggested by Pier Guiseppe Monateri as the basis for understanding the world of legal systems: 'the actual legal world is more to be seen as a world of "contaminations" than a world split up into different families'.[95] He claims that this idea is neither new nor linked to globalization since - with the exception of insulated legal systems such as the English common law - 'practically every system, even in antiquity has grown through "contaminations"',[96] the practice of borrowing having always been normal practice. In his view the 'widespread cross-diffusion of French and German patterns within Civil law, and the overcoming of American models at the present, shape a similar legal landscape all across the world, with a wilderness of local variants'.[97]

Surely what is necessary today is a re-assessment of individual legal systems according to the old and new overlaps and blends and, of how the existing constituent elements have mingled and are mingling with new elements entering them. Hence I propose a scheme which regards all legal systems as mixed and overlapping, overtly or covertly, and groups them according to the proportionate mixture of the ingredients.[98] To do this, it is essential to look at the constituent elements in each legal system and to regroup legal systems on a much larger scale according to the predominance of the ingredient sources from whence each system is formed. Both horizontal and diachronic analyses are called for at all times. The starting point is appreciation of the fact that all legal systems are overlaps and mixes to varying degrees.

Thus some continental systems such as the Dutch are combinations of Roman law, French Law, German Law and indigenous law, and some of Canon Law, Roman Law, *ius commune*, French Law, Austrian law and German Law such as the Italian. Indeed, all European systems can be better understood as overlaps. Then there are other combinations such as common law, religious law and indigenous customary laws as in countries such as India and Pakistan; and French, Socialist, Islamic and indigenous customary tribal laws as in Algeria. It must not be forgotten that French law, German law and common law are themselves all outcomes of overlaps of various ingredients.

The old overlaps on the European continent are of Roman Law, Canon law, various versions of the civilian tradition, the *ius commune* and indigenous local customary laws. The new overlaps in Europe contain in addition, elements of common law, British or American. English Law is becoming more and more an overlap of common law, various civilian systems and European Law. Indeed,

---

[95] P.G. Monateri, ' The "Weak" Law: Contaminations and Legal Cultures' in *Italian National Reports to the XVth International Congress of Comparative Law*, Bristol 1998 (Milano, Giuffrè editore, 1998) 83- 110, at p. 107.

[96] *Ibid.*

[97] *Ibid.*

[98] This topic can be read together with the next Section.

classical English common law itself was an overlap of Roman Law, civilian ideas, canon law, equity and domestic common law.[99] In this new approach the underlays and the overlays must be carefully distinguished, because layers may also shift their positions. For example, in Hong Kong, until 1990, English common law was the overlay, with Chinese customary law as the underlay, but now, it is becoming an underlay alongside Chinese customary law both under a growing overlay of modern Chinese law. In addition, there is the 'knock-on effect' to be considered.

My scheme makes the classification of systems such as those of Malaysia, Singapore, Burma and Thailand particularly easy. The whole of South East Asia would be better served by this approach. Off-shoots and sub-groups can be more clearly seen and catered for. For example Thailand, which was never a colony, has had in its modern texture a real mixture of sources such as English Law, German Law, French Law, Swiss Law, Japanese Law and American Law since the end of the nineteenth century. These sit alongside historic sources in existence since 1283, rules from indigenous culture and tradition, customary laws and Hindu jurisprudence, still to be found in some modern enactments. In addition, Thai Codes were originally drafted in English and French and then translated into Thai.[100] So, where could this legal system be placed in the traditional classification of legal families?

The same question can be posed for Malaysia where first there was the 'native' law of the aboriginal inhabitants still today regarded as positive law by courts. Then came layers of transplanted law: *adat* law (a number of Malay customs), Hindu and Buddhist law, Islamic law, Chinese law, Thai law, the English common law tradition coloured by Anglo-Indian Codes and the USA model. There are further influences in South East Asia: French, Dutch, German, Swiss, Portuguese and Spanish civilian traditions, American law, Japanese law and Soviet law.[101] Andrew Harding demonstrates how the region 'has an abundance of legal traditions, practically all of them having been "received" or "transplanted" in one sense or another, and encompassing all of the world's major legal world views and systems. ... except perhaps for African law and Eskimo law'[102] Which of the commonly used classifications deal with these? It is striking that South East Asia with approximately 500 million people, is consigned 'to a small section of a chapter on the "family" of East Asian legal systems, which we are told, bizarrely, are all "confucian" or "authoritarian" or something equally blasé. Some texts venture cautiously further in

---

[99] For contributions from Islamic and Talmudic laws into common law see the literature mentioned by H.P. Glenn, 'Are Legal Traditions Incommensurable?' (2001) 49 *American Journal of Comparative Law*, 133, at p. 141-142.

[100] I am indebted to my PhD student Jutharat Compeerapap in Erasmus University Rotterdam, working on 'The Reception of Legal Language in Thai Contract Law: A Comparative Perspective' for kindling my interest in Thailand.

[101] Harding, above note 90, pp. 42-43.

[102] *Ibid.*, p. 47.

saying that South East Asia's legal systems are "pluralist", or "evolving from status to contract".'[103]

The civil law, common law and socialist law, as the traditionally accepted legal families, may be regarded now as the forebears of many of the legal systems in the family trees. However, obviously there are other forebears such as Islamic law which must not be ignored.

Then come attempts at tracing transfrontier mobility of law, its paths and consequences. Of special interest are four kinds of encounters: those between systems of socio and legal cultural similarity, those between systems of socio-cultural similarity but legal cultural diversity, those between systems of socio-cultural diversity but legal cultural similarity, and those between systems of both socio and legal cultural diversity. These encounters account for overlaps, interrelationships, mixed and mixing systems and systems in transition, by approaching law as the product of a process of transposition as in music, the concept 'transposition' helping to highlight the crucial importance of the internal tuners who deal with the mix, adapting it to the new instrument, or gardeners who deal with the mix, adapting it to the new soil. My own first attempt in 1987 led to an article, 'An Exercise on the Internal Logic of Legal Systems',[104] the second, to 'Transfrontier Mobility of Law' in 1995[105] and the third, to 'Law as Transposition' in 2002.[106]

The time has now come to consider legal systems more closely as overlaps, marriages and off-spring. Terminology used could include fertilization, pollination, grafting, intertwining, osmosis and pruning, with a view of paving the way for a future understanding of developments of our own day.

In linguistics, the 'tree model' of language development reflecting an evolutionary approach, is the one generally used to explain ramification and divergence. However, the 'wave theory' showing that changes can spread like waves over a wide area, can also handle the equally important forces of convergence.[107] Similarities do not always arise from genetic relationships. Neither does resemblance necessarily indicate common origin. There can be 'horizontal transfers' between adjacent systems. 'Horizontal transfer' can also explain why a borrowed concept or institution does not always exactly retain its original meaning. Areas nearest to or adjacent to the initial change will change first and may even give up their own peculiarities. Subsequent re-groupings may come about on the 'wave model' mentioned above. Thus convergence occurs between concepts or systems

---

[103] *Ibid.*, p. 48.

[104] E. Örücü, 'An Exercise on the Internal Logic of Legal Systems'. (1987) 7 *Legal Studies*, 310.

[105] E. Örücü, 'A Theoretical Framework For Transfrontier Mobility of Law', in R. Jagtenberg, E. Örücü and A. de Roo (eds) *Transfrontier Mobility of Law* (The Hague, Kluwer Law International, 1995) pp. 5-18.

[106] E. Örücü, 'Law as Transposition', (2002) 51 *International and Comparative Law Quarterly*, 205.

[107] See for an analysis of these theories, C. Renfrew, *Archeology and Language: The Puzzle of Indo-European Origins*, (London, Jonathan Cape, 1987), especially pp. 105, 244-248.

originally different. The 'tree model' and the 'wave model' can be used together to explain development. So can the 'knock-on-effect'. It flows from the foregoing that a wave need not start from a fixed centre. Developments can take place in steps with no one locale as the prime innovating centre. It is not necessary to depict one as the donor and the other the recipient. In this perspective, there is no one localized homeland but 'cumulative mutuality'. Interaction is the essence. This combined approach indicates a way forward for an understanding of how legal systems function, change and develop.

Of course, it would be impossible to classify here all the legal systems in the world and place them on the branches of family trees. Instead, it is suggested that a pattern be produced and scholars dealing with individual systems find the places for their specific systems on the family trees. The starting point would be with the ancestors, the seeds, that is 'day one'. Thus, civil law and common law would appear near, but not necessarily at, the roots of their trees, as it would of course be possible to go back further to the laws of Hammurabi, to Greek laws and beyond even before considering Roman law,[108] the ingredients of which possibly included elements of Hindu law through Egyptian and Greek channels.[109]Indeed, some systems of the olden days must have died prematurely, their seeds lost, fallen on barren ground or destroyed. It might even be said that some plants are annual, some biannual and some perennial, that some plants are hardy and some are not; and the hardy survive even bad gardening, poor soil and lack of fertilization!

Comparative lawyers must understand the relationship between legal systems, legal cultures and legal traditions and be able to uncover the rules outside the framework of the formal legal system held by the people to be binding. Both the top-down and the bottom-up models of law have to be appreciated. This broad approach must include 'ordinary' and 'extraordinary' legal systems.[110] I see such a family trees approach as the most appropriate for an understanding in our century where overlaps are the norm. This approach would lead to neutral classification - one which would accord with all the ingredients.

For example, starting the story with the civil law, one could take the working definition suggested by Alan Watson for an all-encompassing approach to the systems that fall under this heading. This definition suits the purposes of my project. It would be 'a system in which parts or the whole of Justinian's *Corpus iuris civilis* have been in the past or are at present treated as the law of the land or, at the very

---

[108] See E. Hondius, 'The Supremacy of Western Law' in L. de Ligt. J. de Ruiter, E. Slob, J.M.Tevel, M. van de Vrugt and L.C. Winkel (eds) *Viva Vox Iuris Romani: Essays in Honour of Johannes Emil Spruit*, (Amsterdam, J.C. Giben Publisher, 2002), pp. 337-342, for his concern that Western lawyers regard Western civilization as superior to other civilizations and his argument that Western law does not have a monopoly.

[109] See Glenn, above note 99, quoting from M. Sharan, *Court Procedure in Ancient India* (1978) on p. 141.

[110] See E. Örücü, 'Comparatists and extraordinary places', Chapter 13 in P. Legrand and R. Munday (eds) *Comparative Legal Studies: Traditions and Transitions* (Cambridge, Cambridge University Press; 2003), 467-489.

least, are of direct and highly persuasive force; or else it derives from any such system.'[111] One can create a working definition for common law systems in a like manner: 'a system in which parts or the whole of the English common law have been in the past, or are at present, treated as the law of the land, or at the very least, are of direct and highly persuasive force; or else it derives from any such system'.

Although it may be claimed and accepted that civil law and common law are the main ancestors of the world's legal systems, there are surely others.[112] These other parents could also be given their working definitions in a similar manner to the above. When one looks at legal cultures and traditions, one sees that civil law and common law are but two of the ancestors, the others being, according to one divide, Chthonic, Talmudic, Islamic, Hindu, and Asian.[113] Even then, Patrick Glenn says that:

> In looking at (only) seven legal traditions of the world, it has been impossible to avoid the existence of other recognizable legal traditions. Some might say the other legal traditions are minor ones, which complement or oppose the traditions which have been examined. This may or may not be accurate, since there are no well established criteria for distinguishing major from minor traditions ... If the traditions in law which have been examined here ... appear presently as the major ones of the world, it may be that this is only a conclusion of first impression, and that there are other legal traditions ... which are still more profound and which await investigation, and recognition, as being of primary importance.[114]

Marriages have taken place between systems and sub-systems of different parentage. Some are cohabitation, some life-long, some passing. It may be difficult to determine with exactitude the degrees of hybridity when there are many overlaps, cross-fertilization, reciprocal influence, fusion, infusion, grafting and the like. The conclusion is that there are no pure systems in the legal world and that there are various degress of hybridity arising from different levels and layers of crossing and intertwining between the roots and branches of adjacent trees.

Some of the off-spring showing clear signs of their different legal cultural, racial, ethnic and religious parentage overtly, have already been grouped as 'mixed jurisdictions', and are usually treated as *numerus clausus*. However, this is not a

---

[111] A. Watson, *The Making of the Civil Law* (Cambridge, Mass. and London, Harvard University Press, 1981), p. 4.

[112] For an intriguing sideline which, if true, would have fundamental impact on our mental framework see, P.G. Monateri, 'Black Gaius / A Quest for the Multicultural Origins of the "Western Legal Tradition"', (2000) 51 *Hastings Law Journal*, pp. 479-555. Also see, M. Bernal, *Black Athena: The Afroasiatic Roots of Classical Civilisation*, 2 vols., (New Jersey, Rutgers University Press, 1987, 1991).

[113] H.P. Glenn, *Legal Traditions of the World* (Oxford, Oxford University Press, 2000).

[114] *Ibid.*, pp. 318-319.

correct approach, as there are many overt and covert mixtures which are the offspring of the same marriages or of other combinations.[115]

As noted above, even within the continent of Europe, it is easy to see sitting on one family tree, crosses between indigenous law, French law, German law and Roman law such as in the Netherlands, and crosses between customary law, neo-canon law, German law, Greek law and Roman law such as in Greece, as well as more complicated crosses such as those in Malta.[116]

In Malta legal history began with the Phoenician settlement and continued with the Roman conquest bringing the *Corpus Iuris*. The Normans invaded and brought feudal law as applied in Spain, Naples and Sicily. The invasion of the Moors had direct influence on the Maltese language. The sovereignty of the Knights of St. John recognized local usage and issued declarations of private law drawing on laws of other countries, mostly Italian. Then came the French with their Napoleonic laws. Finally the British brought the common law. So here in Malta we see a good example of an eclectic Criminal Code drafted under a strong Italian influence but with pervasive English and Scottish impact, and a Commercial Code largely based on the French. Maritime law follows English law. The 1873 Civil Code is predominantly based on the French and Italian Codes and also on the Municipal Code de Rohan, the Civil Code of Louisiana and the Austrian Civil Code. Canon law applies in family law where there is also the influence of English law, German law, Italian law and French law. Constitutional law is mainly British. The official languages are Maltese and English. The ingredients work cumulatively and interactively. How could this legal system be defined and classified with the conventional tools used by comparative lawyers?

There are of course even more extreme and unexpected crosses. Sometimes, seeds are scattered widely. For example Turkey is a cross between Swiss law, German law, Italian law, French law, Roman law, a covert Islamic law and local customary law, as well as more recently, European law and American law. This came about as a result of grafting, pruning and intertwining. It might even be said that germination was 'forced' under green-house conditions by an elite concerned with changing not only the law and legal culture but the people themselves and the way of life from traditionality to modernity by the introduction of radical social reform laws to accompany the forging of the new legal system by receptions from abroad. These social reform laws are still protected under the present Constitution. Parentage varies for different fields, such as Swiss in Civil law, German in Commercial law, Italian in Criminal law and French in Administrative law, all intertwined with each other, with what existed before - the unwanted growth having been cut and pruned - and with the diverse socio-culture, to make up the present

[115] Örücü , above note 94, pp. 344-345.

[116] See J.M. Ganado, 'Malta: A Microcosm of International Influences' in Örücü, Attwooll and Coyle, above note 94, pp. 225-247.

legal system.[117] Where should this system be placed if looked at through the lenses of the old classifications?

It is possible to say that European law today reflects marriages between common law - such as Irish law, English law and American law - and civil law in its many varieties - such as German law, French law, Dutch law and Danish law - as well as mixed jurisdictions such as Scottish law and so on, all with their own diverse historic ingredients. In addition, an enlarged Europe will have even more to accommodate as it will have to engage with socialist law and legal culture and other varieties of the civilian tradition. The status of Islamic law and its impact in Europe is now an important subject of study. As people are on the move in Europe so are legal systems.

This is why it is first necessary for comparative law to move from its exclusive interest in the top-down model, that is, the legal system as laid down by formal law-makers and the appropriate high courts. A broader approach rather than mere normative inquiry is needed. Comparison cannot be limited to classical and faceless civil law/common law comparison, though the 'ordinary' world often appears to be so divided when viewed only from within Europe. Such a one directional approach cannot lead to useful and comprehensive research. One can no longer concentrate solely on what are regarded classically as the great 'parent' systems. However, it has been suggested by Konrad Zweigert and Hein Kötz that only the mature 'parent' systems should be studied:

> Mature legal systems are often adopted or extensively imitated by others; as long as these other so-called 'affiliated' legal systems maintain the style of the parent system, they usually do not possess to the same degree that blend of originality and balanced maturity in solving problems which characterise the 'significant' legal systems. While they are at this stage of development, the comparatist may ignore the affiliate and concentrate on the parent system.[118]

According to this view then, some systems justify intense investigation while others do not! Surely, regions of the world other than Europe and the 'extraordinary' places, even if seen as extensions of the two traditional families, must be studied by comparative lawyers. This is an essential activity with the view of re-placing and re-arranging them on the branches of the appropriate family trees. In the past, the legal world might have appeared to Western comparatists to be largely divided between the heirs of Rome and Westminster, but these heirs are now linked together in various ways both with each other and with those of other parentage, such as

---

[117] Elsewhere I have called this legal system 'hyphenated', since the roots have not been cut off from the parents and the source laws are still referred to with a hyphen, as for example in the case of 'İsviçre-Türk Hukuku' (Swiss-Turkish Law), when referring to the civil law. See E. Örücü, *Critical Comparative Law: Considering Paradoxes for Legal Systems in Transition,* Nederlandse Vereniging voor Rechtvergelijking No: 59, (Deventer, Kluwer, 1999), pp. 80-118.

[118] Zwiegert and Kötz, above note 73, p. 41.

Islamic, Hindu, Jewish, traditional and tribal. Ignoring these developments will not be forgiven in the coming years. Whatever view one takes, one must always be aware of overlaps and cross-fertilizations.

It has been said that 'the last thing we need is "distinctiveness for its own sake".'[119] This is true. However, this should not mean that we can ignore distinctiveness. Even when comparative law is used directly as an instrument of integration one must be aware of the virtues in 'distinction' and 'diversity'. Whereas in classical classifications only 'similarity' mattered, in the new family trees approach 'distinctiveness' matters as well as similarity. The relevant degrees of distinction and similarity give a legal system its place. By adopting this family trees approach, comparativism offers the only way to see legal systems as they actually are, neither cherishing nor denying diversity in order to create a true and reliable map of the legal world. The approach is not an 'either - or' between the integrative and contrastive. It needs and uses both. The family trees approach is initially deconstructive and critical. The aim is to then re-construct a more reliable map of the legal systems of the world.[120]

The strategy for the family trees approach is to look at the picture as objectively as possible with a view of discovering the ingredients and historical antecedents of each legal system together with its current blend. One methodological problem of comparative law research in determining where legal systems sit, is how to decide on what to ignore as accidental rather than vital and what as changeable rather than constant. In addition, certain factors may be deemed irrelevant for the purposes of a particular project. Problems associated with looking at what is changeable rather than constant may cause instability in the research, but the family trees project rests on the assumption of fluidity.

It is worth noting that trees grow in a number of ways. Seeds fall from a chestnut, and a new tree grows. Trees can be grown from cuttings, either directly planted to form a new tree, or grafted on a tree of a different species. New shoots may sprout from the roots of an old tree and grow into new ones. Legal systems can be found as examples for each of these types of generation.

In this attempt at re-aligning legal systems and placing them on their genealogical trees, we must consider transpositions, reciprocal influences and cross-fertilization both horizontally and vertically. This is a very fruitful area of study, and the answers we seek lie here. Transpositions tell us much about the development of the law and allow us to understand cultural and legal navigation as well as the role of tuning in legal development.

Comparative lawyers cannot ignore the function of reciprocal influence, cross-fertilization and pollination by claiming that legal cultures are specific to individual

---

[119] E. Clive , 'Scottish Family Law' in J.P. Grant (ed) *Independence and Devolution: The Legal Implications for Scotland* (Edinburgh, Green, 1976), 162 at p. 173.

[120] The question still remains however, whether this approach could go far enough to embrace legal pluralism and all layers of law such as the global, international, regional, transnational, inter-communal, terrritorial state, sub-state and non-state, in the mapping. See W. Twining, *Globalisation and Legal Theory* (London, Butterworths, 2000), pp. 136-141.

cultures and therefore such studies are fruitless, misleading and even dangerous. Today, within the European Union for example, scholars either assume commonality or, seek for diversity. But we know that legal systems and cultural systems can indeed 'live apart together'. If the function of comparative law is to be the building of bridges, placing legal systems on the branches of family trees can bring them into closer proximity with each other within the boundaries of Europe and around the world. If legal systems can see themselves as part of one large world, part of a fertile forest rather than being divided into isolated copses, the chances of 'living apart together' successfully increases.

Legal systems are looking to each other for law reform. Legal systems that are closely related to each other, legally, politically, socio-culturally and economically, and that sit on the same branch of their family tree are not always the best systems to benefit from each others' experience. The legal systems of today, most of which are in transition, need models which are socio-culturally and/or legal culturally different from their own. History tells us that when legal systems of diverse socio- and/or legal-cultures meet, the diverse elements co-exist side by side in the resultant legal system.[121] Usually it is a law or even a legal institution that moves from a foreign source into a new domestic scene. Sometimes, legal systems themselves shift their positions en bloc. At times, especially in global receptions, it is a whole legal culture that moves.[122]

Some of the terms employed for analysis of such developments today, are 'seepage', 'contaminant', 'irritant', 'underlay', 'overlay', 'cross-fertilization', 'incremental reception', 'competing systems', 'hyphenated' legal systems, 'layered law', 'chance', 'choice', 'prestige', 'efficiency', 'elite' and 'historical accident'. Any one of these terms may be appropriate for the analysis of a specific move and for the explanation of a specific growth.

In the past many shoots sprouted on the family trees through impositions and colonial contact. Indeed, the English common law has been likened by Lord Denning to an 'oak tree' which grows only in English soil, saying that if this tree were to be planted elsewhere, it would need to be severely pruned. In his words:

> ... the common law cannot be applied in a foreign land without considerable qualification. Just as with an English Oak, so with the English common law. You cannot transplant it to the African continent and expect it to retain the tough character which it has in England. It will flourish indeed but it needs careful tending. So with the common law. It has many principles of manifest justice and good sense which can be applied with advantage to peoples of every race and colour all the world over. But it also has many refinements,

---

[121] Örücü, above notes 94 and 105.

[122] Note the Turkish experience between 1926-1930, when secularism and westernisation were embraced through social reform legislation, which, as already mentioned, supported the large scale receptions of Codes from a number of civilian sources.

> subtleties and technicalities which are not suited to other folk. These off-shoots must be cut away. [123]

Today is not a period of imposition; yet neither is it one of voluntary reception. It is a time of imposed reception - a seemingly voluntary activity of import under circumstances in which the exporters hold all the cards. In this market, the exporter packages and labels his model as the one to be preferred over others. Such imposed receptions are to be seen in the Central and East European States, and within the context of European integration. While the Continental civilian systems are trying to impose civilian type Codes on the English common law, the English common law is introducing the system of judge-made law to them. A reaction to codification as top-down centralist legalism has led 'law and economics' scholars to propose the competition of legal rules in a free legal market as opposed to both codification, which is in effect unification, and direct harmonization. The elements of choice and efficiency here are the main criteria. Some advocates of the 'new *ius commune'*, stressing the need for re-systematization of the law and the development of a European legal doctrine, also claim that this could be done without a final synthesis and unification.[124] Whatever the means, the end result will be more transposition, more intertwining and more new shoots. Many new shoots are growing on family trees today and many more will grow there tomorrow.

Past receptions from Civil law and Roman law into English law have been called 'sporadic receptions' or 'injections', with 'civil law based reasoning filtering into common law'[125] ensuring that English law was constantly enriched. However, any rules based on Roman law or the later *ius commune* 'were immediately cut off from their roots', and 'assimilated into the specifically English framework, and given life outside their original context'. The resultant new law 'did not remain in dialogue with the old law from which it derived'; and 'once the borrowings are cut off from their roots they cease to be part of the same culture' as they grow in the

[123] Lord Denning J in *Nyali Ltd. v Attorney General* [1955] 1 All E R 646 at 653. This case and opinion is also quoted by C. Mubirumusoke, in 'Application of the Received Law of Torts in East Africa and the Problem of Transplanting Legal Norms', in T.W. Bechtler (ed) *Law in a Social Context (Liber Amicorum Honouring Professor Lon L Fuller)* (Deventer, Kluwer Law International, 1978),131 at p. 154.

[124] M. van Hoecke and F. Ost, 'Legal Doctrine in Crisis: towards a European Legal Science' (1998) 18 *Legal Studies*, 197 at pp. 211-215.

[125] D.J. Ibbetson, A Reply to Professor Zimmermann', in T.G.Watkin (ed) The *Europeanisation of Law*, United Kingdom Comparative Law Series:18 (London, UKNCCL, 1998), 224 at p. 228.

new soil.[126] Therefore, the influences were not systematic and the solutions did not remain the same. Nevertheless, these affected the growth of the tree. Today, European Law is regarded by many as an 'irritant' or a 'contaminant' of the common law. Again, the results will become apparent in the manner of the tree's growth.

We can detect a pattern in the growth of family trees. If legal systems continue to be grouped in the same manner, then there is a constant pattern; however, when the legal systems are grouped in a different manner, a new pattern emerges, as was suggested above. So we should be looking anew at what we have looked at before, look at others we have never or seldom looked at and look at them all from different perspectives, and try to detect new patterns. Some new patterns may look familiar, some may be the old shapes seen from a different angle, and some others be totally new. Each different grouping however, must be regarded as temporary and fluid. This is the time for a fresh approach to the grouping of the legal systems and the making of new patterns; a time of re-thinking. It is submitted that we are witnessing the actual growing and intermingling.

When we look at systems such as Malta, Thailand and Turkey and place them on the appropriate branches of the appropriate trees, or look once again at well-studied legal systems such as the German, French, Italian, Dutch and English horizontally and vertically from this new analytical standpoint, we will see many new and more vibrant patterns emerging.

Lawrence Rosen has recently put his concerns thus:

> The point, surely, is to get away – as most natural scientists have – from thinking of our subjects of study as organized like a stamp album or a set of pigeon-holes, ask whether we can see connections by trying out various combinations of associations and appreciate what the non-comparatists may ignore, that by widening our categories we see associations others have been missing.[127]

To sum up: as comparative lawyers, our main work now is to deconstruct the conventionally labelled pattern of legal systems and reconstruct them with regard to parentage, relationships, overlaps and interrelationships, and the diverse fertilizers,

---

[126] *Ibid.*, p. 229. Here I would like to quote from A.Watson, *Legal Transplants and European Private Law*, Ius Commune Lectures on European Private Law (2000 METRO, Institute for transnational legal research), p. 14: 'I am a tomato grower. I have plastic trays each with 24 small containers filled with a soil mix. Into each container I place a tomato seed, which I proceed to water and fertilise. When the plants are about six centimeters tall, I sell them. A buyer takes one, pinches it out of its container, and plants it in his yard. The plant soon stretches out its roots into the surrounding, very different soil. The purchaser fertilises it with his own, different from mine, fertiliser. The tomato plant is in a very different ethos on which its future depends. Even the sun strikes it differently. The tomato plant may flourish or even wither.. … Is the tomato plant the same plant as it was under my care?'

[127] L. Rosen, 'Beyond Compare', in: Legrand & Munday (eds.), above note 110, 493-510, at p. 507.

that is, the social and cultural context, and the grafting and pruning used in their development. In this way the comparative lawyer can draw up family trees, leaving ample space for newly forming growths.

4. THE REALITY OF MIXED AND MIXING SYSTEMS

At the outset let us note that the adjective 'mixed' now has much more frequent use than previously and with many meanings: a 'combination of various legal sources', a 'combination of more than one body of law within one nation, restricted to an area or to a culture', 'the existence of different bodies of law applicable within the whole territory of a country' and 'legal systems that have never had a single dominant culture'. In this Section we will talk of 'mixed legal systems' but also indicate the importance of the ongoing 'mixing' of legal systems. Instances of mixing are complicated as they may be overt or covert, structured or unstructured, complex or simple, blended or unblended; and often difficult to define. Mixing systems present themselves to comparative lawyers in diverse forms. There are ongoing states of 'mix', and a wide scope of knowledge is required to fully analyze this phenomenon, since many systems are shifting and in transition, and new types of mixes are constantly coming into being.

Being prone to using culinary metaphors, I envisage the new 'mixes' as 'cake mixes' where the outcome is not precisely known until the cake is fully cooked. There is always the chance of the cake being spoilt by under- or over-cooking. Moreover, whether the final taste of the cake is equal to the taste of the ingredients in combined form, whether the cake feels 'right' in the mouth and whether the recipe is a good one cannot be determined until the cake is eaten. However, in legal mixes the degree of success cannot be measured as easily. Neither can 'success' be defined from a single standpoint. Pre-determined economic, social, cultural, religious or ideological ends can all be factors by which success is measured. Efficiency, internalization, cultural shift, and the actual use of the new legal structures can all be criteria for measurement. Despite all this, the conclusion is that all law is mixed and there are no exceptions. It is only that the ways of mixing and the ensuing mixtures are different, and the levels of combinations and therefore the extent of the mix varies.

Given what has been said, certain questions arise: Do 'purist' categories work in analyzing legal systems? Can it be said that one fibre runs through the whole length of a thread? Which fibre alone is strong enough to denote the overall character of a legal system? Elspeth Attwooll ends her book, 'The Tapestry of the Law'[128] with a comment on a quotation from Wittgenstein: '... we should therefore accept that "as in spinning a thread we twist fibre on fibre. And the strength of the thread does not reside in the fact that some one fibre runs through its whole length,

[128] E.M.M. Attwooll, *The Tapestry of the Law: Scotland, Legal Culture and Legal Theory*, (London, Kluwer Academic Publishers, 1997), p. 250.

but in the overlapping of many fibres".' She concludes that there may be many different types of thread in the tapestry of the law.

Before one considers this 'tapestry' for any legal system it is worth considering the importance of both 'separateness' and 'distinctiveness' when studying legal systems, especially those we regard classically as mixed systems. The first point to remember is that all systems are in fact separate and distinct whether considered as mixed or not, noting that separateness may be a handicap but distinctiveness an asset. All systems differ in the way they have been formed as their histories show. All have elements from different sources. Systems also differ in the way the legal elite have reacted to their mix, handled it and tuned the incoming legal elements and moulded them into the legal system. In addition, systems differ as to how the mix has been sustained, nurtured or killed.[129] In all these senses each system is unique. However, as well as having features that are unique, each has features shared with others and features common to all. This enables us to study mixed systems both separately and together.

There is also the factor of 'temporal relativity'. A study of a legal system fifty years ago and again today may reveal considerable changes in its structure, context and conceptual infill and also in the attitude of lawyers, academics and people to it and its 'mix'. This leads to another point, which is the question of how the legal elite approach the system and assess it. Do they favour the 'mixedness' and try to further it or do they try to eradicate it in the name of convenience? Are legal systems in fact dominated by the so-called 'purists', 'pollutionists' or 'pragmatists'?

Sometimes 'mixedness' can be the manifestation of a transition. If 'mixedness' is regarded as a transitional phase on the road to a different end, then 'transitional jurisprudence' tells us that we should study the role and contribution of law and legal institutions to this process. Yet 'mixedness' can be a permanent state. When 'mixedness' is the end result of transition and is there to stay, this state of 'mixedness' itself could have been the aim. If 'mixedness' is a state of existence, then what should we study? The answer may lie in the fact that we should study the contribution and the role of the tuners of the law, that is the judge and the jurist.

Thus far then, it must be recognised that each mixed system is unique in its formation, the degree of 'mixture', the state of the blending and the end product. 'Mixedness' is usually a result of historical accident and accidents can lead along unexpected paths to unexpected outcomes. However, it must also be recognized that mixed systems share their 'mixedness' to a higher or lower degree with those other mixed systems which have been called 'mixed jurisdictions'.

Mixed systems can be viewed along a spectrum. As a general observation, one can start with simple mixes[130] where the blend is mainly between two traditions - the

---

[129] See J. du Plessis, 'The promises and pitfalls of mixed legal systems: The South African and Scottish Experiences' (1998) 3 *Stellenbosch Law Review*, 338.

[130] See for an analysis of mixed systems, E. Örücü, 'A Theoretical Framework for Transfrontier Mobility of Law' in Jagtenberg, Örücü & de Roo (eds) above note 105, and E. Örücü, 'Mixed and Mixing Systems: A Conceptual Search' in Örücü, Attwooll & Coyle (eds), above note 94.

civilian and the common law. This blend is as to content and substance, and not necessarily as to structure, although some of these systems have codified their civil laws, such as Louisiana, and some have not, such as Scotland. At the substantive level however, all legal systems are mixed whether we regard them as mixed legal systems or not.

Let us take a brief look at Scotland. Scotland, designated as a classical 'mixed jurisdiction', has one of these simple mixed systems, a system 'mixed' only at the substantive level.[131] Its history is unusual. The path of the migration of law from different sources into Scots law was seepage, imitation, inspiration, voluntary reception and imposed reception. The starting point was Scots customary law, which was then overlaid by Anglo-Norman law, Canon Law, Roman Law and European Civil Law and later in modern times by English law. Further, the system now has to absorb European Community law and European Human Rights law.

The Scottish mix did not 'result from the imposition of the Common Law upon a Civilian system by a colonial power, as in Louisiana or South Africa,' but rather from the close cultural and political ties with the jurisdictions of both traditions 'at different stages of its history'.[132] Thus the Scottish legal system can be regarded as being a system 'mixed from the very beginning.'[133] It has also been claimed that Scottish jurists created the 'mix' by selecting 'the best' of the ingredients from various sources.[134] However, the exact balance between the elements of this 'mix' in modern Scots law has long been and still is the subject of constant controversy at home and abroad. I have dubbed this blend elsewhere, a 'mixing bowl' and not a 'purée',[135] since the desire on the part of the legal elite has been to preserve its particular distinctiveness. Yet this desire was not always consistent in the past, nor is it today.[136] Nor is this distinctiveness always appreciated by the legal elite. It should also be pointed out that 'separateness' and 'distinctiveness' do not always coincide.[137]

---

131 See A. Rodger 'Thinking about Scots law' (1996) 1 *Edinburgh Law Review,* 3.

132 E. Reid, 'Comparative Law: Perspective from a Mixed Jurisdiction', in *HLS Cahier Nr.2 Methodology and its application* (Groningen, Facilitair Bedrijf, 2001), p. 49.

133 W.D.H. Sellar, 'Scots law – mixed from the very beginning? A tale of two receptions' (2000) 4 *Edinburgh Law Review,* 3

134 For a challenge to the view that the mixture was created by choosing deliberately from the 'two great pillars of the Western legal traditions', see R. Evans-Jones, 'Mixed Legal Systems, Scotland and the Unification of Private Law in Europe', in J. M. Smits (ed) *The Contribution of Mixed Legal Systems to European Private Law* (Groningen, Intersentia, 2001), 39, especially pp. 44-45.

135 See Örücü above note 105.

136 For example, neo-civilians underplay the strong and lasting influence of English law today, while some claim that Scotland is a common law country.

137 See T. Weir, 'Divergent legal systems in a single member state' (1998) 6 *Zeitschrift fur Europaisches Privatrect,* 564

Scots law, like any other, must be looked at historically and again today[138] through her judges and jurists, the actors and the tuners of her laws.[139] As legal elite vie with each other today, as they have done in earlier centuries, we find two different strands of interest in Scots law emerging as is typical of discussions that take place in all mixed systems. The first strand can be summarised through the views of Lord Hope of Craighead, the one time Lord President of the Court of Session who said that, 'The Scottish legal system is as much a part of Scotland as its landscape', and that since 1707 when it was preserved in the Act of Union, it has remained 'one of the essential pillars upon which Scotland has been able to base its separate identity. Far from withering under the influence of English law and English institutions, the legal system of Scotland has gone from strength to strength' and not only that but that 'Scotland's own legal system provides the essential structure for whatever may lie ahead.'[140]

We see the second strand as Scots law copes with contemporary technological and social developments. For instance, it is the opinion of another one-time Lord President of the same Court that we need to be pragmatic. He says that: 'Whether we find the appropriate solution to those problems in the classical Roman law of Julian, in the writings on Grotius, in the opinions of Lord Chancellor Brougham or in an article by some Australian academic seems to me to be, almost, a matter of indifference.' He is happy to belong to 'a legal world which stretches not only backwards for more than two thousand years but onwards across the globe.' The proviso is to 'abandon any notions of false superiority and go forward in that spirit', his prediction being that 'the future state of Scots law is likely to be happy.'[141]

We know that interest in Scots law and the Scottish legal system is growing in Europe today, where it is sometimes regarded as one of the models for the newly developing *ius commune*.[142] This interest has led to substantial contributions from Scottish scholars to a number of European Commissions and groups involved in creating General Principles in some fields of private law within the context of the European Union and also to renewed research activity into legal history at home.[143]

---

[138] See L. Farmer and S. Veitch (eds), *The State of Scots Law: Law and Government after the Devolution Settlement*, (Edinburgh, Butterworths, 2002).

[139] David Walker makes an apt point when he says that the word 'jurist' has no clearly defined meaning and is sometimes used 'as a rather grandiloquent synonym for a lawyer of any kind, or sometimes for a judge' D. M. Walker, *The Scottish Jurists* (Edinburgh, Green, 1985), p. 1.

[140] David Hope, Foreword to Derek Manson-Smith, *The Legal System of Scotland* (Edinburgh, HMSO, 1995), p. xi.

[141] Roger of Earlsferry, 'Preface' in Farmer and Scott, above note. 138, p. vi.

[142] See A. Watson 'A Common Private Law for Europe?' 9 *Maastricht Journal of European and Comparative Law* 4 (2002), for a contrary approach where he doubts the use of the intermediate position of mixed systems as a model for the future of European private law.

[143] K. Reid and R. Zimmermann (eds), *A History of Private Law in Scotland* (Oxford, New York, Oxford University Press, 2000); D.L Carey-Miller and R. Zimmermann (eds), *The Civilian Tradition and Scots Law: Aberdeen-quicentenary essays* (Berlin, Duncker & Humbolt, 1997).

It is possible to claim that since through cross-fertilization and horizontal transfers all legal systems within the European Union will eventually mix to some degree, a study of legal systems already mixed can teach valuable lessons to these mixing systems, and therefore the study of how they work is vital. In fact, mixed legal systems have always been the 'laboratories' of comparative lawyers. Now they have gained a special place in the process of European integration.

The existence of 'mixed legal systems', the creation of new mixes, and the present process of mixing may prove to be problematic for those who adhere to the definitive role of the cultural context. As mixing is beyond mere communication and conversation, how can the new blends be analyzed? This question needs an answer, but, difficult questions cannot be posed and answered in one breath!

Unless one starts from the premise that 'mixedness is itself the culture', there is no easy way forward. Even if one does start from that premise, one has to probe into the generation of the 'mixedness'. This is related to 'horizontal transfer', the possibility of which in turn is refuted by those who state that 'legal transplants are impossible'.[144] So we end in an impasse.

Obviously the mixed legal systems that attract attention in the European integration process are the simple ones, the 'mixing bowl' type, with only a limited number of ingredients. For the seekers of a new *ius commune*, one of the obstacles is that the ingredients to be blended or interlocked come from two different legal cultures - the common law and the civil law – and this, notwithstanding the variety that exists among the systems that belong to the so-called civil law tradition. Jan Smits for example, says that the mixed legal systems will provide 'inspiration' and the experiences of South Africa, Scotland, Quebec and Louisiana are consequently of great importance for the future developments of European private law.[145]

In this context, it is worth reading what Kenneth Reid and Reinhard Zimmermann have to say on this issue:

> If, therefore, the establishment of an intellctual connection between civil law and common law is regarded as an important prerequisite for the emergence of a genuinely European legal scholarship, it should be of the greatest interest to see that such connection has already been established ... in a number of

---

[144] See for example, P. Legrand, 'The Impossibility of "Legal Transplants"', 4 *Maastricht Journal of European and Comparative Law* (1997), 111; also see P. Legrand, 'What "Legal Transplant"?' in D. Nelken and J. Feest (eds), *Adapting Legal Cultures* (Oxford, Hart Publishing, 2001), 55-69.

[145] J.M. Smits, 'Introduction: Mixed Legal Systems and European Private Law', in J.M. Smits (ed) *The Contribution of Mixed Legal Systems to European Private Law* (Groningen, Intersentia, 2001) p. 9, and J.M. Smits, 'How to Take the Road Untravelled? European Private Law in the Making: A Review Essay', 6 *Maastricht Journal of European and Comparative Law* 1 (1999), 25-46, at p. 35.

> "mixed" legal systems. Such systems provide a wealth of experience of how civil law and common law may be accommodated within one legal system.[146]

In contemporary terms, law is the fruit of cross-fertilization and direct transposition. This is made clear by the fact that many legal systems are interrelated, such as those within the European Union. We must not limit our view of the world of 'mixing' to the confines of the European Union however. When looked through the lens of history, we see that many of the mixes of the past were formed by strong movements of transmigration of legal institutions and ideas, mostly in the form of impositions, and of divergent linguistic, communal or religious traditions. Legal systems are constantly mixing, blending, melting, then solidifying into new shapes as they cool down while transposition and tuning take their effect. There will always be new movements, new transposition and further tuning. Law is the outcome of a series of transpositions and legal systems are born out of overlaps.

As a consequence of transmigration of law problems arise. Systems that are mixing are evolving, are in transition, are inter-related or are in the process of becoming mixed systems. Particular attention must be paid to legal-cultural convergence and non-convergence that may come about as a result of legal import, and to any ensuing socio-cultural non-convergence. In this context, cultural pluralism, clash of diverse cultures, and the consequences for the importing legal system are of particular contemporary interest and legal pluralism is another significant concern. When elements from different internal logics come together, the usual outcome is a mixing system.

As already observed, mixed systems can be visualized along a spectrum. At one end of the spectrum of mixed systems is the position where transposition has not worked and the official legal system has 'curdled' and is dysfunctional, as is the case in Burkina Faso and Micronesia. At the other extreme is the position where the transmigration works smoothly, either because of extensive similarities in structure, substance and culture and fine 'tuning' such as in the Netherlands, or under the pressure of a ruling elite and the legal profession, that is, the actors of the law, as is the case in Turkey. Between these extremes lies the range of 'extraordinary' places. The composition of each depends on conditions such as the size of the transmigration, the characteristics of legal movement, the success or otherwise of transpositions and 'tuning', the element of 'force' or 'choice' inherent in the move and the social culture of the new environment.

At times, elements from socio-culturally similar and legal-culturally different legal systems come together forming 'mixed jurisdictions' of the 'simple' kind, the so-called 'mixing bowls', the ingredients being still in the process of blending but in need of further processing if a 'purée' is to be produced. An example of this type is Scotland as seen above. Next come the 'complex' mixed systems, 'extraordinary' places where the elements are both socio-culturally and legal-culturally different. This type can be called the 'Italian salad bowl' where, although the salad dressing

---

[146] K. Reid and R. Zimmermann, 'The Development of Legal Doctrine in a Mixed System', in Reid & Zimmermann, above note 143, p.3.

covers the salad, it is easy to detect the individual ingredients clearly through the side of the glass bowl. A good example of this is Algeria. Then there is the 'English salad plate', the ingredients sitting separately far apart on a flat plate with a blob of mayonnaise at the side into which the different ingredients can be dipped before consumption. Examples of this are the Sudan and Zimbabwe which lie towards the far end of the spectrum, the examples becoming more 'extraordinary' along the path, ending in 'curdling', with a dysfunctional legal system, as already mentioned.[147]

By 'extraordinary' place is meant a place not ordinarily covered by conventional comparative lawyers. In this sense 'ordinary' would be civil law and common law, usually limited to France, Germany, Italy and recently Spain, and England and the USA. Any system outside these would be a system in an 'extraordinary' place. This place could be one where the legal system or the law is based on, or heavily determined by, religion or belief. It could also be a place in which extraordinary events are taking place. Examples are Hong Kong, where in its relationship with China there is talk of 'one country two systems', Hungary, where there was a civilian tradition with no civil code, a socialist era with freedom of sorts for the civilian tradition to live on and where there is now a new era of transformation, and Turkey, where the dominant elite had a 'vision' which entailed changing not only the legal culture but also the socio-culture by employing foreign legal models leading to the erasure of the indigenous, and ending up in a 'limping marriage' with the European Union. An 'extraordinary' place could also be a place where there has been transmigration of laws between legal systems of both legal and socio-cultural diversity creating either legal pluralism, a mixed jurisdiction or a hybrid system, or unexpected results under pressure from an '*élite dominante*'. Sometimes there are overlaps between these meanings and a place could be 'extraordinary' in any or all these senses.[148] These places obviously defy the traditional theory of 'legal families', classical paradigms being totally inadequate.[149] One thing to remember however, is that legal systems in 'extraordinary' places are not necessarily the so-called 'exotic' legal systems.

Juxtaposing legal and socio-cultural systems of 'ordinary' and 'extraordinary' places, the comparative lawyer may find that the 'extraordinary' place is in some ways similar to the 'ordinary' one, the similarity being socio-cultural and legal-cultural, or legal-cultural only. When there is socio-cultural similarity but legal-cultural diversity between the two systems under review, then the comparative lawyer can seek refuge in historical explanations or the term 'historical accident'. In cases of such similarity, her task is to analyze the reasons for the similarity. However, even after very successful transpositions, an evolutionary dynamism emerges and systems go their own way. There can never be sameness. Concepts or

---

[147] See also E. Örücü, ' A Theoretical Framework for Transfrontier Mobility of Law' in Jagtenberg, Örücü & de Roo (eds) above note 105; and E. Örücü, 'Comparatists and extraordinary places', in Legrand & Munday (eds) above note 110.

[148] I discuss the issue of an 'extraordinary' place also elsewhere. See *Ibid.*

[149] The reader might be inclined to read this Section together with the previous Section on deconstruction of classifications.

institutions coming into different environments begin to change and internal 'contamination' occurs. Here the 'wave theory' of linguistics already referred to, which shows how change spreads like waves over a whole area and which can handle both resemblance and difference, may aid our understanding.[150]

What can the comparative lawyer do beyond trying to explain the reasons for the difference or divergence when the 'extraordinary' is totally different to the 'ordinary', both socio-culturally and legal-culturally, or socio-culturally only, or legal-culturally only. When the divergence is socio-cultural and yet there is legal-cultural similarity, again the term 'historical accident' may have to be resorted to.

Transmigration from a system of an 'ordinary' place into the system of an 'extraordinary' place may cause incompatibility or mismatch, and the deeper values and purposes of the two may be seemingly irreconcilable.[151] If reciprocity and mutuality were to be achieved between legal and cultural systems, then all would become 'contaminants' and 'irritants' of each other. In this case, comparative lawyers would be the bridge-builders between traditional cultures and Western style expressions of norms and standards. When the Eurocentric spectacles are discarded, the comparative lawyer immediately sees that indigenous law rarely consists of a single homogenous system. Dozens of indigenous legal orders as well as social orders can live side by side. To find, understand and re-present this law can be extremely difficult, especially when some of this law is unwritten and, some written but imperfectly translated. In many Asian systems for example, Western law was added to the religious laws of Hinduism, Buddhism, Confucianism and Islam, which themselves co-existed prior to colonization. The mixture was also complicated by the fact that not all laws were applicable to all peoples, where there was in fact division into different legal groups, different parts of the population being classified as 'foreign Orientals', 'assimilated Asians', 'Europeans', 'non-natives' or 'natives'. The resultant mixture continues to give rise to problems in countries such as Indonesia, Taiwan and Malaysia even today. The comparative lawyer must understand the relationship between these layers of systems in order to depict such systems in transition today.

Transmigration of law has followed the paths of colonization, re-settlement, occupation, expansion, and inter-relationship. The methods of these migrations were imposition, reception, imposed reception, co-ordinated parallel development, infiltration, imitation and variations and combinations of these. The consequences have been the birth of systems in transition and mixing, mixed jurisdictions, inter-related systems, evolving systems, layered-law, hyphenated legal systems, harmonization, unification and standardization. There are conceptual implications in all this. Comparative lawyers must now re-define law, legal concepts, legal rules and legal system, re-assess clashes between culture and law (legal cultures in diversity,

---

150 See Renfrew, above note 107, p. 105.

151 D.S. Berry, 'Interpreting Rights and Culture: Extending Law's Empire' (1998) IV *Res Publica – A Journal of Legal and Social Philosophy*, 1 at p. 14.

legal cultures in affinity), explain top-down and bottom-up law-making, law reform, legal systems in transition and adopt a new approach to legal families.

In the past the main emphasis was on historical transplants. Today, one must assess the consequences of encounters within the European Union, for example, as instances of reciprocal influence, horizontal transfers or cross-fertilization between adjacent systems, rather than only consider them as the transplant or contamination of common law by civilian input into European Community law.

In our day, many legal systems, both in 'ordinary' and 'extraordinary' places, are in transition to differing extents. Most are, and will continue to be considering the re-shaping of their social as well as their legal systems. Comparative law will be asked to provide answers. Comparative lawyers must concentrate on the way in which legal institutions are connected, disconnected and transposed, and extend their subject beyond the traditional and 'ordinary' geographic and substantive borders into the 'extraordinary'.

Reciprocal influences must be examined in new ways since the emphasis, the consequences and the means are different to those of the past. Most obvious 'reciprocal influence' today is in Europe within the European Union, but transpositions from the Western legal traditions to the Central and East European legal systems will in future be of greater importance. Beyond Europe, other cross-fertilizations are taking place. One such is that between China and Hong Kong. The consequences are the birth of a 'new genre of *mixité*', more 'extraordinary' places, the blurring of the demarcation lines between the generally accepted classifications of legal families, and the emergence of new clashes between legal cultures themselves, or legal cultures and socio-cultures. The means are apparently voluntary reception rather than colonization and imposition as in the past, though imposed receptions are more prominent in some places.

At present many legal systems are experiencing fundamental upheaval. Some are re-shaping themselves with the help of outside models chosen from competing systems. This is so in social, economic and legal terms. They are systems in transition. Some, living within certain regions or groupings, are fundamentally effected by reciprocal influences. Some others are swayed by globalization, a term much used in our day. How should comparative lawyers approach this new world?

It has been suggested by Vernon Palmer that we should be talking of a new 'third legal family' alongside the common law and the civil law families with the name 'Mixed Jurisdictions' to include a number of historically determined mixes which he regards as sharing certain characteristics. This means that these systems 'are built upon dual foundations of common-law and civil-law materials', that is, there is a 'specificity of the mixture'; the mix is obvious to both insiders and outsiders, that is, 'obvious to an ordinary observer'; and the private-law sphere has 'the outward appearance of a "pure" civil-law system', whereas the public law sphere 'will appear to be typically Anglo-American', that is, there is a 'structural allocation of content'. According to Vernon Palmer, these 'are the lowest common denominators of a mixed jurisdiction.'[152]

Although the idea is presented as a comprehensive world-wide study of 'mixed jurisdictions', Vernon Palmer uses the concept of 'mixed jurisdictions' in a narrow and conventional sense, considers only co-existing and commingling between the civil law and the common law and talks of a 'closed family' of fifteen members, with seven of them studied in the volume. This is only a partial answer, as clearly not all 'mixes' can be pooled together and not all the existing members of such a family would have the same or similar ingredients. In addition to the fact that all legal systems are mixes to some degree and that they continue to mix, I see many more mixed systems of different parentage and moreover, many more becoming mixed. It would be extremely difficult to place Quebec, Hong Kong and Algeria, all mixed systems, into one family, for example. Simple mixes, complex mixes, as well as dual systems and systems adhering to legal pluralism cannot be all grouped together. Even if we were to accept that Vernon Palmer's fifteen individual legal systems share certain characteristics to justify placing them together and to give this conglomeration the status of a 'Third Family of Mixed Jurisdictions', what would stop us from creating yet a fourth and a fifth family for other mixed systems? What of contemporary mixing systems and systems in transition? How would these be grouped and analyzed? We need to ask ourselves whether comparative lawyers are any better off by viewing the new world with its increasing number of mixtures through this approach. Vernon Palmer's attempt may be an elegant method of re-grouping but it does not solve the problems of understanding and analyzing the world we live in today. At a time when the classical groupings are proving to be inadequate for such understanding, other approaches must be sought.[153]

One other approach is that offered by Anthony Ogus who looks at mixed or 'hybrid' systems through the lenses of a 'law and economics' scholar and places them into three categories.[154] In his first group are those systems 'where a culture was imposed by a colonialist power, but where a native culture persisted to some degree'. In this category the native culture 'competes' with the imposed culture. Many African countries are shown here as examples.[155] In the second category are 'countries which have experienced successive colonialist or other occupation'. Here, each successive foreign culture has had a major impact on the legal culture and competes with the other. The examples he chooses for this category are Quebec, Louisiana and South Africa.[156] Countries 'which experienced industrial and commercial development relatively late and where rulers recognised the need to look elsewhere for more sophisticated legal input than the domestic legal system could

[152] Palmer, above note 78, p. 7-9.
[153] See for example, the previous Section.
[154] A. Ogus, 'The Contribution of Economic Analysis of Law to Legal Transplants', in: J.M. Smits (ed.), *The Contribution of Mixed Legal Systems to European Private Law* (Groningen, Intersentia, 2001), pp. 27-37.
[155] *Ibid.*, p. 35.
[156] *Ibid.*

provide' form his third category, his examples being Japan, Turkey and Greece. Anthony Ogus says that in this category 'there were effectively "tenders" from several major legal cultures to supply the necessary set of specifications'. East European States using Western models for law reform are also regarded as falling into this category, though 'in somewhat different circumstances'.[157]

Anthony Ogus goes further and offers some predictions for the future. He is of the opinion that the three categories share characteristics which separate them from legal systems with one dominant culture. The first characteristic is that these systems have more than one 'specification set' which should make it easier – that is, cheaper – for them to incorporate foreign legal concepts in the future. Then, unlike single-culture systems where a high degree of formalism is expected, in these systems it is less likely that there will be 'inefficient levels of formalism and complexity'. Even if there is collusion – that is, cartellization - in these mixed jurisdictions between the representatives of the different cultures, 'some degree of rivalry can be expected'. When such competition exists, then the lawmakers and the consumers can compare the 'performance of the areas of law subjected to the different specification sets'. The expected outcome is that mixed systems will be 'more efficient, and adapt more readily to changing external variables, than those with a single dominant culture', though much depends on how the competition works. Of course, there is always the possibility that optimal selections may not be made from between the different 'tenders'; the 'rents' to be enjoyed by a particular foreign legal system may be too attractive for domestic lawyers trained in that system, for example. Despite such problems however, from the 'law and economics' point of view, the future is quite bright for mixed systems. His general conclusion is that they should, 'unless obstructed by private interest groups allied to a particular culture, adapt more readily to efficient legal reform'.[158] Comparative lawyers need to consider what contribution, if any, does a 'law and economics' approach have in assessing 'mixed systems' over and above other approaches.

We could ask ourselves whether the three examples given in the previous Section on the 'Deconstruction of classifications' can be better understood using the approaches suggested by Anthony Ogus or Vernon Palmer.

The first example given there was Malta. As already indicated, its legal history started with the settling Phoenicians. The *Corpus Iuris* was brought to them by the Roman conquest and feudal law as applied in Spain, Naples and Sicily by the Norman invasion. The Moors invaded and had direct influence on the Maltese language. Local usage was recognized by the Knights of St. John who issued declarations on private law drawing on the laws of other countries, mostly Italian. The French conquest brought with it Napoleonic laws. Then the common law arrived with the British. An eclectic Criminal Code drafted under a strong Italian influence but with pervasive English and Scottish impact is one result, and a Commercial Code based on the French Code (except in the field of Maritime law which follows English law) is another. The 1873 Civil Code is predominantly based

[157] *Ibid.*, p. 36.
[158] *Ibid.*, p. 36-37.

on the French and Italian Codes and also on the Municipal Code de Rohan, the Civil Code of Louisiana and the Austrian Civil Code. Canon law applies in family law where there is also the influence of English law, German law, Italian law and French law. Constitutional law is mainly British. Maltese and English are the official languages. All ingredients apply cumulatively and interactively. In addition, Malta is now poised to join the European Union. What kind of new mixing can we expect? How is it possible to fit this mixture into any of the suggested categories?

The second example was Thailand which was never a colony. Its modern texture has been formed from many sources such as English Law, German Law, French Law, Swiss Law, Japanese Law and American Law, all since the end of the nineteenth century. Laws from historic sources in existence since 1283, such as rules from indigenous culture and tradition, customary laws and Hindu jurisprudence, still to be found in some modern enactments, sit alongside modern ones. In addition, Thai Codes were originally drafted in English and French before being translated into Thai, and the legal system of today still grapples with problems of translation and connotation.[159] How then are we to categorize Thailand?

Turkey was our third example. Turkey was placed by Anthony Ogus in his third category. It might fit there. But does that aid our understanding of the system as it works? Further still, can his predictions for future success apply here? As we have seen, Turkey as a cross between Swiss law, German law, Italian law, French law, Roman law, a covert Islamic law and local customary law, and more recently, European law and American law, is a more extreme mixture. This legal system was brought about by grafting, pruning and intertwining. An elite concerned with changing not only the law and legal culture but the people themselves and their way of life from traditional to modern by the introduction of radical social reform laws, forged the new legal system solely by receptions from abroad. Swiss law is the basis of Civil law, German law of Commercial law, Italian law of Criminal law and French law of Administrative law. These have intertwined with each other and with the diverse socio-culture, to form the present legal system.[160] Turkey is now trying to assimilate many European Community directives and the '*acquis communautaire*' in the hope of joining the European Union. There are also the demands of the International Monetary Fund and the World Bank. One of their conditions is the 'improvement of the legal system' and further 'modernization' of the law, 'modernization' being understood to mean further elimination of 'traditional values'. What does the future hold for this mixture?

The above three are not classical 'mixed jurisdictions' in the sense that there is no underlay and overlay of laws from different sources as in Hong Kong, where until 1990, English common law was the overlay with Chinese customary law the underlay, and where now English common law is itself an underlay alongside Chinese customary law under a spreading overlay of modern Chinese law. Although

---

[159] The information is from Jutharat Compeerapap, See above note 100.

[160] Since the roots have not been cut off from the parents and the source-laws are still referred to as, for example, in the case of '*İsviçre-Türk Hukuku*', when referring to the civil law, I have called this legal system 'hyphenated'. See Örücü, above note 117, pp. 80-118.

not 'mixed jurisdictions' in the classical sense, the three examples above are certainly 'mixed' and 'mixing' systems, the various elements from different sources being woven into the tapestry of their laws.

All legal systems are born of different parentage, from marriages between systems and sub-systems of such. Some parents cohabited, some had life-long and some passing relationships. It is difficult to determine the exact level of hybridity in each case. What is clear, however, is that combinations of disparate legal and social cultures give birth to mixed systems. Later formations of such systems are by horizontal transfer. Overlap, cross-fertilization, reciprocal influence, fusion, infusion, grafting and the like are all responsible for the coming into being of mixed and mixing systems. As now widely acknowledged, there are indeed no pure systems in the legal world and various degrees of hybridity arise from various degrees, levels and layers of crossing and intertwining.

It is obviously easier to handle such legal systems when there are clear signs of their different legal cultural, racial, ethnic and religious parentage. Some of these systems have already been grouped as 'mixed jurisdictions' and are treated as *numerus clausus* as noted. However, as pointed out, there are many other overt mixes with different parentage. There are also some covert mixtures, the results of the same or of other combinations. It is the covert and the ongoing mixes that really tease the comparative lawyer.[161]

It follows from the foregoing that awareness that law is not static, that it moves and changes and that legal systems today are at a crossroads, is essential. Irrespective of whether the future holds confluence or divergence for legal systems, one thing is certain: more and more systems will be mixed and mixing be they in Europe, in South East Asia or the Middle East. In line with these developments, comparative law research is also at a crossroads, and the new starting point is to study 'mixedness' in order to facilitate an understanding of current and future patterns of legal development. It is the study of this 'mixedness' that can illuminate the path towards the comprehension of the interaction of law and culture as no other study can.

5. LIMITS OF COMPARATIVISM?

When one talks of 'limits' one may mean borders, boundaries, frontiers, margins, edges, perimeters or obstacles, restrictions and restraints. Some of these are rigid, some are not.

When one talks of 'limits of comparativism' one is referring to certain factors that may restrict the 'comparative law enterprise'. One could be talking of the limits of the comparative lawyer herself – intrinsic limits; the limits of the context and the environment in which she works – extrinsic limits; the limits of the purpose of

[161] Örücü , above note 94, pp. 344-345.

comparativism; the limits of its use; the limits of its methodology; the limits of topics to be compared and so on. Some of these are severe, some are not.

In this Section, I regard 'limit' as a 'not so rigid restriction' and question the existence of some of the factors regarded by some as insurmountable. Spelling this out, I will consider below the 'limits of comparativism' as I see them in two categories. The first is related to the comparative lawyer herself and the second arises from factors extrinsic to her. In each category there are a number of issues to look at, some more serious than others.

Before I venture into the first category however, it is important to note the importance of the comparative lawyer herself. I will do this by reference to other forms of cognizance by an audience.

A painting, though an interpretation of the world by a painter, can be directly seen when hung on a wall, and a book can be read in direct contact with a writer. Obviously it can be said that a picture may be enhanced or obscured by the place where it is hung, under what light and so on. So for a book, clearly printed on good quality paper and published with care. Nevertheless, the contact is direct in both cases. However, in music three factors come together, the composer where the composition starts, the player-interpreter through whom the piece is heard and the listener where it ends. The composition reflects the personality of the composer and the re-presentation of the interpreter.

So it is in comparative law. In comparative law we start with the foreign law - the composition - reflecting the society for which it is envisaged in internal and external contexts,[162] the composer being the actor of the law, in a 'top-down' sense, the legislature, and a 'bottom-up' sense, the judge. The comparative lawyer is the interpreter and the target audience is the listener. Since law must be considered by the comparative lawyer in the context in which it lives, she, as the interpreter, is the middleman. The target audience is exposed to the law through the comparative lawyer's conception of that law.

It follows from the foregoing that since foreign law passes through the interpreter raconteur, the comparative lawyer, the first limit of comparativism is of course, the comparative lawyer herself. Hence we can now delve into the first category of limits. A number of issues will be dealt with here.

Our first question is, 'Can she find the law, understand it, interpret it in keeping with the original meaning and faithfully represent it?' It can be said that in our day most comparative lawyers do possess the technical equipment to meet any demand made upon them, the necessary language skills, cultural appreciation and the tools of social science methodology. But are they all sufficiently familiar with the totality of the legal system and the context of the foreign jurisdiction? Do they all have that keen eye for detail and the willingness to see both similarities and differences and the skills for transmitting this to the audience?

---

162 For a discussion of mirror theories, and what mirrors society, what law mirrors and the three versions (mirror, reflection and connection) of the metaphor see W. Twining, 'A Post-Westphalian Conception of Law: Review essay' (2003) 37 *Law and Society Review*, pp. 206-208.

A comparative lawyer's florid addenda to basic facts without sufficient confirmation may mislead the audience and even take on a life of its own; it may even start a new narrative. This first limitation then, can only be approached with 'trust' in the integrity and meticulousness of the comparative lawyer. For example, I would regard myself as having a 'deep level knowledge' of Turkish law and the Turkish language and am at times amazed at passing remarks made in the works of comparative lawyers which misrepresent Turkish law and its socio-cultural context. Incorrect dates given for pieces of legislation, bizarre explanations for certain legal developments, mis-spelt words and postures of unfounded authority are frequent.[163]

The comparative lawyer may be forever confronted with the problem of how closely she can keep to the actual. We expect a high level of legal intelligence and sensitivity from comparative lawyers. However, some exaggeration and generalization of findings may be inevitable. Also we must keep in mind that there will always be a number of different interpretations, since law is a living thing capable of being seen in different lights and from different angles at different times even by the same comparative lawyer.

Remembering that to a large extent interpretation is a matter of emphasis, the audience must know the interpreter as well as the law. The comparative lawyer must be faithful to the original material, but her personality, views and approach will inevitably colour her interpretation. For example, a comparative lawyer whose views generally coincide with the first Variations in the Chapters of this work will re-present reality differently to the one following the second Variations of the sub-themes of the theme 'Comparative Law'. Each comparative lawyer thinks differently, has different emotional attitudes and a different philosophy of life. It is only to be expected that they handle material differently. There could even be exaggeration or even falsification of material by the comparative lawyer. The target audience must be aware of the comparative lawyer's input to what they are being presented with. As a point of reference the audience needs some idea of the legal systems under consideration and be able to sense the contribution of the comparative lawyer to it. What is needed is an intelligent body of audience who also must have a sense of responsibility. This requires a broadened base. It is insufficient to be involved only in the conventional aspects of the normative legal order.[164] The target audience must develop an unprejudiced broad taste for the different. Above all, the comparative lawyer and the audience must both 'hear' and 'listen'.

As pointed out above, interpretation, re-creation and re-presentation are delicate tasks. In these processes we see other limits of comparativism related to the comparative lawyer. A major one is a lack of a deep knowledge of language. A comparative lawyer's most important tool is language, the language of the foreign law, the 'original language' and the language of the target-audience. Grammar,

---

[163] I am not giving any references here to avoid embarrassing some of my colleagues!

[164] See H.T. Klami, 'Comparative Law and Legal Concepts' in *Oikeustiede Jurisprudentia,* ((1981) XIV Suomalaisen Lakimiesyhdistyksen Uosikirya (Vammala 1981), pp. 67-166, for an intriguing and thorough discussion of the role and limits of comparative law, as well as the theoretical problems, legal dogmatics and contexts.

structure and vocabulary can hide a host of relationships between law and the language in which it is expressed. The same relationship exists between law and the language into which it is interpreted. Law is expressed in language but until law has been constructed and applied, it remains merely words on paper. Meaning must be given to language and there is never one single meaning but permutations of meaning. Especially in relation to concepts that do not exist in the target language, any translation made by the comparative lawyer, however well she may know both languages, may remain at the level of the idiosyncratic.[165]

In addition, when dealing with customary law, the comparative lawyer must remember that it is not always explicit or written and is often known only by word of mouth. She must re-present this in explicit language, at times abstracted from the facts. Here a further danger may arise from a misunderstanding of what is 'said', or a misinterpretation of what is 'not said', leading to analytical conclusions or even universal truisms. My example for this is simple. Most people who have travelled to Turkey tell me: 'Turkish coffee is awful, it is so sweet, so strong and so gritty! I could never drink that.'[166] Coffee cannot be sweet by nature and personally, I always have my coffee without any sugar in any country. Turkish coffee is sweet, strong and gritty only for the half-enlightened and is the result of misunderstanding and confusion between what is 'said' and what is 'not-said'.[167] A Turk when ordering coffee would never ask for, '*kahve*', but would say '*sade*' (without sugar) or '*şekerli*' (with sugar) with gradations such as '*az*', '*orta*' or '*çok şekerli*' (meaning a little, some or a lot of sugar). Thus when the foreigner ('other') asks for 'coffee', the waiter makes his own judgement on what is being asked for. He assumes that, 'foreigners like sweet things' and brings a very sweet cup of coffee. Neither would a Turk drink the coffee grains in the bottom of the cup, thus the coffee itself is neither strong nor gritty. Whereas the 'other' drinks her coffee, notices that a lot of coffee is still sitting in the bottom of her small cup and swallows the grounds which should have remained at the bottom, and from which she might even have her fortune read! Misunderstanding, misinterpretation and misrepresentation! If this can happen in so simple an act as drinking coffee, imagine the perils at the door of a comparative lawyer facing oral law!

Another acute problem is translation. This we observe even when comparing the name of our theme, Comparative Law, its English version, with French, Italian, German, Dutch or Turkish versions. Then there are well known and frequently observed problems with terms such as public policy and *ordre public*; rule of law,

[165] See the PhD thesis in Tai law, above note 100, and some concepts made up in Turkish while translating the foreign Codes.

[166] This example was inspired by the one provided by M. de S. –O, -l'E Lasser, 'The question of understanding' in P. Legrand and R. Munday (eds*) Comparative Legal Studies: Traditions and Transitions* (Cambridge, Cambridge University Press, 2003), p. 237.

[167] For the novice: A cup of Turkish coffee is individually made to personal taste. It is not filtered but cooked. The grounds fall to the bottom and stay there, and are not meant to be consumed. Sugar, if asked for, is added while the coffee is being cooked.

Rechtsstaat and due process; law, *droit*, *recht*, rights and so on. Bernhard Grossfeld, analyzes the relationship of law and language and asks the questions:

> All this is very alarming for the comparative lawyer: if law lives in and through language, what happens to it when it is transferred to another language? If the structure of a language influences, or even determines, the mode and content of thought, might it not be that any language can only express certain thoughts, and that these thoughts differ from culture to culture?[168]

This concern is even deeper than that voiced by Harold Gutteridge in 1938: 'I would, in fact, be disposed to assert that pitfalls of terminology are the greatest difficulty and danger which the student of comparative law encounters in his novitiate.'[169] Not only the novice but also the seasoned comparative lawyer is at risk here.

Let me complement Bernhard Grossfeld's observations of the Japanese language by giving another example. In the Turkish language, the verb is always at the end of the sentence; the subject need not always be mentioned but be understood; there are no separate personal pronouns for 'he', 'she' and 'it', and the word 'o' may mean he, she or it. A sentence may be extremely long, cut across by a number of clauses carrying the thought from one subject to another. So for example, in a translation from English, say a judgement by the late Lord Denning, usually consisting of one line long sentences, the directness and the crispness of the English language could be totally lost and the idea become fuzzy. If we agree that limits of the language mark limits of understanding,[170] then either certain legal ideas are untranslatable, or altered in the process. Therefore the comparative lawyer would be advised to keep the original terminology and offer a description and an explanation of it in the target language in a footnote.[171] Since comparative lawyers will in future be going more often to more 'extraordinary' places and to cultures beyond the Western, the limits for comparative lawyers will be reached more quickly, the fundamental difficulty being the overcoming of conceptual differences. It might be worth remembering that, 'A word denoting an object, an institution or, if such exists, a psychological characteristic peculiar to the source-language culture is always more or less untranslatable – everything else is more or less translatable.'[172]

---

[168] B. Grossfeld, *The Strength and Weakness of Comparative Law*, trans. T. Weir (Oxford, Clarendon Press, 1990), p. 101.

[169] H.C. Gutteridge, 'The comparative aspects of legal terminology', (1938) 12 *Tulane Law Review*, 401-11, at p. 403.

[170] Grossfeld, above note 168, p. 101.

[171] See M. Weston, *An English Reader's Guide to the French Legal System* (New York / Oxford, Berg, 1991) for a most valuable contribution, specifically the first three chapters, pp. 9-42.

[172] *Ibid.*, p. 9 where Weston quotes P.P. Newmark, 'Twenty-three restricted rules of translation', (1973) 12 *Incorporated Linguists*, p. 12. Also for the 'translation theory' and some problems that may arise see N. Jamieson, 'Source and Target-Oriented Comparative Law', (1996) 44 *American Journal of Comparative Law*, 121.

Connotations, as well as words themselves can pose problems. For example, the British think in terms of 'reasonableness' and assess an administrative action in relation to administrative action taken by a 'reasonable administrator'. 'Reasonableness' would apply to all professions. However once, while giving a paper on English administrative law and judicial review in a Seminar in Turkey, I talked of 'Wednesbury reasonableness' and the 'reasonable administrator'. This caused a lot of mirth and I was asked whether there could ever be a 'reasonable administrator' and what would he be like, a question seldom asked in Britain since the connotation of 'reasonable' is well internalized. I was then told by one Turkish judge that a Turkish 'reasonable judge (!)' could never base a decision on such vague criteria as the 'Wednesbury test'!

In addition, many foreign legal terms do not have a directly corresponding translation. Therefore, even bilingual legal dictionaries cannot be relied on exclusively. They can even be dangerous.[173] When there is a translation, meanings often may not be the same. Examples abound and one finds lists of these in most books and articles on comparative law. As to definitions, to find internationally acceptable definitions is very difficult indeed. Generality and vagueness can make such definitions almost useless. These are some of the problems faced by comparative lawyers when involved in the preparation of international Conventions or in creating multi-language legal texts. Comparative lawyers working for the enlarged European Union will face considerable problems. Those of us who are also interested in other regions of the world encounter even more significant difficulties. There is a growing need for explanatory bilingual glossaries and dictionaries.[174]

At the most basic level, a simple warning to students of comparative law is, 'beware of words which are similar in two languages or two cultures'. One example I give at the very beginning of my comparative law classes is the word 'sheriff'. It goes thus: A serious Scottish student of comparative law is on holiday in the deep South in the USA. He wants to carry out a small piece of empirical research by interviewing a judge of a court of first instance, for him a 'sheriff'. However using the vocabulary of his domestic legal culture and with the assertion that he is in an English speaking country, he asks his friend whether he could be introduced to a 'sheriff'. Imagine his amazement when he meets the American 'sheriff' with all his paraphernalia! Had he asked to meet a judge from a court of first instance, he would have had no such surprise and been able to carry out a meaningful survey. Moral of the story: dangers arising from similar or related languages may be the most acute! A complete misunderstanding is the worst possibility, but just as bad is the meaningless or unnatural use of language for the target audience. Then, more subtly of course, there is the apparent correspondence of terms that have different meanings which one finds in the various so-called civil law countries.

---

[173] See for severe criticism put forth, G.R. de Groot, 'The quality of bilingual dictionaries' 7 *Maastricht Journal of European and Comparative Law* 4 (2000) 331-335, who says that out of approximately one hundred bilingual dictionaries only six can meet the requirements of the comparative lawyer.

[174] See *Ibid.*, p. 139.

Up to this point, the limits of comparativism have been related to the comparative lawyer herself: the possible lack of a deep level of language, problems related to listening and hearing, and the pitfalls related to translation, especially translation of culture-specific concepts. This last leads us into one more limit related to the comparative lawyer, that of cultural deficit. The comparative lawyer must be able to understand the context well in order to approach a legal system in context confidently before she can re-present what she finds. The context - mainly the culture and therefore localism - may sometimes escape even an academic looking at her own law. It is often said that an outsider at times sees more clearly than an insider, but the question is whether seeing is understanding. It is in some ways comparable to hearing and listening noted above.

The wood may not be visible because of the trees and yet a knowledge of the wood is essential for the identification of the trees. This becomes an occupational hazard for comparative lawyers who may pay close attention to formal and substantial detail but lose sight of the text as a whole, let alone the context. The cultural deficit can only be closed if one is aware of its importance and impact, and if one is humble enough to correct possible misunderstandings by using the experience of domestic academics, practicing lawyers and judges in the confirmation stage of one's research in order to check the correctness of one's understanding, insight, imagination and creativity. However, even the best intentioned comparative lawyer will have great difficulty in tackling law as a bottom-up phenomenon. The top-down approach is easier to cope with since the material is to hand, it is easier to understand and re-present. But the apparent bottom can prove to be bottomless and the re-presentation can become idiosyncratic, and unreliable. This ties in with yet another limit of comparatavism related to the comparative lawyer herself, and that is, her conception of law itself.

If the comparative lawyer believes that reporting formal rules of the foreign law and signalling differences and similarities between the laws studied are the sole aims of her research, and her conception of law is the normative legal order found in legislation, regulations, judicial decisions and doctrinal writings, then of course, this black-letter-law approach would have already restricted the comparative lawyer and prevented her from entering into any discourse of context, or show any interest in the bottom-up approach to law. This comparative lawyer would be happy to limit herself to descriptive translations and information on foreign law. She may not even need a specific methodological approach and definitely no theory. In this case, the cultural deficit remains but is regarded as of no importance in comparative law. Issues of cultural pluralism let alone legal pluralism would not even arise in the normative context of 'law'.

The question 'What is law?' however, is as hotly contested as the question 'What is comparative law?'. The term 'comparative law' has been bisected and the discourse taken to an inquiry into the meaning of both 'comparative' and of 'law'.[175]

---

[175] See G. Samuel, 'Epistemology and Comparative Law: Contributions from the Sciences and Social Sciences' in M. Van Hoeche (ed) *Epistemology and Methodology of Comparative Law* (Oxford, Hart Publishing, 2004).

Obviously, before one can 'compare' one must determine what one is comparing, that is 'what is law'.

The law then is the 'composition' of which the comparative lawyer is the 'interpreter'. The composition must be grasped with all its intricacies, textually, contextually, with its form and content, and the environment within which it lives. Legal scholars approach 'law' in many different ways. Some analyze law as rules, as norms, as system, as virtual facts, constructed facts or actual facts, as cases, as culture or as tradition. Some analyze law in relation to history, to economics, to legal theory, to sociology or even to anthropology. I once said for example, that 'law is transposition'.[176] In addition, one can consider law as coming from the 'top', from the 'bottom', from the 'side', from the 'back' or moving 'forward'. In fact, there is no agreement on what 'law' is or on its properties! There are arguments about the nature of law and further, arguments on the nature of the arguments about the nature of law.[177] Thus, as Joseph Raz says: 'The list of the essential properties of law is indefinite',[178] and as pointed out by Robert Alexy, the 'essential properties of law are topics of a seemingly never-ending dispute. The number of arguments put forward in this dispute are, as always, even greater than the number of problems that they deal with'.[179] Having already dramatically oversimplified the issues, I will not try to rehearse the whole debate here.

The last limit of comparativism in this first category of limits, all related to the comparative lawyer herself, is her methodological tools and how she uses them. The problems with social science methodology and the failure of mainstream comparative lawyers to avail themselves of this methodology have already been discussed in Chapter 5. Listening to a piece of music many times does not necessarily bring an understanding of it and might actually have a dulling effect to nuances; neither does reading material over and over again necessarily bring enlightenment. For a fuller picture, the reader should now consult Chapter 5 on 'How to compare?' and read both Variations in it. This limit is also related to the comparative lawyer's conception of the law, how far she is going into context and what is the level of her comparative venture.

All the above limits of comparativism relate to the interpreter, her conception of law, the depth of her knowledge of languages, translation skills and the possibilities of listening and hearing, and to the audience of comparative law. Hearing but not listening is also a limitation of the audience though obviously not as significant as for the comparative lawyer. A cultural deficit is a further problem.

The second category of limits of comparability is related to nationalism, specific national visions and the 'contrarian challenge'. The 'contrarian challenge'

---

176 Örücü, above note 106.

177 See R. Alexy, 'The Nature of Arguments about the Nature of Law', in L.H. Meyer, S.L. Paulson and T.W. Pogge (eds.), *Rights, Culture, and the Law* (Oxford, Oxford University Press, 2003), 3-16.

178 J. Raz, 'On the Nature of Law', *Archives for Philosophy of Law and Social Philosophy*, 82 (1996), 1-25, at p. 6.

179 Alexy, above note 177, p. 4.

straddles the two categories since it is also related to the interpreter, her personality and philosophy. So, let us start with this. The so-called 'contrarian challenge' advocates that the comparative lawyer be only interested in difference. However, in its extreme form, assuming an epistemological pessimism, there could even be denial of comparativism. Cultural differences in this extreme position would bar comparative law research. The 'other' would remain a mystery, since any attempt at understanding the 'other' would only lead to misconceptions and misleading results. We seem to be living in 'closed worlds'. In its more flexible form however, comparative law works, but must be involved only with differences between systems. There is a natural link between the 'contrarian challenge' and the 'difference theory'.[180]

Pierre Legrand invites the comparative lawyer,

> to place herself firmly in opposition and to pursue the *contrarian challenge*. Indeed, there is no more pressing research and teaching programme for a comparatist to undertake in this historical juncture than actively to promote the merits of the *contrarian challenge* for comparatists themselves, for comparative legal studies, and for the European legal order.[181]

He states that,

> From the moment he [comparative lawyer] ascribes meaningful meaning to law through tradition or culture and accepts that nothing can be explicated without the support of historical narratives arising over the *longue durée*, the comparatist naturally engages in interdisciplinary studies. He also spontaneously privileges the idea of difference as *principium comparationis*.[182]

The next limit in this second category is nationalism. A lawyer from the legal system of a country where nationalism is a pronounced philosophy will have little room for developing an interest in comparative law or an understanding of foreign laws. The official position may even be to direct any interest in comparative law research towards proof of the superiority of the domestic legal system. This could only be frustrating for the comparative lawyer and be an impasse for comparative law. Today, it might be difficult to find many examples to illustrate this limit but in the past it was commonplace. 'We have nothing to learn from elsewhere' was the common attitude of many practicing lawyers, judges and even academics. In such a culture there is little scope for comparative law.

A more subtle version of nationalism is the possession of a specific 'national vision' or a political or religious ideology. A State may have a goal, an inbuilt mission. In the realization of this goal, only certain ideas can be furthered. This also

---

180 R. Hyland, 'Comparative Law', in D. Patterson (ed) *A Companion to Philosophy of Law and Legal Theory* (Oxford, Blackwell, 1996), pp. 193-197.
181 P. Legrand, *Fragments on Law-as-Culture* (Deventer, W.E.J. Tjeenk Willink, 1999), p. 13.
182 *Ibid.*, p. 18.

means that comparative law research must be carried out between the domestic legal system and legal systems that have served as models, or legal systems with the same vision or ideology. Usually these visions are specific to a nation State or a cluster of States. One such obvious case is that of the socialist camp prior to 1989 which regarded the carrying out of comparisons as only valid if taking place 'within the family'. So, we see the denial by socialist comparative lawyers of the possibility of comparative law across legal families, possibly regarding the term 'comparable' to mean 'similar'. However, there are other instances, such as that of Turkey, earlier discussed, where the official vision was to create a State, a law and a people with a forged socio-culture which was introduced by the reception of laws of western origin and social reform legislation. Here also, comparisons could be given value if carried out with the 'source-laws', however, later developments in the source-laws in unwanted directions would be ignored. This could create an isolationist approach with 'separateness' and 'distinctiveness' valued as good in themselves. In Turkey the comparative lawyer's role is greatly diminished in the eyes of the target audience who cannot see the relevance of being exposed to the 'other'. To consider the 'other' might even be regarded as detrimental to the vision.

What about the limits of comparativism regarding the topics to be dealt with? As far as I am concerned, there can be no limits to comparativism as to the topics that can be compared. Although it has been sometimes claimed that system-oriented topics are incomparable or culture-specific topics should not be covered, I believe personally that it is part of the comparative lawyer's duty to expose all. I do not accept that certain topics 'do not lend themselves to comparison'. Family law, previously regarded by many as not appropriate for comparison, is one area in which a commonality in certain of its aspects has now emerged in Europe to an extent that harmonization is necessary and feasible. Areas of public law likewise used to be regarded as 'no go areas' for comparative lawyers, but today there is vigorous comparative activity in such areas. The Constitution for Europe, presently under construction, requires thorough comparison of the constitutional traditions of all the Member States and of the US Constitution if it is to build a Europe 'united in its diversity'.

I would say that the interest of the comparative lawyer determines her choice of topic. She can inquire into any subject matter. She might want to show for example that 'never the twain shall meet' in a certain area, but she could only determine this by first carrying out comparative research. The only limit here might be when an institution is unique, but how would a comparative lawyer discover this if she did not undertake comparative research?

Chapter 11

MORE CURRENT DEBATES

Among the many current comparative law debates now taking place, a few stand out. Some of these have been referred to already as sub-themes of the Theme Comparative Law. Alongside these, there are two others that occupy most comparative lawyers. One relates to the question, 'What is the field of study for comparative law?' Comparative lawyers stand on either side of the private law/public law divide, though the dividing line is itself becoming slightly blurred. The second debate, which is related to the convergence debate, is on how to regard the creation of *ius commune novum* and the common law of human rights. This sub-theme looks at these two debates. Both are handled through our customary two Variations.

1. PRIVATE LAW ONLY - PUBLIC LAW NOW?

Mainstream comparative lawyers have always been private lawyers. Mainstream comparative law has studied aspects of private law, usually excluding family law, and the most frequently covered areas of private law have been contracts and obligations. Indeed the traditional classification of legal systems into legal families springs from private law. It has even been said that the best comparative lawyers are private lawyers and often, in continental Europe, comparative law professorships and private international law professorships are combined.

However, there is nothing in the logic of comparative law, apart from its history and tradition to indicate that comparative law should only deal with private law. Thus, recently there has been growing interest in comparative public law, comparative constitutional law, comparative human rights, comparative criminal law and comparative procedural law. In spite of this, it is still the case that most comparative lawyers of our day are private lawyers.

Variation I below makes the case for public lawyers and for the widening of the scope of comparative law and criticizes the established views. Variation II however, regards comparative law as the exclusive domain of private lawyers and is sceptical of the widening of this horizon.

VARIATION I

Comparative law cannot be regarded as the most sophisticated analytical branch of social science and at the same time be utilized exclusively in the study of private law. The fact that it has been tied to private law for at least a century does not mean that it is only capable of dealing with that branch of law. It is true that the presently used classification of legal systems into legal families was created by private law comparatists with private law in mind, and is used extensively by private lawyers. It is also true that the modern *ius commune* for Europe is regarded as desirable for integration in areas of private law. These areas have been to date predominantly contract, obligations and tort law (delict). Family law followed later. Nevertheless save for these historic reasons, there is nothing in the logic of comparative law that tells us that it is the preserve of private law. Indeed, in an integrated Europe, the areas of procedural law, administrative law, constitutionalism and human rights are proving to be the more significant fields where reciprocal influence is at its widest and therefore, where extensive comparative law work is most needed.

'Comparative law in the 20th century omitted almost entirely to deal with public law topics such as constitutional law, administrative law, and even criminal law. Many scholars doubted the possibility of meaningful comparative law scholarship in these areas.'[1] In the new climate of a global shift towards democracy, rule of law and human rights, it is now necessary to examine public law concepts and institutions comparatively. In the past, comparative public law may have been in the research domain of public lawyers, but now it must move into the domain of comparative law studies.[2] Not only that, but public law has such a pervasive influence that many fields of private law are now changing under the impact of public law.

Most 'law as transposition' once stood firmly in the area of private law. Now, one area where transposition and cross-fertilization can be analyzed with advantage is in the construction of constitutions, since most developing constitutional systems have adopted from elsewhere institutions, norms and constitutional models comprising institutions of democracy, the rule of law and human rights and related issues as bases, and principles such as the rule of law, equality, legal certainty, fairness and non-discrimination - both as to content and to structure.

Within the context of Europe, many fields of law are acquiring a '*mixité*' and certainly public law is one of these. Although public law has been traditionally regarded as nationally specific, it is in public law that we see most of the fundamental cross-fertilization in our day. Does the resultant change justify regarding a public law system as 'mixed'? This is one of the main questions comparative lawyers have to deal with. The extent of reciprocal influence may justify the use of the term 'a mixed system of public law'. Would a 'mixed' public

---

[1] A. Harding and E. Örücü, 'Preface' in id (eds) *Comparative Law in the 21st Century* (London, Kluwer Law International, 2002), p. ix.

[2] See the plea by A. Harding, 'Comparative Public Law: Some Lessons from South East Asia' in *Ibid.*, pp. 254-256.

law be a cross between the French and the American, or the German and the Irish? Would it be mixed in substance, in structure, or way of thinking? Much of the future of comparative law study will address public law and particularly public law as a 'mixed system'. In the area of public law, there is a vast amount of transmigration of ideas and reciprocal influence, for example between the USA and Europe, within Europe and between the USA, Europe and South East Asia. So the end result will be the birth of a mixed public law system.[3]

Certainly within the context of the European Union, both current and future developments in law, whether understood as 'law as rules' or 'law as context', are predominantly approached within the 'convergence' debate. The European Community concept, 'the freedom of movement of ..', can be extended to embrace the 'freedom of movement of laws and legal institutions'. The results of this freedom of movement may be 'mixes', but not all 'mixes' produce major change - change which would qualify a whole area of law to be called 'mixed'. In the first place, mixes as to content and mixes as to structure have different outcomes. Secondly, how much of a mix is necessary to transform a system in such fundamental ways as to justify the use of the word 'convergence'? Would the introduction of principles such as 'legitimate expectations' or 'proportionality' into English law for example - these being the main illustrations used by scholars - have an impact so far reaching that public law in the common law world would change its character? Or is it only structural change that would have such implications as for example, the introduction of a separate court hierarchy for administrative law disputes or a written constitution or written procedure (a Code of Civil Procedure)? When can we talk of 'cultural re-orientation' or 're-alignment'?

The use of comparative law study in areas of public law has a different purpose, context and subject matter from its use in private law. The contexts are wider, institutional settings more complex and history has a more poignant place in the development of public law. 'The comparators and the similarities of setting which may be appropriate for comparing private law may well not be the same as for public law'.[4] Notions such as privatization, decentralization, sovereignty, subsidiarity, autonomy of the nation State, accountability and transparency are acquiring new meanings. The comparative study of these is imperative if we are to be prepared for the world awaiting us.

In the area of judicial review of constitutionality, for example, Mauro Cappelletti has analyzed the different traditions in the contemporary world, given examples of the classical models and of mixes, and has shown that whereas in the past the distinctions were clear, today they are blurred [5] The established traditions in judicial review of constitutionality can be studied as two broad types: The first type is the decentralized, diffuse, *incidenter*, *inter partes*, concrete, legitimating and

[3] I have treated this subject also elsewhere. See E. Örücü, 'Approaching Public Law as a Mixed System' (2002) *Juridical Review*, 131-142.

[4] J. Bell, 'Comparing Public Law' in Harding & Örücü (eds), above note 1, p. 246.

[5] M. Cappelletti, *Judicial Review in the Contemporary World* (Indianapolis, Bobbs-Merrill, 1971).

retroactive *ex tunc*, and the second centralized, concentrated, *principaliter*, *erga omnes*, abstract, invalidating and prospective *ex nunc*. According to Mauro Cappelletti, all others are intermediary systems developed under the influence of these two original models. A spectrum of possibilities would include no review, constitutional review by a special court (the Germanic model for post-review, and the French model for pre-review), constitutional review by all courts (the American model), and constitutional review in respect of the European Convention on Human Rights only (the Netherlands and the peculiar system of positive construction of legislation by courts to avoid incompatibility and restricted to a declaration of incompatibility, set up by the 1998 Human Rights Act in the United Kingdom). Systems could also be viewed as preventative, consultative, indirect or explicit. These are not all pure 'ordinary' models. There are some 'mixed' systems here too. Today more and more 'mixed' and intermediary systems are forming in addition to the original intermediary systems such as the Mexican, Irish and Israeli. So, which of these new ones are 'mixed' and what are their characteristics? How much have they influenced each other? Review of constitutionality is one area of inquiry for comparative lawyers as they look at cross-fertilizations and mixed legal systems and mixed areas of law.

In addition to judicial review of constitutionality, another subject of inquiry in this context is the place of human rights in the different constitutional frameworks. The way in which the highest courts or the Constitutional Courts derive support and guidance from the courts of other jurisdictions and the decisions of the Strasbourg Court, for example, has become a productive field of inquiry for comparative lawyers.[6] This inquiry is far reaching - there is cross-fertilization between the legal systems in the Commonwealth and Europe, between Europe and the USA, between legal systems of the States in transition in Central and East Europe and Western Europe and the South East Asia and the USA.

Now, as already noted, transposition and cross-fertilization can also be analyzed within the area of constructing constitutions, since most developing constitutional systems have adopted institutions, norms and constitutional models from elsewhere both as to content and to structure. Constitutions may epitomise national aspirations, but democracy, the rule of law, human rights and related structures, though born out of different philosophical and cultural antecedents, are now at the core of all modern western constitutions. Even the word 'western' has been changing its meaning since the 1990s. The most striking rapprochement is the acceptance of principles such as the rule of law, equality, legal certainty, fairness, non-discrimination and all rights and freedoms protected by the European Convention on Human Rights. Such a rapprochement indicates 'mixing' or '*mixité*'. In the areas mentioned this rapprochement is mostly as to content but sometimes as to structure. It has already been noted that the transposition of substance or content rather than of form or structure does not necessarily lead to a 'mixed' legal system however, but only to mixed areas of law.

---

[6] See contributions to E. Örücü (ed) *Judicial Comparativism in Human Rights Cases*, United Kingdom Comparative Law Series Vol: 22 (London, UKNCCL/BIICL, 2003).

Until recently, administrative law was closely linked to nationalism, and comparisons here were considered useless. But, the view that administrative law is rooted in the political and social traditions of each nation State is not correct. Recent studies have shown that, 'in the public law sphere 'borrowings', 'importations' and 'transplants' can be detected since the diffusion of the Napoleonic model in continental Europe.'[7] Especially since the 1970s, reciprocal influence between administrative law systems has been further emphasized by public lawyers. This has been brought about mainly under European Community law developments. The traditional methods of controlling the administration were by ordinary courts or a separate hierarchy of courts, and by 'ordinary remedies' or 'special remedies'. Are these still pure 'ordinary' models? If so, what is a mixed model of administrative law? Is a special ordinary court, such as the Queen's Bench is becoming in England, not 'ordinary' and therefore a 'mix'? Does the birth of new structures in France in the area of '*service public*' under challenges from European competition law justify talking of a '*mixité*' as for instance, in the area of 'liability of public bodies'? Without doubt, administrative law is another rich area of research for comparative lawyers of our day.

John Bell, looking at different administrative law traditions in Europe and trying to identify the principal features of convergence, first establishes four such traditions: French-influenced systems, Germanic systems, common law systems and those of the Netherlands, and Scandinavia.[8] The first challenge of this depiction is to the classical legal families theory. Obviously the traditional map of legal families drawn up for private law, and specifically for the private law of obligations, does not apply here. We can critisize the classification into the present legal families even as we see them crumble when considering other areas of 'private law' such as company law or labour law. John Bell moreover notes that, 'Public law is anchored firmly in a national setting, whatever wider trends also impinge on it.'[9]

He then determines four areas of convergence in administrative law: in values, in changes under pressure exerted by European Community law and European Court of Human Rights case law, in increased legalization of administrative relations, and in terminology and concepts.[10] As to the dynamics of this convergence, he points to legal education (Socrates programme), the involvement of judges and practitioners, international conventions, European Community Directives and European Court of Justice/European Court of Human Rights case law, and common social problems.[11]

In the realm of administrative law, public law as a mixed system in Europe comes to life through the contemporary focus on the protection of legitimate

---

[7] G. della Cananea, 'Beyond the State: The Europeanization and Globalization of Procedural Administrative Law' (2003) 9 *European Public Law*, 563 at p. 564.

[8] J. Bell, 'Mechanisms for Cross-fertilisation of Administrative Law in Europe' ch. 11 in J. Beatson and T. Tridimas (eds) *New Directions in European Public Law* (Oxford, Hart Publishing, 1998) p. 149.

[9] Bell, above note 4, p. 247.

[10] Bell, above note 8, pp. 153-154.

[11] *Ibid.*, p. 158

interests, the regime of governmental liability for the non-implementation of European Community rules and for the restitution of unlawfully paid monies, and proportionality.[12] These elements are found in many legal systems in Europe together with the direct transposition of foreign concepts into legal systems. As already noted, the administrative law principles with continental origins most talked about in the United Kingdom are legitimate expectations and proportionality, which are both included in the Government's guide to judicial review of administration, 'The Judge Over Your Shoulder'.[13]

At the European level, the European Court of Justice selects the 'most advanced' legal approaches to problems, and thereby eventually, through the binding nature of Eueopan Court of Justice decisions, all Member States receive these principles. Thus the European Union acts as a catalyst and a mediator in the process of producing public law of a 'mixed' nature. It is said that a 'Eurostandard' serves as a point of reference that can be accepted or rejected by the legal systems of the Member States. However, as this standard applies to all European Community institutions, there will always be mutual influence. Though European principles may only be used to fill gaps and act as correctives, the reality of 'seepage', and the force of 'infiltration' and 'cross-fertilization' is always present.

In addition, the Court of Justice of the European Communities has laid down common standards for judicial protection against public power through cases such as the *Fasctortame II*,[14] and *Zuckerfabrik Süderdithmarschen.*[15] So, this is another field where European administrative law systems are converging.

For example, the examination of the balance between public and private interests, an issue rejected for so long by British judges, is now being established as one of the tasks of the British courts, following the European practice. Recently, the Court of Appeal explained this task as: 'not to impede executive activity but to reconcile its continuing need to initiate or respond to change with the legitimate interests or expectations of citizens or strangers who have relied, and have been justified in relying, on a current policy or extant promise'.[16] This shows the widening scope of 'legitimate expectations' from procedure to substance and a departure from the strictly common law stance. This is the heyday of comparative lawyers involved in public law comparisons.

---

[12] J. Schwartze (ed) *Administrative Law under European Influence* (London, Sweet & Maxwell, 1996) and J. Schwartze, 'Towards a Common European Public Law' (1995) 1 *European Public Law*, 232.

[13] *The Judge Over Your Shoulder: A Guide to Judicial Review for UK Government Administration* (March 2000, Treasury Solicitor's Office), available at htpp://www.open.gov.uk/tsd/judge.htm

[14] *Factortame Ltd.* v *Secretary of State for Transport* Case C-213/89 [1990] ECR 1-2433,; note by A,G. Toth, 27 *Common Market Law Review* (1990), 573.

[15] Joined Cases C-143/88 and C-92/89 *Zuckerfabrik Süderdithmarschen AG* v. *Hauptzollamt Itzehoe*, and *Zuckerfabrik Soest GmBH* v. *Hauptzollamt Paderbon* [1991] ECR 1-415; case note by H.G. Schermers, 29 *Common Market Law Review* (1992), 133.

[16] *R* v *North and East Devon Health Authority, ex. p. Coughlan* [2000] 2 W.L.R. 622 at 647.

Another development having an impact on the public laws of the Member States of the European Union, is the establishment of the European Ombudsman, one of the most important achievements of the Maastricht Treaty. This institution was originally to be based on a Spanish proposal supervising the rights of European citizens under Community law at national, regional and municipal levels, but it was eventually based on the Danish proposal. Hence, the European Ombudsman does not supervise Member States, but 'pollinization' and convergence will inevitably occur with the setting up of principles of good administration for the supervision of European Institutions. The Code of Good Administrative Behaviour prepared by the European Ombudsman lays down a long list of the principles in developing a European administrative law. The list includes lawfulness, absence of discrimination, proportionality, absence of abuse of power, impartiality and independence, objectivity, legitimate expectations (legal certainty) and consistency, fairness, courtesy, reply to letters in the language of the citizen, acknowledgement of receipt and indication of the competent official, obligation to transfer to the competent service of the Institution, right to be heard and to make statements, reasonable time-limit for taking decisions, duty to state the grounds of decisions, indication of possibilities of appeal, notification of the decision, data protection, keeping of adequate records, and public access to information, to documents and to the Code. The assumption is that most of the Member States already have these principles at national level. Nevertheless, standards, especially those related to transparency issues, are expected to rise and discretionary powers be more effectively controlled in the Member States as a result of the existence of this overarching Code.

Institutions of public law in the European Union change under European and national political pressure. Outside the European Union, the change comes under national and international political pressure alongside obvious reasons for change, such as, efficiency, chance, prestige and affiliation to certain models for political or economic reasons. The convergence, both in constitutional and administrative law, reflects elements of both transposition and cross-fertilization. In administrative law most changes are contentual rather than structural. In constitutional law they are both structural and contentual. Change is also apparent in procedural matters and there are common influences in this area. The clearest common development is to be seen in the area of values.[17] Comparative lawyers are again active in all these areas. Their work in public law is manifested in studies of globalization, regulation, agencies, rule-making and transparency.

Comparative law reveals that public law in Europe today is indeed a 'mixed system', civilian in origin, enriched by common law principles and innovations and true cross-fertilization. Among the common law innovations, one could mention corporate governance which has influenced both German and EC laws and led to market-driven convergence, and 'the law of professional privilege' and 'the right to be heard', both exported to the European Court of Justice. Again under British

[17] Bell , above note 8, p. 166.

influence, the continental emphasis on the privilege of the administration undertaking public services is moving towards the stressing of individual rights, and yet the protection of the individual under a human rights framework in the United Kingdom in fact springs from a continental understanding. In the United Kingdom, the 1998 Human Rights Act, democracy, majority rule and the notion of limited government are all now fundamental areas of study - study undoubtedly influenced by continental thinking, as is also the principle of 'proportionality' which will be predominantly employed in the area of human rights.

Most important cross-fertilizations, horizontal transfers and transpositions take place at the level of basic ideas in the field of public law, and in future, comparative law research will be obliged to deal with public law and the vast amount of transmigration of ideas and reciprocal influence in this field. The areas will expand to cover influences within Europe, between the USA and Europe, between the USA, Europe and South East Asia, and within the South East Asia. Public law developments in South East Asia and South Africa are major areas of research today by 'regionalists' - comparative lawyers working in hitherto neglected regions - while research within Europe gathers momentum. So our century will witness a major shift from private law to public law.

VARIATION II

The most important area of law is private law. Throughout history this has been the area which regulated relationships between individuals, and most everyday contacts in society are concentrated in areas such as persons, obligations, contracts, property, tort or delict, and family. Some continental Civil Codes even include commercial relationships. The 'pride of place' in academic studies must be given to comparative private law, 'the heartland of all comparative law'.[18]

The promotion of world trade and international business, and today at least in Europe, the creation of an ever closer common market, demand private law integration which in turn requires more comparative work to be undertaken in various aspects of private law.

The best and the best-known comparative lawyers are private law comparatists. Many of them are at the same time private international lawyers. This is especially the case in continental Europe. In fact, although the two areas are distinct, they interact and there is further and strong correlation between comparative lawyers and private international lawyers. It can be said that comparative lawyers are usually pluralists but 'reluctant integrationists'. Busying themselves with differences is in their interest both as academics and as practitioners. Academics are interested in differences in order to make the case for identity and non-convergence or mentality or law in context. However, most become integrationists when working for projects such as the General European Principles, though even then, they advocate the

[18] K. Zweigert and H. Kötz, *An Introduction to Comparative Law*, 3rd edn., trans. T. Weir (Oxford, Clarendon Press, 1998), p.3.

preservation of 'identity in harmony'. Practitioners are on the whole interested in differences in order to find divergent solutions so that they can bring these solutions to the notice of the courts in the interest of their clients. Conversely, private international lawyers are integrationists - though in a different sense to comparative lawyers - but 'reluctant pluralists'. By using doctrines such as '*ordre public*', 'equivalence' or '*accord procedural*', they try to concentrate the cases they are involved in on *lex fori* and only reluctantly work out problems of foreign law. Even then, when they do address such problems, they tend to revert back to *lex fori*. Private international lawyers must also be comparative lawyers in order to function properly.

One of the most important roles comparative law plays is in harmonization and unification activities and comparative lawyers are involved in the preparation of many projects to achieve these ends. Such activity is of ever increasing significance not only in Europe but internationally. Whether the starting point is 'common core' studies or 'better law' studies, the areas prepared for harmonization and unification are all private law areas. 'It is in private law in the widest sense that the world forces tending towards the integration of law are at their strongest.'[19]

Comparisons in public law and related fields where politics and policy are the prevalent forces, cannot be undertaken. The purported results of such research would be misleading and futile. Factors other than law are at work here. The classification, the methodology and the conceptual framework of comparative law are created by private lawyers specifically for private law and are not suitable for use in the public law field. This would remain the case even if it were regarded as desirable to carry out comparative law research in public law.

Meaningful comparability and functional equivalence can only make sense and be relied upon in the area of private law. The historical 'unity of common law' and 'European *ius commune*' were in the area of private law. European integration can only safely take place related to the private interests of private parties.

2. CONVERGENCE OR NON-CONVERGENCE? - THE 'NEW *IUS COMMUNE*'? - 'UNITY OF COMMON LAW'?

On the one hand, it is claimed that only convergent or similar systems can benefit from each other's experience; hence, for example, the attempts to enlarge the catchment area of systems covered by the 'new *ius commune*' within the context of a wider Europe. On the other hand, it is claimed that it is differences that must be stressed for their value in enhancing our understanding of law in society, since it is only by observing differences that we can learn lessons, but that such models cannot be used for domestic law reform.

Most 'theoretical comparativism' is dominated by the 'sameness and difference debate'. It is legitimate to ask whether comparative law is indeed an instrument of

[19] *Ibid.*, p.24.

integration and whether 'the last thing we need is "distinctiveness for its own sake"'.[20] However, do such strong views defy the virtues of 'distinction' and 'diversity'? 'Are we identifying difference, and cherishing it, or are we trying to suppress it, by effective same-ness?'[21] It is claimed by many that at present comparative law within Europe is used predominantly 'as a means of effecting same-ness and suppressing difference',[22] and therefore, comparative lawyers are seen as 'powerful players' and not as 'neutral observers'.[23] However, some others prefer to stress non-convergence and difference. Thus, comparativism could be seen as a threat with only a limited role. The question is: 'Should our approach be an either/or between the integrative and contrastive trends in comparative law?'

Surely, to compare means to look for similarities as well as differences. It is true that within the framework of a nationalist movement for example, only the differences will be underlined, with the aim of stressing the individual worth of a particular legal system. Since individual legal systems all have their own decisive characteristics and unique institutions, this can be done with ease. But it is equally plausible and possible to stress the similarities between the legal systems under comparative survey. This is the target of the researcher who wants to encourage a movement of integration and harmonization.

A researcher involved in the Scottish nationalist movement, for instance, might prefer to stress the differences that exist between the English and the Scottish legal systems - and there are many - in order to prove that they are insurmountable for even partial harmonization of the legal systems. Whereas a Scottish researcher believing in the unity of the UK and perhaps also wanting to pave the way for western European unity, might pick on the similarities between the English and the Scottish legal systems - and again there are many - in the hope of generating a unification movement at home as a first step to a harmonization movement within Europe. Thus it is possible to claim, according to this type of political choice, that the Dutch and the Scottish legal systems are quite different in their approach to and use of European law and 'never the twain shall meet'. But, it is also possible to stress the similarities between the two if there is the will to facilitate European co-operation within the European Union. So, in the course of her work, the researcher may look at similarities or differences, or similarities as well as the differences.

These are all legitimate research strategies as long as the strategy is clearly laid down at the start of the project. Which strategy is chosen depends on the political and theoretical orientation of the researcher. In a sense, it is reminiscent of a court deciding to follow one line of precedent rather than another, the choice being dictated by policy considerations rather than by legal considerations. Methodologically however, there is a problem in this two way choice, since each

[20] E.M. Clive, 'Scottish Family Law', in J. Grant (ed) *Independence and Devolution: The Legal Implications for Scotland* (Edinburgh, Green, 1976), 162, at p. 173.
[21] I. Ward, 'The Limits of Comparativism: Lessons from UK-EC Integration (1995) 2 *Maastricht Journal of European and Comparative Law*, 23 at p. 31.
[22] *Ibid.*
[23] *ibid.*, p. 32.

will lead to different results. These are operational choices tied up with the comparative lawyer's strategy.[24]

In the early part of the last century the utopian idea of 'one law for the civilized nations' if not 'one law for the world' was expressed from time to time. Whether this was envisaged for private law only or for other areas of law is not clear. What can be said is that feelings of fairness and justice were seen to demand uniform laws for all. That this was a dream was soon realized, but still, there were many who aspired to it. In times of peace it is commonplace to wish to get closer together and the reverse is true in times of conflict. Variations of this dream came to life in certain regions such as in the Nordic Union and the Benelux countries in the harmonizing the laws. Convention law, model laws and the like were all attempts to create uniform standards, often for the sake of convenience and to ease the way for economic integration as part of a political agenda. Some comparative lawyers have aligned themselves with this agenda.

In the context of Europe today, there is an effort to create 'ever closer union', and although some see this only as a means of facilitating economic ties, others regard legal and cultural integration as the ultimate goal. World-wide unification is no longer discussed and, at a time when there is even talk of 'clash of cultures', it does not seem to be the dream of our century. The 'new *ius commune* seekers' are mainly interested in private law. Yet, the boundaries of private law have been widened for this purpose to include family law, which classically and traditionally was not part of that common world. To date areas such as commercial law, trade and labour law, transport by rail, sea and air, copyright and industrial law and procedural law have been brought closer together and in some cases unified. Moreover, there are moves to create a 'common law of human rights' as well as a criminal law for Europe, particularly for crimes that extend beyond the borders of a single nation State. Such entities as the European Union and the Council of Europe are regarded as facilitators for the realization of such aspirations. 'I submit', says Thijmen Koopmans, 'that a new *ius commune* for Europe is taking shape before our eyes.'[25]

There are also those of course, who see this rapprochement as a nightmare. These anti-integrationalists have their own political agenda and talk, if not of divergence, of non-convergence. Cultural identity, mentality, difference, and 'living apart together' are stressed as the important tenets of nation States within which cultural pluralism, and, further than that, legal pluralism are discussed. Some comparative lawyers have aligned themselves with this. Though they would not deny the existence of a historic *ius commune* in continental Europe, they do not recognize the existence of a *ius commune* involving both the common law and the

---

[24] Another slant to the above would be to stress differences arising from similarities or similarities arising from differences. From this the comparative lawyer can move on to generalization.

[25] T. Koopmans, 'Towards a New "Ius Commune"', in: B. de Witte and C. Forder (eds.), *The common law of Europe and the future of legal education* (Deventer, Kluwer; Metro, 1992) p. 49.

civil law in the past and are totally opposed to attempts at the creation of one now, even for the members of the civilian tradition, seeing this as impossible.

Before delving into the two Variations on this sub-theme, it may be wise to observe what Vivian Curran says:

> It should be remembered in this context that the perception of the cultural and the incommensurable as primordial to comparative law ... never in and of itself implied a necessary rejection of the search for cross-cultural unification, including of a legal nature, in a project undertaken by peoples choosing to unite and to search for coexistence and community, such as in the European Union.[26]

We might therefore ask ourselves the question whether privileging difference in cross-cultural study requires rejecting an undertaking such as the European one? Again we might further ask whether in globalizing encounters cultural differences can be preserved intact?

Below, the two Variations take up these two positions.

VARIATION I

It is true that when comparing closely related systems it is usually more rewarding to analyze differences, while in two entirely unrelated, or apparently unrelated, systems it is more rewarding to explain similarities.[27] In practice, it seems a matter of preference or policy, whether the comparative lawyer highlights the one or the other. Comparative law can only benefit when it interests itself seriously in searching for and explaining divergences, especially those between the apparently similar,[28] with a 'constructive' attitude in order to develop further a 'critical comparative law', rather than with the 'negative' attitude of stressing 'irreducible differences in *mentalité'* or '*summa differentia'* within the context of a 'contrarian challenge'.[29]

Since the term 'to compare' can be taken to mean simply to observe and explain similarities and differences, the emphasis will be sometimes on differences and at other times on similarities. Rudolf Schlesinger talks of periods of 'contractive', or 'contrastive' comparison with the emphasis on differences, alternating with periods of what might be called 'integrative' comparison, that is,

---

[26] V.G. Curran, 'On the Shoulders of Schlesinger: The Trento Common Core of European Private Law Project' Vol. 2 [2002] No.2 Aricle 2 *Global Jurist Frontier* (The Berkeley Electronic Press), p. 18.

[27] M. Bogdan, *Comparative Law* (Göteborg, Kluwer Tano, 1994), p. 18.

[28] See V.G., Curran 'Dealing in Difference: Comparative Law's Potential for Broadening Legal Perspective', (1998) 46 *American Journal of Comparative Law*, 657, and N.V. Demleitner, 'Challenge, Opportunity and Risk: An Era of Change in Comparative Law', (1998) 46 *American Journal of Comparative Law*, 647.

[29] See E. Örücü, 'Unde Venit, Quo Tendit Comparative Law', in Harding & Örücü (eds), above note 1, pp. 9-10.

comparison with the main accent on similarities.[30] He concludes that the future belongs to 'integrative comparative law'.[31] The 'new *ius commune* seekers' in Europe are trying to integrate legal systems, while looking at a legal world which includes differents - the UK and Ireland. In the common law world however, the unity of common law is of similars as far as legal systems are concerned, though it is now generally accepted that this unity may be enhanced by diversity, and the Privy Council has somewhat loosened its hold on the commonwealth jurisdictions.[32]

Once reciprocity and mutuality between legal and cultural systems have been achieved, all will become 'contaminants' and 'irritants' of each other. When elements from different interpretive communities combine, they can tap into each other and mesh, bringing 'cultural conversation' into the broader narrative. This is the factor of 'fit'. To realise this 'fit', tuning at the time of 'transposition' and understanding law as transposition are crucial.

This Variation supports the view that in the past there was a *ius commune* in Europe deriving its authority not from political power but from its scientific character, that it included the common law as well as the civil law, that there will be a new *ius commune* which is now being developed to include the common law, that the 'ever closer union' will go far beyond private law, that we can already see developments towards a common law of constitutional law and human rights law, and that the catchment area of this *ius commune novum* is getting wider and wider within an enlarging Europe. Similar circles can be observed in the 'unity of common law' and in the Islamic world which in fact has no nation State boundaries. The legal systems of some African States may also be converging. The ultimate vision may be represented as a number of overlapping circles of various sizes sitting within an all-encompassing circle of human rights.

Let us now consider these issues. In the past, there was a *ius commune* and England was part of it, as part of 'European culture'.[33] As pointed out by Luigi Moccia, whose working hypothesis is that 'Continental (Civil) law and English (Common) law stood together in past centuries as component parts of a same cultural context not yet affected by legal nationalism and positivism',[34] these are two traditions on a path of convergence. In many parts of the world, as well as at home, English law met the civilian tradition and happily lived with it: the two have never been strangers.[35] English law borrowed from the civilian tradition, internalized

---

[30] R. Schlesinger, 'The Past and Future of Comparative Law', (1995) 43 *American Journal of Comparative Law*, 477 at p. 477.

[31] *Ibid.*, p. 481.

[32] See *Invercargill City Council* v *Hamlin* [1996] 1 All ER, 773 (PC).

[33] R. Zimmermann, 'Savigny's legacy: Legal history, comparative law, and the emergence of a European legal science', (1996) 112 *Law Quarterly Review*, 557, at p. 602. Later published in: T.G. Watkin, *The Europeanisation of Law*, United Kingdom Comparative Law Series Vol: 18, (London, UKNCCL/BIICL, 1998) pp. 1-38.

[34] L. Moccia, 'Historical Overview on the Origins and Attitudes of Comparative Law', in: Witte & Forder (eds.), above note 25, p. 609.

[35] See Zimmermann, above note 33.

various Roman law concepts into equity and common law, and thus enriched its common law. It had no problems with Codes and indeed it introduced common law to some of its colonies in an already codified form. In addition, in the fields of contract law, commercial law and criminal law there were attempts at home to codify the law in the nineteenth and twentieth centuries. So it is clear that, common law and codification can co-exist. Examples can be found in other common law jurisdictions such the United States where there is a variety of Codes such as the Uniform Commercial Code and the Californian Civil Code, and in Australia where one talks of Code States with codified Criminal Law.

Today, the newly growing *ius commune* will include England. The path leads towards an integrated Europe. Integration will be in many fields. It will extend far beyond the limited number of fields of private law. Therefore, to speak of a *ius commune* only in private law is inappropriate and does not do justice to the vision. Integration will surely extend beyond private law, commercial law and procedural law. To start with, the mere existence of the European Union itself implies an active role for comparative lawyers in the development of general principles of private law at least. The number of 'common core' projects and Commissions set up to prepare European Codes, European General Principles, European Case Books, Restatements, and to develop theories of 'competing legal systems', in addition to regulations, directives and conventions of the European Union and the Council of Europe, and the European Convention of Human Rights bear witness to a plethora of activity in building the groundwork for convergence. We see also the development of a *communis opinion doctorum novum*, to supply answers to shared problems from this new pool of 'rule of reason'.

Starting with a quotation from the Opinion of Advocate-General Warner of the European Court of Justice, indicating the existence of a common 'legal heritage', one reads:

> This Court, in developing the general principles of Community law, draws on what has been termed "the legal heritage" of all the Member States. It seems to me that, if one considers, for instance, the Danish law as to "*stiltiende afkald*", the English law as to estoppel, the German law as to "*Rechtsverwirkung*", the Italian law as to "*legittimo affidamento*" and the Scots law as to personal bar, as well as the French law as to "*renonciation implicite*", there emerges a general principle (applicable to a public authority except where that would be irreconcilable with its public duty) that one who, having legal relations with another, by his conduct misleads that other as to a material fact (including the existence of a right) cannot thereafter base on that fact a claim against him if he (that other) has acted in a relevant way in reliance on what he was led by that conduct to believe. What matters here, of course, is the existence of the principle, not the scope or mode of its application in the law of any particular Member State. The principle exists also in public international law where,

> although it is generally given its English name of "estoppel", it is considered to have its origin in Roman law.[36]

Let us continue with a more recent statement of Advocate-General Geelhoed specifically mentioning the resort to *ius commune*:

> Both these cases concern the interpretation of Council Directive 85/374/EEC of 25 July 1985 on the approximation of the laws, regulations and administrative provisions of the Member States concerning liability for defective products. ... regard must be had to the changes which have occurred in the legal systems of Western Europe over the last 50 years. Those changes are characterised by the almost continual attention which legislatures have paid to protecting interests which in social terms have been shown to be vulnerable. This led, firstly, to special laws on collective agreements granting special private-law protection to employees. Subsequently, in the majority of Member States, it also led to special protection for tenants and lessors. In recent decades, legislatures have also paid special attention to the position of consumers. ... The aforementioned legislation, which is tailored to the specific needs of the individual – employee, tenant, consumer etc,: - is characterised by the precision with which it defines its scope, *ratione materiae*, *ratione personae*, and, sometimes, *ratione loci*. Individuals and interests not included in the scope of the legislation may not rely on the special protection provided by it. Therefore, they must rely on general rules of private law, such as *ius commune*.[37]

It is true that in the past *ius commune* was partly private law based and was originally seen to be in the field of obligations. In fact, it was more extensive than that. Although when we speak of Roman law today we tend to think of private law, 'this restriction dates only from the 19th century; it is not true of the *ius commune*. The *ius commune* was universal in the sense that it included all fields of law: criminal law, procedure and to a certain extent, even public law.'[38] The main sources of the *ius commune* were Roman law in the form given to it by Justinian (dubbed in the middle ages the *Corpus Iuris*), canon law (forming the second *Corpus*, *Corpus Iuris Canonici*), and some medieval institutions such as feudal law, rules developed by jurists, and commercial law as developed during the Middle Ages. Furthermore, the moral-theology of the Middle Ages and, from the middle of the 17th century onwards, rationalistic natural law and the *ius commune* were mutually influential.

---

[36] *Boizard* v *Commission* 63+64/79 [1980] ECR 3002, (Advocate-General Warner).

[37] The Advocate General's opinion is for both *Gonzalez Sanchez* v *Medicina Asturiana SA* Case C-185/00, para 66+67, and *Commission of the European Communities* v *French Republic* Case C-52/00.

[38] H. Coing, 'The sources and characteristics of the ius commune', (1986) 19 *Comparative and International Law Journal of Southern Africa*, 483-489, at p. 487.

'The *ius commune* was in force in all countries west of a line drawn from Venice to the Baltic sea, including Hungary and Poland.'[39]

Now in the search for a closer integration in Europe, a number of hitherto neglected areas are being looked at. For instance, although as yet there is no uniform family law for Europe, there are efforts to create standardization in some aspects of family law through European law and Conventions related to respect for family life, the equal treatment of men and women, the equal treatment of legitimate and illegitimate children and the recognition of divorce, maintenance and custody judgements. There is lively comparative law research activity in this field. The belief that family law, being culture bound, does not lend itself to comparison, let alone harmonization, has been refuted.[40] Obviously, some of these efforts are academic but European norms enunciated through the European Convention on Human Rights in relation to Article 8 on the right to family life, for example, have had a substantial impact on the legislation of countries such as the UK, France, the Netherlands. This is apparent in areas such as parental authority in marriage and after divorce. A number of Council of Europe Conventions such as the 1967 Convention on adoption and the 1975 Convention on the legal status of illegitimate children are among other harmonizing agents. In addition, the rights of the child and the protection of minors have been specifically targeted at the European level.

Hence, an increasing number of areas of law are designated as 'European' today, including areas such as European competition law, European contract law, European tort law and European family law with European Commissions of academics working to produce general principles in these fields either using the 'common core' or the 'better law' approach.[41] Treaty law also brings together rules in various branches of substantive law and private international law.

Now that so many harmonization and unification projects have been completed and a European private law is being developed, the questions of necessity, feasibility or even desirability do not need further discussion. It was necessity that led to these efforts towards the creation of European private law. The very fact that European private law is being developed indicates its feasibility. Desirability is tied to political agenda, and the views in this Variation indicate a positive answer to the question of desirability. What is really needed is discussion on how best to achieve this end and on what is the right course of action.

To wait for a gradual development of a *ius commune* however is not practical. One way forward towards uniformity is through codifying basic principles in these fields, and thus attaining uniformity. As put by Alan Watson:

---

[39] *Ibid.*, p.488.

[40] See for instance, P. de Cruz, 'Legal Transplants: Principles and Pragmatism in Comparative Family Law', in: Harding & Örücü (eds) above note 1, 101-120; K. Boele-Woelki (ed) *Perspectives for Unification and Harmonisation of Family Law in Europe* (Antwerp-Oxford-New York, Intersentia, 2003) and contributions to that volume.

[41] Much has been written in this field. See for instance, contributions in de Witte & Forder (eds), above note 25.

> A satisfactory private law for Europe is not primarily to be sought for in the most common solutions, themselves the result of borrowing. Nor in established rules, themselves the result of longevity, and lack of governmental incentive in innovating. Nor should it be sought in immediate positions of various mixed systems. ... Rather it is to be found in the need for authority. ... This means that a common law for Europe requires the acceptance of a uniform system of adjudicating differences within a standard framework of the necessary sources of law, Authority is paramount, because it alone can constitute the common element.[42]

He then suggests that a standard system of authority can only be created by legislation which alone can be authoritative. 'A *ius commune* will not suffice ... aggressive action is needed', he says. 'Despite the usual lack of legislation for private law, a uniform law for Europe demands it. And this can only be achieved by a common civil code. The idea may be unpalatable in some jurisdictions, but it alone is workable.'[43]

Indeed in 1989 and 1994 the European Parliament adopted Resolutions calling for the codification of European Private Law, the call being based on the belief that 'unification can be carried out in branches of private law which are highly important for the development of a Single Market, such as contract law ...'.[44] Since then, the study of private law has faced a new challenge. Whether at present a European Civil Code is practicable, or even desirable, is under debate. The project has found support in some quarters.

Short of a European Civil Code however, there are other options. First, a European Code of Contracts might be a slightly watered down version of a European Civil Code. Another possibility was to unify the General Principles of Contract law and this has in fact been achieved. The Commission set up in 1980 for this purpose has completed its work, which can be seen as the first step towards the production of a future Code. Such projects on unifying General Principles which can then be used as Restatements, are being undertaken in other fields also, thus another way forward is in American style Restatements. The case-books approach has already produced its first fruits[45] and 'law and economics' scholars suggest that when legal systems

---

[42] A. Watson, 'A Common Private Law for Europe?' *9 Maastricht Journal of European and Comparative Law* 4 (2002), p. 330.

[43] *Ibid.*, p. 332.

[44] The Preamble of the Resolution of 26 May 1989, OJEC No. C 158/401 of June 26 1989.

[45] See for some of the results: W. van Gerven, J. Lever and P. Larouche (eds.), *Tort law, Common Law of Europe Casebooks* (Oxford, Hart Publishers, 2000); H. Schulte-Nölke, R. Schulze and J. Jones (eds.), *A Casebook on European Consumer Law* (Oxford, Hart Publishers, 2000).

are in competition in a 'market of solutions', the 'best solution' will always win the day.[46]

Even an 'evolutionary theory' has been suggested, as a variation of the 'law and economics' approach, whereby gradual and organic convergence could take place based on spontaneous 'cultural evolution' without any compulsory principles.[47] At worst, transnational rules could function alongside national rules and eventually become congruent with them.[48] At the level of private law at least, legal education embracing both European and national principles should become compulsory and text books be produced to this end. Today, European Law Schools are being set up and new relationships between universities forged.

All the above approaches[49] indicate that convergence is inevitable and this Variation supports the view that the end result will be a *ius commune novum*. Analysis also reveals that convergence does not stop at private law. For instance, administrative law systems in Europe are also converging and common rules, common principles and a common mentality are emerging. However we have not yet reached the stage where we can talk of a *ius commune* of public law.

Turning again briefly to England, we see that English law, for example, has already been contaminated and therefore purity is not in question here. Nevertheless, as an expression abstracted from its literal meaning, the term 'contaminant' could be neutralized as 'leaving a mark', as in the cross-dying process that takes place when two garments of different colours are accidentally put in the washing tub together and the colours run. Even then, one of them may be regarded as the culprit, unless of course, the dying is reciprocal, in which case we have a new hue for both! This may be regarded as true convergence. One could also think of fugitive colours such as blue, which may gradually fade in the wash and finally disappear! This can happen even before there is time for it to become an 'irritant'!

When English common law co-exists with an uncodified jurisdiction, it can seep into that other but find it harder to penetrate into Codes where judges tend to

---

[46] See for instance, A. Ogus, 'Competition Between National Legal Systems: A Contribution of Economic Analysis to Comparative Law', (1999) 48 *International and Comparative Law Quarterly*, 405.

[47] See J.M. Smits, 'The Harmonisation of Private Law in Europe: Some Insights from Evolutionary Theory', (2002) 31 *Georgia Journal of International & Comparative Law*, pp. 79-99.

[48] Also see T. Hartlief, 'Towards a European Private Law? A Review Essay', *Maastricht Journal of European and Comparative Law* 1 (1994), 166 at p. 175.

[49] For an overview of the methods and the achievements so far see, E. Hondius, 'Towards a European Ius commune: The Current Situation in other Fields of Private Law' in: Boeke-Woelki (ed) above note 40, pp. 118-140; and for an assessment of various methods proposed for creating a European private law, see J.M. Smits, 'How to Take the Road Untravelled? European Private Law in the making: A Review Article', 6 *Maastricht Journal of European and Comparative Law* 1 (1999), pp. 25-46.

adhere to the actual wording of the Code itself when deciding cases.[50] According to 'convergence theories', English law can live with codification of the law. There are historical examples of this. 'Divergence theories' covered in the next Variation are opposed to any involvement of the UK in any pan-European Code however.[51]

It is not surprising that the UK straddles two worlds. It has one foot in the *ius commune novum* with legal systems of the continental Europe, and the other in the 'unity of common law' with the legal systems in the Commonwealth and the USA.[52] The UK which also comprises Scotland, a mixed jurisdiction, can be regarded as a point of confluence. This position can best be illustrated by recent cases. For instance in the *Fairchild* case,[53] inspiration was drawn from other common law jurisdictions such as Australia, New Zealand, Canada and the USA, from Scotland, a mixed jurisdiction, from civilian jurisdictions such as France, Germany, the Netherlands, Greece, Spain and Norway, as well as from Roman law.

Lord Bingham, delivering his opinion in *Fairchild,* made this most pertinent observation:

> This survey shows, as would be expected, that though the problem underlying the cases such as the present is universal the response to it is not. ... But ...most jurisdictions would, it seems, afford a remedy to the plaintiff. Development of the law in this country cannot of course depend on a head-count of decisions and codes adopted in other countries around the world often against a background of different rules and traditions. The law must be developed coherently, in accordance with principle, so as to serve, even-handedly the end of justice. If however, a decision is given in this country which offends one's basic sense of justice, and if consideration of international sources suggests that a different and more acceptable decision would be given in most other jurisdictions, whatever their legal tradition, this must prompt anxious review of the decision in question. In a shrinking world (in which the employees of asbestos companies may work for those companies in any one or more of several countries) there must be some virtue in uniformity of outcomes whatever the diversity of approach in reaching that outcome.[54]

---

[50] An interesting example of common law penetrating a civilian Code is St Lucia however. See D. White, 'Some problems of a hybrid legal system: a case study of St. Lucia' (1981) 30 *International and Comparative law Quarterly*, pp. 862-881.

[51] See for instance P. Legrand, 'Against a European Civil Code' (1997) *Modern Law Review*, 44.

[52] For past encounters of English common law with the civilian tradition see, E. Örücü, *Critical Comparative Law: Considering Paradoxes for Legal Systems in Transition*, Nederlandse Vereniging Voor Rechtsvergelijking No: 59 (Deventer, Kluwer, 1999), pp. 34-43.

[53] Joined cases of *Fairchild* v *Glenhaven Funeral Services Ltd and other*; *Fox* v *Spousal (Midlands) Ltd* and *Matthews* v *Associated Portland Cement Manufacturers (1978) Ltd and others* [2002] UKHL 22 , [2002] 3 All ER 305.

[54] *Ibid.*, at 334.

It is true that the circle in which the English law predominantly lives is the 'unity of common law' born of a process of colonial expansion with English common law rivalling the civilian tradition based on Roman law in the creation of a legal Empire. English law laid the foundation stones of most of the legal systems in North America, Australia, New Zealand, India and large parts of Africa and South East Asia. English common law also played a crucial role as the basis of harmony in the common law world maintaining this harmony by laying down paths of cross-fertilization, the Privy Council bringing the laws of the individual jurisdictions of the Commonwealth into line with others within their specific regions on many occasions. For instance, in *Cheali* v *Equiticorp Finance Group Ltd and another*, Lord Browne-Wilkinson stated that, 'It is manifestly desirable that the law on this subject should be the same in all common law jurisdictions.'[55]

The different socio-cultures within this circle face the same legal culture - the common law. Specific to this circle, there is still a consciousness that common law is a whole and provides a real tie between the several jurisdictions within the 'unity of common law'. 'Whatever differences there may be between the legal systems of South Africa, the United States, New Zealand and this country, many of the basic principles to which they seek to give effect stem from common roots.'[56] Judges use cases from other jurisdictions within this unity, attributing to them persuasive effect and sometimes preferring one such decision over the domestic one: the citing sometimes for 'help' or 'comfort' but at times as authority. It is most striking that, 'the feeling of oneness is so strong that in one case the [British] judge found it difficult to refer to New Zealand as foreign and apologised to his New Zealand friends for using the word "foreign".'[57]

Beyond these two circles there are of course other worlds some of which also live in unity. For instance, such a 'commonality' exists in the Islamic world, where Moslems living in many of the jurisdictions in the Islamic world are first and foremost members of '*ummet*'(*ummah*)[58] rather than 'nationals' or 'citizens' of their respective States since Islam has no national boundaries. However Islamic law has never been applied as a uniform code of law and does not aim at uniformity though it is comprehensive. So, similar to the unity of the common law, there is a 'unity of Islamic law'. The reception of Islamic law was the spreading of a global doctrine which, in historical terms, had a wider catchment area than that of Roman law in Europe.

In our day, peoples of the world are on the move and an increasing number of Moslems live in parts of the world within other circles, other communities and other unities than their own. Islam, being a way of life, has laws that govern every aspect of life providing a self-contained and self-regulating legal order. With its primary

---

[55] [1991] 4 All ER, 989 (PC).

[56] See *Bennett* v *Horseferry Road Magistrates' Court and another*, [1993]3 All ER, 138 (HL).

[57] E. Örücü, 'Comparative Law in British Courts', in: U. Drobnig and S. Van Erp (eds.), *The Use of Comparative Law by Courts*, (London, Kluwer Law International, 1999), at p. 257. For the case see *Attorney General of New Zealand* v *Ortiz and other* [1082] 3 All ER 432

[58] Community of the same religion.

and secondary sources emanating from divine revelation, this legal system unites all Moslems regardless of where they live. Its most important aspect is that Moslems have the duty to live according to Islamic law, as law is part of religion. Thus, since a Moslem must regulate his/her life according to Islamic law, a man-made law which contradicts divine law should not be obeyed. This can create problems for Moslems living in jurisdictions other than the Islamic, especially when the official legal system of the country concerned regards Islamic law as customary law.[59] However, as the Nigerian Justice Wali stated, 'Islamic law is not the same as customary law as it does not belong to any particular tribe. It is a complete system of universal law, more certain and permanent and more universal than the English common law.'[60] Thus, communities cannot shape Islamic law, Islamic law shapes Islamic communities. It follows from the foregoing that this unity of the Islamic world is another circle in overlapping relationship with the '*ius commune*' and the 'unity of common law' in the Western world, and more poignantly, in those parts of the world where the post-colonial independent States with inherent cultural and religious pluralism have accepted legal pluralism.

It has also been suggested that it is possible to talk of an emerging convergence in African law. Maybe what we see here is more of a possibility of convergence of laws, a natural and spontaneous process, rather than harmonization of the law which is a plan and an applied technique. As Gardiol van Niekerk points out, Africa presents a more complex case than Europe in this regard.[61] The first obstacle is that legal pluralism prevails in most of the African continent and therefore the achievement of convergence is much more difficult. The second obstacle is that in some countries such as Cameroon, Mauritania and Somalia, the colonial heritage has meant that there is not one single overarching colonial legal system but two: a complex and multifaceted indigenous underlay with two overlays side by side. Nevertheless, in Southern Africa there is convergence with regard to private law, the focus so far being 'on the unification of the imposed Western law and the indigenous laws within individual African countries'.[62] Two groups of countries have been considered by Gardiol van Neikerk: countries belonging to the South African Law Association and the States belonging to the Southern African Development Community (SADC). His analysis of developments reveals that the focus is 'not only on economic integration and the facilitation of free trade in the region.' Programmes are sectorial and include, 'environment and wildlife, energy, illicit drug trafficking, transport, education and training, health care, law enforcement and legal affairs, and matters pertaining to "gender and development".'[63] What is striking here is that there is room for both convergence

[59] See, A.A.Oba, 'Islamic Law as Customary Law: The Changing Perspective in Nigeria', (2002) 51 *International and Comparative Law Quarterly*, pp. 817-850.
[60] Uwais CJN, Kutigi, Ogbweghu and Onu, JJSC, reported by *ibid.*, p. 839.
[61] See G. van Niekerk, 'The convergence of legal systems in Southern Africa' (2002) XXXV *Comparative and International Law Journal of Southern Africa*, pp. 308-318.
[62] *Ibid.*, p. 309.
[63] *Ibid.*, p. 312.

and divergence, thus hope for congruous development. Natural convergence must be the ultimate aim. A loosely connected unity may be developing in Africa which may lead to the formation of another circle.

Beyond these circles, human rights is yet another area where a 'common law' is forming. Many concepts developed on the basis of the European Convention of Human Rights have seeped into domestic legal systems either directly or by way of European Community law. Mentalities, cultures and legal constructions are mixing to bring about such a common law. This is extremely significant. A 'common law of human rights' is developing fast and this *ius commune* of human rights is intended to cover all the circles mentioned above as an outer shell. It is an all-embracing circle. Such a unity already exists within the context of Europe between both the Member States of the European Union and the jurisdictions subject to the Council of Europe Conventions. However, the repercussions are wider. Today it is commonplace to talk of 'globalization' of human rights.

Within the European Union, both the European Court of Justice (ECJ) and the Court of First Instance (CFI) have jurisdiction - limited though it be – to ensure respect for fundamental rights arising 'from the constitutional traditions common to the Member States, as general principles of Community law.' Human rights or fundamental rights are constitutive elements of European integration, part of a pre-existing 'common heritage'. These general principles now extend to the relevant rights arising under the European Convention on Human Rights. According to Advocate-General de Lamothe, these principles:

> contribute to forming that philosophical, political and legal substratum common to the Member States from which through the case law an unwritten Community law emerges, one of the essential aims of which is precisely to ensure the respect for the fundamental rights of the individual. In that sense, the fundamental principles of the national legal systems contribute to enabling Community law to find in itself the resources necessary for ensuring, where needed, respect for the fundamental rights which form the common heritage of the Member States.[64]

Though some talk of 'globalized localism' rather than 'localized globalism' when referring to human rights, seeing it as arising from Western tradition, this view can be challenged. It is first of all a development based on the formulation of common principles which allows a degree of diversity and differing domestic applications yet at the same time provides coherence and consistency: a standard setting. 'Freedom, security and justice' and institutionalizing 'balance of power' cannot be the exclusive reserve of Europeans. All societies strive towards these ends regardless of geographical boundaries. As stated by Upendra Baxi, once the 'authorship' to human rights is pluralized, it follows that 'human rights are not gifts of the West to the Rest'.[65] In addition, today's multi-cultural societies can only survive under an

---

[64] Case 11/70 *Internationale Handelsgesellschaft* [1970] ECR 1125 at 1146-7.

[65] See U. Baxi, *The Future of Human Rights*, (Oxford, Oxford University Press, 2002), p. vi.

overarching framework of 'fundamental rights' which also makes intercultural communication possible.

Overlapping circles of four or more worlds living in interrelationship, congruous with each other if not interlocking, and surrounded by an outer circle of human rights, is the ideal to be worked towards in this globalizing world of ours.

The place of comparative law in all this is crucial. First, comparative law is one of the fundamental sources of any Europe-wide project, in fact, of European law. It is the main tool for working towards European integration. It aids in overcoming exclusive nationalism and shows that the *ius commune novum* must be based on intercultural communication leaving room for diversity. This can be called with William Twining, 'rooted cosmopolitanism'.[66] The mere existence of the European Union implies that comparative law has a serious role in the developing of principles at least in private law.[67] Second, the kind of comparative law that facilitates intercultural communication is the one which goes beyond juxtaposing, contrasting and comparing. This strengthens the call for comparative lawyers to be trained in interdisciplinary research problems, to have knowledge of and familiarity with different legal cultures, to have a good command of languages, knowledge of history, economics and politics, and also to receive training in methodology. The third point is that the work of comparative lawyers in facilitating the achievement of this interrelationship between the overlapping circles and to bring about an intercultural understanding is vital.

The fact that there are few overt references to comparative law in the judgments of the courts of the Community in no way reflects the true position. This work is undertaken primarily by the Advocates-General, the Commission, national courts, academics and practicing lawyers. In fact both the ECJ and the CFI have been called the 'laboratory of comparative law',[68] and the comparative approach in the activities of the Community judge has been hailed as 'a "quasi-compelling" method of interpretation of Community law intrinsically linked to the continuous integration process which characterises the European construction.'[69] As put by Koen Lenaerts, the European Union,

> has its own variant of *E pluribus unum*, that is a set of interlocking legal orders, showing mutual respect for each other based on equivalent levels of judicial protection of the rule of law. That constitutes the common platform for the

[66] See W. Twining, Globalisation and Legal Theory (London, Butterworths, 2000) pp. 47, 50, 88.

[67] Cf. R. Zimmermann, *The Law of Obligations, Roman Frontiers of the Civilian Tradition* (Oxford, Clarendon Press, 1996).

[68] M.Hilf, 'The role of comparative law in the jurisprudence of the Court of Justice of the European Communities" in: *The Limitation of Human Rights in Comparative Constitutional Law* (Cowansville, Les Edition Yvon Blais, 1986), p. 550.

[69] K. Lenaerts, 'Interlocking Legal Orders in the European Union and Comparative Law', (2003) 52 *International and Comparative Law Quarterly*, 873-906, at pp. 878-879

> legal underpinnings of European integration, a *ius commune* built with the bricks of the comparative law method.[70]

Within Europe today, 'common core' projects in areas such as contract, property and tort, regard legal systems as being multi-level and consider comparative law as an 'integrative' enterprise.[71] Regarding cultural diversity in law as an asset while not taking a preservationist approach for the sake of taking it, the aim must be to work towards building European culture on a map of multi-level legal systems. As already noted, this building of a common culture puts strong emphasis on legal education - education that recognizes the crucial place of comparative law teaching.

One important such project at the level of university education aims towards the forging of links between European universities in order to integrate qualifications, and at creating a European higher education area (EHEA) by 2010. This project is supported by 38 countries which have agreed to set up a common pattern distinguishing undergraduate and postgraduate courses, systems of credits and credit transfer, diploma supplements that enable each qualification to be 'readable' in all parts of the EHEA, a structure for quality assurance, joint degrees and integrated programmes for training and research. This movement is obviously not exclusive to law but has the potential to have an impact on the education of future lawyers. The project which started in Bologna in 1998 covers the greater Europe of the EHEA comprising the European Union countries, the remaining European Free Trade Area countries, the European Union accession States and the five Balkan nations. The overall theme is convergence in research and quality assessment. The most remarkable aspect of this development is that, despite the entrenched autonomy and traditions of disparate universities and national sensitivities, the universities have arrived at the principled acceptance of convergence and persuaded governments and the European Commission to back them. The challenge is to collaborate so as to match and surpass the quality of American universities and play as effective a role in the international arena. The European Commission through its Erasmus Mundus programme is poised to spread its Erasmus programme model worldwide while at the same time developing 'Knowledge Europe', working towards the European Union's European Research Area in parallel with the EHEA. These are most welcome developments.

Let us reiterate. Any 'unification' project is integrationist and based on the search for 'common cores'. Whereas, at the other end of the spectrum, difference and distinction are used to create and defend national legal identity by an 'insulation' project. The drive should be towards a common 'European identity' which is achievable by massive cross-border import and export of ideas and collaboration to create a *ius commune novum*.

However, a *ius commune* cannot materialize if Europeanization is restricted to new legislation and scholarly publications. Can we go so far as to say that the rules

---

[70] *Ibid.* p. 906.

[71] For example see M. Bussani, 'Current Trends in European Comparative Law: The Common Core Approach' (1998) 21 *Hastings International and Comparative Law Review*, 785.

of national legal systems should be regarded as local variations of uniform European subject matter? If not, as all comparative lawyers know, when the point of departure is national legal systems and national rules, the outcome always remains biased. Only further integration in Europe can rescue the European nation States from decline.

It can of course be claimed that what is at risk here is traditional values. Variation II is based on this fear.

VARIATION II

As has been pointed out, between the sixteenth and the nineteenth centuries comparative legal history, the comparative law of the time, was interested in similarities only, and it was with rising nationalism and positivism that comparative law discourse began to stress differences, especially those between the civil law and the common law.[72] In the first decades of the twentieth century differences between common law and civil law traditions were emphasized, whereas today, within the European Union, common elements are again sought rather than differences stressed.[73] Since legal systems and cultural systems can indeed 'live apart together',[74] should the function of comparative law be then, the building of bridges? In this Variation the answer to this question is a firm 'No'.

Some of the terms employed for analysis of legal movements and the ensuing convergence today, such as 'seepage', 'contaminant', 'irritant', 'underlay', 'overlay', 'cross-fertilization', 'incremental reception', 'competing systems', 'hyphenated' legal systems, layered law, 'chance', 'choice', 'prestige', 'efficiency', 'elite' and 'historical accident' will be put to the test in the new century.

Is there strong evidence that legal systems are indeed converging as a result of the above processes? The answer is that there is no such evidence. Legal systems are not converging. Though convergence may be the aim of legislatures, true convergence could only come about through 'internalization' of received law by the people themselves and this is not possible. Comparative law must pay attention to identity, non-convergence and difference, not to convergence or similarity.

The 'contrarian challenge' for example, advocates that comparative lawyers must be interested only in difference. Cultural differences may even be bars to comparative law research. The 'other' is a mystery and will remain so since attempting to understand the 'other' would only lead to misconceptions and misleading results. We are living in a world of 'differents'. If comparative law work is to be undertaken, then it must be involved only with differences between systems.

---

[72] L. Moccia, 'Historical Overview on the Origins and Attitudes of Comparative Law' in de Witte & Foster, above note 25, 609 at p. 618.

[73] *Ibid.*, p. 619.

[74] P.C. Müller-Graff, 'Common Private law in the European Community', in de Witte & Foster, above note 25, 239, at p. 254.

There is a natural link between the 'contrarian challenge' and the 'difference theory'.[75]

Pierre Legrand for one, invites the comparative lawyer,

> to place herself firmly in opposition and to pursue the *contrarian challenge*. Indeed, there is no more pressing research and teaching programme for a comparatist to undertake in this historical juncture than actively to promote the merits of the *contrarian challenge* for comparatists themselves, for comparative legal studies, and for the European legal order.[76]

He further states that,

> From the moment he ascribes meaningful meaning to law through tradition or culture and accepts that nothing can be explicated without the support of historical narratives arising over the *longue durée*, the comparatist naturally engages in interdisciplinary studies. He also spontaneously privileges the idea of difference as *principium comparationis*.[77]

As regards the old *ius commune* which included the common law, this Variation denies its existence, regards this old *ius commune* as irrelevant to today's problems, sees the creation of a new *ius commune* as an impossibility, desires no convergence in any areas beyond maybe commercial law and the already existing '*lex mercatoria*', and views Europe as divided into distinct segments. At a time when the 'unity of common law' is breaking down, the clash of cultures blocks the formation of any overlaps between different cultural spheres or of new identities being forged. Equally important is the fact the *ius commune* was the product of a common language, Latin, which does not exist as a common language today. At best we can live in 'harmony of diversities', at worst jealously cling to our own worlds and live in peaceful isolation.

The *ius commune* as we knew it, is past and has been dead for a long time. It seems bizarre to hanker after a past that was given up in favour of national codifications and national legal systems with their own peculiarities and specific features to fit the needs of the socio-cultures they serve. If the nation State in its present form is to be abandoned, it should be for the benefit of legal pluralism and not for further centralist development. Now is the time for appreciation of cultural identity and cultural difference and recognition of multi-layered law. The creation of a *ius commune novum* would be an unacceptable and forced development.

Even when the old *ius commune* was alive, English common law was not part of it. At that time, there was no convergence between the civilian tradition and the common law, and comparative law research today would be hard put to it to show

[75] R. Hyland, 'Comparative Law' Chapter 11 in D. Patterson (ed.) *A Companion to Philosophy of Law and Legal Theory* (Oxford, Blackwell Publishers, 1996) pp. 193-197.
[76] P. Legrand, *Fragments on Law-as-Culture* (Deventer, W.E.J. Tjeenk Willink, 1999) p. 13.
[77] *Ibid.*, p. 18.

that there is such convergence developing now beyond simple responses to the demands of the European Union. The laws of the Member States are not synchronized in any field, nor are they fully reconciled with the requirements of the European Union, let alone with each other.

Modern European Law out of which integrationist European lawyers, many legal historians and some comparative lawyers are trying to glean a developing *ius commune novum*, has a 'fiercely regulatory nature'[78] which is in total contradiction to the 'classical' *ius commune* that existed prior to the codifications in the civil law world.

As the first point then, it must be said that as far as common law and civil law convergence is concerned, the *ius commune novum* is a non-starter. Neither does it make any sense on a wider scale such as bringing the English common law, which is already within the 'unity of common law', closer to the civilian tradition - itself not monolithic - or indeed any rapprochement with the Islamic world. Under the guise of embracing a wider world, *ius commune novum* is isolationist. Its claim is false.

In spite of the fact that the EC is not equipped with the competence to legislate in the field of private law - or in any other field - it has introduced laws in the fields of tort law (delict), commercial contracts and consumer contracts. Though integration itself is not a value worth fostering, the legal systems of the Member States inevitably interact and a degree of cross-fertilization does occur. The courts of the European Union have been developing a conceptual body of law in certain areas of private law and, with the help of the European Court of Human Rights, in a limited area of human rights law, but this work is piecemeal and could not operate as a *ius commune* without the positive laws of the Member States.

What is often presupposed in this development is that, since the laws of the countries in continental Europe are not so very different after all - though this is a fallacious assumption - they will be pressed more closely together and the ensuing cross-fertilization will of itself lead towards integration. However what is ignored or forgotten is the matter of interpretation. Stephen Weatherill rightly poses the question: 'Is "Europeanisation" likely to occur more profoundly than merely on paper, in the shape of the text of an adopted Directive?' He doubts that any such thing as a 'common approach' to meanings given to words such as 'good faith' for example, is 'culturally feasible (let alone desirable).'[79]

Even if such body of law were to develop further, this would only be welcome to those who believe in the desirability of a coherent, logical legal order for Europe. In addition, if the historic links are an example, there would be no place in it for the common law, thus England and Ireland would remain outside. Expansion of harmonized law would in fact be an erosion of traditional values.

If a *ius commune novum* were to be built on historical foundations, then as David Ibbetson says 'the *ius commune* of medieval and early-modern Europe is on the face of it the best candidate based on the intellectually sophisticated groundwork

---

[78] D.J. Ibbetson, 'A Reply to Professor Zimmermann' in Watkin (ed), above note 33, p. 224.

[79] S. Weatherill, 'Can There be Common Interpretation of European Private law', (2002) 31 *Georgia Journal of International & Comparative Law*, 139 at pp. 159, 160.

laid down by the Roman lawyers',[80] as 'in nearly all of Europe, the medieval and early modern commentaries on Roman law which we group together under the title of the *ius commune* had some part to play in the formation of the national laws of individual States.' A conceptual vocabulary was thus provided for lawyers to use in order to communicate, *ius commune* being a kind of uncodified modern Roman law, based on Justinian's compilations as developed in case law.

Seeing England as part of this tradition however, creates a genuine problem. David Ibbetson says that English law has been regarded by most historically minded English lawyers as different from, and better than, continental law.[81] However, he attempts to identify parallel movements between the *ius commune* and the English common law which was at times influenced by Romano-canonical law especially during the fourteenth and fifteenth centuries. Yet, later, the influence faded rapidly, so that from the nineteenth century onwards English law's contact with continental law was minimal except at the Court of Admiralty, whose influence however was marginal. So, though English common law was enriched by ideas drawn from the civilian tradition, and did not develop in total isolation, 'nonetheless, we must beware of going too far in the opposite direction in characterising English law as just another emanation of the Western European legal tradition based on the *ius commune*.'[82] In any event, any laws drawn from Roman law, were cut off at their roots immediately upon reception and the new laws did not remain in dialogue with those from which they derived.

Attempts at identifying a common culture of European private law are pointless because historical facts do not support it. Neither is there at present any indication that legal systems even on the European continent are moving in this direction. Those supporting a new *ius commune* are living in an idealized past where private law provided identical answers to legal problems wherever such problems occurred. In our day legislative efforts to meet the demands of the European Union may create similar rules in certain areas where European directives so require. However, this does not mean that these laws will necessarily be internalized by the local cultures imbedded in the general culture of the separate peoples in Europe.[83] Neither can we say that there have been successful steps to produce Europe-wide Codes in any area. Efforts have all remained private, with various Commissions and academic groups producing 'General Principles' or 'Restatements' in a limited

---

[80] Ibbetson above note 78, p. 225.

[81] *Ibid.*, p. 225.

[82] *Ibid.*, p. 229.

[83] See generally, P. Legrand who makes six claims that ius commune is largely irrelevant to the debate on contemporary problems of European legal integration, that what integration is to occur will take place only through legislation, that this will only highlight further the summa differentia between the common law and the civil law, that this is epistemological rather than substantive, that this shows itself in systematization, the nature of rules and the role of facts, and that this summa differentia is irreducible., 'Legal Traditions in Western Europe : The Limits of Commonality', in: R. Jagtenberg, E. Örücü and A. de Roo (eds.), *Transfrontier Mobility of Law* (Deventer, Kluwer Law International, 1995), pp. 63-84..

number of areas, and scholars coming up with ideas such as the 'competition of legal systems' or 'the creation of case books' in the hope of facilitating choice by the judges in domestic cases as the 'best rule' from the array of cases so published. It must be remembered that even when one does encounter common conceptual vocabulary, the specifics of legal systems - even on the continent - have 'either diverged or failed to converge'.[84]

David Ibbetson concludes by saying: 'If Europe is to include England, we will have to look beyond *ius commune* to the deeper principles which lie behind it, and also to come to terms with the English lawyer's historical concentration on matters of procedure at the expense of matters of substance'.[85] A truly European legal history which would justify creating a new commonality, even if only in private law, involves an approach different to that advocated by integrationalists. This Variation does not regard such a move as feasible, necessary or desirable in any way. Harmony in diversity is the best to be achieved. If we do get closer, then a programme which retains diversity and which does not introduce compulsory principles is the preferred one. An organic rapprochement may materialize and the best way to accommodate this may be through the 'evolutionary theory' whereby legal uniformity can come about by a competition of rules in a 'market of legal cultures'.[86] The future must be left to chance.

As to public law, this was not part of the 'classic' *ius commune* and could have no place in a new one. Public law, even more than private law, is specific to the social and ideological aspirations of each individual nation and, though in our day there is talk of values such as 'democracy', 'rule of law' and 'free market' as universals, the meanings of these concepts differ in different cultures and their manifestations are not identical by any means. To talk of a 'common law of human rights' is misleading since the concept of human rights is not a universal but a 'globalized localism', a hegemonic interference on the part of the western world, an imposition, the importation of which by the non-western world can only be described as 'imposed reception'. As Boaventura de Sousa Santos points out, this successful 'globalisation of a given localism', a particular expression of Western interests, has reproduced 'the hierarchy of the world system and the asymmetries among core, peripheral and semiperipheral societies' and therefore cannot be regarded as 'genuine globalism'.[87] This surely creates problems for those who regard human rights - a 'globalized Western localism' - as universal. Furthermore, Upendra Baxi points to the dangers of the paradigm shift, saying that the United Nations Declaration of Human Rights 'is being steadily, but surely, supplanted by

---

[84] Ibbetson, above note 78, p. 235.

[85] *Ibid.*, p. 238.

[86] See J.M. Smits, 'A European Private Law as a Mixed System' (1998) 5 *Maastricht Journal of European and Comparative Law*, 328; J.M. Smits, 'The Harmonisation of Private Law in Europe: Some Insights from Evolutionary Theory' (2002) Georgia. Journal of International & Comparative Law, p. 81.

[87] B de Sousa Santos, *Toward a New Legal Common Sense*, 2nd edn. (London; Butterworths, 2002) p. 271.

that of trade-related, market-friendly human rights' through the dominant narratives of globalization.[88]

Most comparative lawyers when talking of the 'unity of Islamic law' or 'convergence of African law' rely on information provided by regionalists or orientalists alone, and are not themselves in a position to ascertain all the facts. At a time when there is talk of 'clash of cultures', comparative lawyers would be well advised to keep to what they know best, that is private law in the Western world!

The most one can say is that there is some kind of common European history - though classical English law is excluded from this. In some areas harmonization has had some effect and a weak synthesis may be possible. But national barriers, the political, socio-legal and cultural, are strong. Diversity and difference are more common features than similarity and convergence. Moreover, as common European developments take place, it is possible that there will be even more diversity since modes of transposition and absorption differ. In addition, it is the belief of Guiseppe Monateri, for example, that in this development, the distinction between Western and non-western will become more pronounced and the west, by insisting that the non-west receives democracy, the rule of law and the free market from the west as a necessity for their development, will try to impose a 'clear conventional evolutions paradigm'. In this, the emphasis is on a 'common economic and political structure' and as Guiseppe Monateri indicates, comparative law thereby becomes 'purposive'.[89] This Variation would see such a role for comparative law as political and extremely dangerous.

Given what has been said so far, let us now make an assessment of the three elements: necessity, feasibility and desirability.

First, a comment on necessity. There is no such thing as a universal legal science and no need to create a unified law even at the level of the European Union. Legal systems, each reflecting the legal culture and the general cultural framework within which it lives, are different to each other. Incommensurability is not defeatist nor is it parochial. It is the belief in unique and self-contained entities co-existing. Comparative lawyers must accept that the 'others have different truths.'[90] Searching for a 'better solution' to replace what we individually have is unnecessary. Nor is there any need to search for non-existent 'common cores'.

When it comes to the feasibility debate, it must be said that even if it were regarded as necessary to re-create a *ius commune* in Europe, the rekindling of an interest in such a project would face a number of serious problems related to feasibility. First of all, no one body has the legal authority to proceed. The EC Treaty does not confer formal general power to make law and therefore all such efforts indicate a distortion of the articles of the Treaty.

---

[88] Baxi, above note 65, p. 132.

[89] P.G. Monateri, 'The "Weak" Law: Contaminations and Legal Cultures' in *Italian National Reports to the XVth International Congress of Comparative Law*, Bristol 1998 (Milano, Guiffre, 1998), 84 at pp. 89-90.

[90] V.G. Curran, 'Cultural Immersion, Difference and Categories in U.S. Comparative Law', (1998) 46 *American Journal of Comparative Law*, 43, at p. 91.

The second feasibility problem is both a practical and a contextual one: the insurmountable differences between the civil law and the common law. To state otherwise is a falsification of historical and present facts. The respective legal premises and structures of the civil law and the common law are so different that their coming together would mean for one to be swallowed by the other: common law by civil law. This would never be acceptable nor would it work. In addition, even the various legal systems in continental Europe are incompatible in many respects. They may share a number of fundamental principles but have many differences. Civil law cannot be taken as a monolithic bloc.

In the context of feasibility, anachronism is a third problem. Going back in time, hankering after a lost past and asking legal historians to re-discover *ius commune* is not healthy and is a waste of time. We should be forward looking and there is no legal unity in that future. One cannot create a new tradition. It is a contradiction in terms. The concept of *ius commune novum* is therefore flawed.

A fourth obstacle is the lack of a common language. The *ius commune* was the product of a shared language. There is now no shared language even on the continent of Europe and unless one language were to be chosen as 'the' language there could be no real harmonization let alone unification, since the related problem of interpretation would immediately lead to a new diversity. This would be the case even if a single language were to be adopted for legal work, since interpretation always reflects the cultural framework of the interpreter. The problem is already becoming more and more acute as the European Union enlarges. To create a *lingua franca* in law is as fanciful as using Esperanto. We cannot realistically expect that even the judges should share the same language.

Another obstacle is the enormous task of re-writing text books for every legal subject within a European context. Some think of this as an inevitable hurdle.[91] This is not a hurdle but a real barrier devoid of practicality. Who would write these books? Who would be the teachers? Which 'European law schools' would be chosen as the elitist? Who would decide?

Finally, it is obvious that integration hampers natural development, so is self-defeating.

When it comes to the matter of desirability, then this Variation is squarely on the side of 'No'. Unification or even harmonization could only mean loss of sovereignty, identity, flexibility, certainty and above all, quality. If market mechanisms create a degree of inevitable unity, that we can live with, but we can go no further. Suggestions concerning competing rules or an evolutionary theory whereby there might be natural and gradual convergence, are more palatable for this Variation than any other forms proposed by integrationists. Yet, even that is but a

---

[91] See, A-W. Heringa, ' Towards a European Law School! A Proposal for a Competitive, Diversified Model for Transnational Co-operation', in: M. Faure, J. Smits & H. Schneider (eds.), *Towards a Ius Commune in Legal Education and Research* (Groningen, Metro: Intersentia, 2002), pp. 3-13.

pious hope on the part of the proponents.[92] American style non-binding Restatements are acceptable as long as there are no compulsory elements attached to their use. They can act as guidelines for the European Court of Justice as do various international Conventions. Pragmatism should prevail at all times. Searching for common roots and tradition is counter-productive. Obviously academics can amuse themselves with any project they may devise as long as they are not taken seriously!

[92] Wouter Snijders considers this hope for the 'invisible hand' as he calls it, as the second of his 'Castles in Spain' and says that though as a metaphor the theory seems interesting, it is unrealistic. See W. Snijders, *Building a European Contract Law; five Fallacies and two Castles in Spain*, Ius Commune Lectures on European Private Law No: 9 (Maastricht, Metro, 2003), pp. 7-8.

Chapter 12

FINALE: WHERE ARE WE GOING?

Having entered the twenty first century, comparative law must now take stock of important issues arising from the above picture and then move on. The shifting and changing horizons of comparative law must be critically analyzed.

What can contemporary comparative law say to a world that will be radically different to the one hitherto covered? Can comparative lawyers enter this new and different world with their existing strategies, and accommodate differences by building on or modifying them and so extend the scope of comparative analysis beyond the jurisdictions and topics traditionally dealt with?

We have seen how some comparative lawyers understand comparative law to be a subject in its own right, the only reliable way of accumulating deep-level knowledge of the reality of law and assessing problems that may arise out of the proposed marriages between comparative law and legal theory, economics, sociology and anthropology and giving warning signals where need be. One of the tasks is to analyze fully the underlying phenomena of most of the interest in comparative law in our day, that is, the transfrontier mobility of ideas and institutions and reciprocal influence. Several points must now be addressed.

The first point is that the current concerns of comparative lawyers on convergence versus divergence, mismatch in borrowings, and problems for the importer and the exporter of legal ideas and institutions should be constructively approached as 'Critical Comparative Law'. The term 'Critical Comparative Law' can be used as the direct opposite of the terms 'Traditional Comparative Law', 'Mainstream Comparative Law' or 'Conventional Comparative Law'. The future entails changes both in the perception and practice of comparative law, and its interaction with other disciplines investigating the phenomena of legal and social cultures. Comparative law will remain independent and develop new visions and new agenda while still continuing to serve other disciplines thereby also broadening its vista.

The second point is that comparative law needs a fresh approach to the classification of legal systems. In Chapter 10, I suggested 'a family trees' approach within which legal systems would be classified according to their constituent elements and grouped according to the principle of predominance. It is totally unsatisfactory in our so-called globalizing age to group localisms as previously under the broad headings of civil law tradition, common law tradition and, begrudgingly, socialist laws, others being regarded either as derivatives of the civil or common law traditions.

Recently there has been increasing interest in mixed systems. It has been suggested that some mixed jurisdictions that are crosses between the civil law and common law traditions could be covered in a 'Third Family'[1] and there is talk of a *Ius Commune Europaeum* as a mixed legal system.[2] I regard all legal systems as mixed, whether covertly or overtly, and suggest grouping them according to the proportionate mixture of the ingredients. All systems are better understood as overlaps. My scheme also makes it easier to classify systems such as Malaysia, Singapore, Burma, Thailand and others long neglected by Eurocentric comparatists. The whole of South East Asia is better served by this approach. Off-shoots and sub-groups can be catered for, and the overlaps are clearly seen, all being the outcome of transpositions.

The third point is that a large number of legal systems are in 'extraordinary' places.[3] The problems facing comparative lawyers today will not be solved by hiding behind phrases such as 'law is culture and lawyers cannot understand any culture other than their own', 'legal history is the only path for comparative lawyers', 'the only true explanation of legal change is through economic analysis of law', or 'comparative law must be legal theory, therefore we must be "comparative jurisprudents" in order to understand other laws', 'comparative law as we know it cannot cope with renewal', or 'transplants are impossible'. We cannot ignore the reality of transmigration and of 'difference'. Whatever our stance, we must be prepared to go out to these 'extraordinary' places. 'Comparison in extraordinary places' is vital in our 'extraordinary times'. These places should not be the sole domain of regionalists and anthropologists or the subject of cultural studies alone.

Many of these 'extraordinary' places are looking towards legal systems socio-culturally or legal-culturally very different from their own either for the purposes of law reform or integration. Differences in legal cultures may be as to sources of law, methods of legal reasoning or legal institutions. Obviously, the more fundamental underlying differences are those related to socio-cultures and values. We have to live with the fact that there can never be a tailor-made model; a perfect match between model and recipient is not possible and a degree of mismatch is inevitable. So, the major question is: 'How is this mismatch to be addressed?' Can it be dealt with by the power of the reception on the imagination and creativity of the recipient, the 'tuning'? What is the measure of success? Alan Watson claims that

[1] V.V. Palmer (ed), *Mixed Jurisdictions Worldwide: The Third Legal Family* (Cambridge, Cambridge University Press, 2001).

[2] J.M. Smits, *The Making of the European Private Law: Towards a Ius Commune Europaeum as a Mixed Legal System* (Maastricht, Metro, 2002).

[3] For 'extraordinary' places, see E. Örücü, 'Comparatists and extraordinary places' in P. Legrand and R. Munday (eds), *Comparative Legal Studies: Traditions and Transitions* (Cambridge, Cambridge University Press, 2003), pp. 467-489.

legal rules can be equally at home in many places,[4] but such models cannot work unless they are delicately transposed and 'tuned'. Comparative law as the science of the new century must be deeply involved here.

Have differences been overstated in the past and similarities overstated today? Can it be said that showing the similarity of some selected single rules in detail as to their substance or function, is enough to negate the 'difference approach' and confirm the 'convergence approach'? Whatever the findings, the function of comparative law is the building of bridges, with the understanding that legal systems and cultural systems can indeed 'live apart together'.[5] Comparative law in 'extraordinary' places can perform this 'bridging' role by analyzing and adjusting any mismatch, and so easing transposition. There are however, serious bridging problems when legal systems from diverse traditions such as the socialist, religious or traditional, look towards civilian or common law systems. This must be of particular concern for legal systems which have never been part of a single legal tradition. Imagine for example the US Uniform Commercial Code in Uzbekistan, or the German Code of Bankruptcy in the Kyrgyz Republic. Such issues are of great importance for legal and social systems in 'extraordinary' places that have for centuries been at the receiving end of movements from the civilian and the common law, that is, 'ordinary' models.

How is the obstacle of the so-called *mentalité* to be bridged? Within Europe, this obstacle is related to the nature of what is accepted and the technique of how it is accepted, rather than to the principle of the acceptance of a rule or solution, on which there is little room for negotiation, such as for example, the putting into effect of an European Union directive. So, the real question is not about refusing the medicine, but how one takes it. Should it be chewed or swallowed whole, with water, with another juice, in a thimble, in a cup?

The fourth point is that many models from 'ordinary' places are competing to sell their particular product to 'extraordinary' places. We know for example, that the new Dutch Civil Code has won the competition as a favoured model in Russia for the preparation of the Russian Civil Code, and that the systems of the USA, the European Union and the individual Member States of the European Union now compete according to their 'power profile' and their previous contacts with the systems in Central and East Europe now in transition. Maybe Dutch law appears to be the favourite being well equipped to fulfil its exporting task since in the past the Netherlands was itself an importing country, and the new Dutch Civil Code of 1992 is itself influenced by German, French and English laws. It is the outcome of

[4] A. Watson, *Legal Transplants: An Approach to Comparative Law* (Edinburgh, Scottish Academic Press, 1974).

[5] See P.C. Müller-Graff, 'Common Private Law in the European Community', in B. de Witte and C. Forder (eds.), *The common law of Europe and the future of legal education* (Deventer, Kluwer, Metro, 1992), p. 254.

thorough comparative studies.[6] These factors are part of its attraction as an ideal model and as a source of inspiration.[7] As a consequence, Dutch legal advice is playing a more important role than that of American, German and Italian experts. For example, in Armenia, a most 'extraordinary' place, Dutch, American and Armenian experts were all involved in the drafting of the new Penal Code and Code of Criminal Procedure in co-operation with the Council of Europe under a predominant Dutch influence.[8]

So we see how the legal systems of 'ordinary' places are today competing to become the ones selected for import to 'extraordinary' places, even as they themselves are trying to modernize. For Central and East European, Asian and African systems the process of import can create acute problems. For example, how will the Dutch model fare in Russia? It could be that a jurisdiction with an existing 'mixture' is the better model and would be more acceptable to recipients.

The legal systems of 'extraordinary' places should be studied as 'layered systems' or 'hyphenated systems', 'limping marriages', or simply 'mixed systems', depending on the pervasiveness of the seepage and the degree of resolution of internal contradictions between layers of law and culture.

Fifthly, we must note that successful transposition and fruitful cross-fertilization do not require similarity. In future comparative lawyers will be more concerned with the question of whether similarity is in fact necessary for successful and fruitful cross-fertilization. We know that socio-cultural and legal-cultural differences are the most serious causes of mismatch. Yet differences between national rules do not seem to restrict their import and even the misunderstood can be transplanted though there is a danger that legal-cultural and socio-cultural differences may effect their internalization and efficacy.[9] Internalization of norms and standards by the people of a recipient system is crucial for success. This can be aided by the 'tuners'. Harmony as a possibility of conversation can be achieved through the appreciation of diversity as well as by the elimination of diversity. 'When elements from two different interpretive communities combine', 'one drawing its understanding from culture and the other from law' for instance, they may be able to tap into each other and mesh, bringing 'cultural conversation' into a broader narrative.[10] This in fact is the 'fit', and creative 'tuning' at the time of 'transpositions' is the key to this 'fit'. When communication and conversation are on the move, then cross-fertilization between seemingly incompatibles is facilitated and

---

[6] J.M. Smits, 'Systems Mixing and in Transition: Import and Export of Legal Models: The Dutch Experience' in E. Hondius (ed), *Nederlands Reports to the Fifteenth International Congress of Comparative Law* (Antwerp, Groningen, Intersentis Rechtswetenschappen, 1998), p. 63.

[7] *Ibid.*

[8] *Ibid.*, p. 57.

[9] V. Gessner, Global Legal Interaction and Legal Cultures' (1994) 7 *Ratio Iuris*, 132.

[10] D.S. Berry, 'Interpreting Rights and Culture: Extending Law's Empire' (1998) 4 *Res Publica – A Journal of Legal and Social Philosophy*, 1 at p. 10.

even the misunderstood can be successfully transposed. If unexpected developments ensue, they are also part of the progress.

Shared human problems require similar responses from legal systems, hence legislatures and courts look to other jurisdictions for inspiration in an effort to improve these responses.[11] Global problems of our day need global solutions or interrelated local solutions. Legal ideas and institutions are crossing borders. The new forms in these systems challenge the established conceptual and analytical frameworks of law, the role and value of receptions, theories of convergence and divergence, the dynamism of comparative law, the classification of legal families, and the concept of the legal system itself.

It must be remembered that our time is one of imposed reception - a 'voluntary' activity of import under circumstances in which the exporters hold the trump cards. As this activity accelerates, systems in 'extraordinary' places will become the 'ordinary' systems of tomorrow and laboratories for comparative lawyers. There will be more harmony though not necessarily more integration. The future lies in 'diversity' and 'unity in diversity' rather than 'unity through uniformity. As 'ordinary' places cease to be the main focus of attention, the new 'genre of *mixité*' in 'extraordinary' places will be the focus of 'system-watching'. It is in 'extraordinary' places that comparative lawyers can best observe, analyze and understand the interaction of legal- and socio-cultures, and appreciate the value of 'tuning' in transpositions. Paradoxically, it is in these 'extraordinary' places that the present comparative lawyers are least equipped to work. Comparative lawyers of tomorrow must have education appropriate to the new age.

The sixth point to consider is that, as newly emerging democracies search the pool of competing models available in Western Europe and America with the purposes of re-designing and modernizing their legal, economic and social systems, a whole new world of research possibilities opens up for comparative lawyers. Comparative law will be tied theoretically and practically to enhanced legal science, convergence and integration as well as the appreciation of diversity, the use of foreign models in law reform, and law and culture studies. New approaches to harmonization, receptions, mixing systems and the re-designing of systems, a new European *ius commune*, and a new emphasis on regional comparative law such as European, Central and East European, Common law, African and Far Eastern, will be the main concerns of comparative lawyers. Comparative law will be recognized as an indispensable tool of construction for the European Court of Justice of the Communities, for national courts and for law reform bodies.

It has been pointed out by Thijmen Koopmans that:

> In the nineteenth century history was very much the fashion, in particular on the Continent: history of the codes, pre-existing Roman law traditions, Poitier on obligations, etc. Our own century discovered society; it wondered how the

[11] In the area of human rights, see the contributions in E. Örücü (ed), *Judicial Comparativism in Human Rights Cases*, United Kingdom Comparative Law Series Vol: 22 (London, UKNCCL/BIICL, 2003).

> law works, what its economic context is and how legal decisions can be adjusted to social needs; and it saw the judge as a kind of decision maker, or even a "social engineer". The twenty first century may become the era of comparative methods. ... Our problems in society increase as our certainties in religious, moral and political matters dwindle; and more and more problems are common problems. The search for common solutions is only slowly beginning.[12]

In our new century, comparative law will be pressed to create blue prints for importers of models to aid law reform, and to provide a better understanding of changing concepts. It will be used by courts in resolving disputes as one method of construction and interpretation, particularly in the field of human rights. Thus comparative law, by providing models of legal reasoning, will supply systems in transition, both within and outside Europe, with the possibility of structured change. Its role in this field will strengthen. Comparative law can no longer be regarded merely as an instrument of integration or an instrument of construction and statutory interpretation however, though the knowledge gained through comparative law studies may be thus used. Comparative law is about communication. By providing the language of that communication, it allows legal scholars to enter into holistic communication.[13] Comparative law research also reveals how legal institutions are connected, diversified and transposed. Comparative lawyers will extend their subject beyond the traditional areas, both geographic and substantive, and re-assess legal systems and legal families. Comparative law now has an even broader intellectual agenda, and will remain an essential instrument for legal understanding.

The seventh observation is that a number of distinct approaches to comparative law became prominent towards the end of the twentieth century. These approaches will enhance the prospects of comparative law. Some such distinct trends in comparative law discourse today are comparative law and legal history (historical comparative law or the historico-comparative perspective); comparative law and legal philosophy (comparative jurisprudence); comparative law and culture (comparative legal cultures and law and culture studies); comparative law and economics; and comparative law and regions or subjects not hitherto covered. Public law, whether administrative or constitutional, criminal law and human rights demand that comparative lawyers consider these areas urgently rather than putting all their efforts into private law which dominated the scene in the past. In addition, attention should be paid to regions neglected until recently, and comparative lawyers should not see the world as simply divided between the common law and the civil law traditions. Comparative law should sit comfortably within these combinations.

As noted, one such combination is that between comparative law and legal history. The legal historians, 'legal transplant scholars' and the 'new *ius commune*

---

[12] T. Koopmans, 'Comparative Law and the Courts' (1996) *International and Comparative Law Quarterly*, 545 at p. 555.

[13] W. Ewald, 'Comparative Jurisprudence (1): What Was it Like to Try a Rat?' (1995) 143 *Pennsylvania Law Review*, 1889 at p. 2149.

seekers' are all interested in this combination. Legal historians look at past legal transplants and transfrontier mobility of ideas and institutions in an effort to provide an understanding of, and an explanation for, the development of the law and to help justify future legal development by suggesting law reform through the use of foreign models. In the context of Europe, legal historians also work to rediscover a *ius commune novum*. The third thesis of the Trento Manifesto is: 'Comparison turns its attention to various phenomena of legal life operating in the past or the present, considers legal propositions as historical facts including those formulated by legislators, judges and scholars, and so verifies what genuinely occurred. In this sense, comparative law is an historical science.'[14] According to Rodolfo Sacco, 'Comparative law examines the way in which legal institutions are connected, diversified and transplanted from one country to another'.[15] It has even been asked: 'Is comparative law anything more than legal history?'[16]

Another combination is one of comparative law and legal philosophy with the claim that only with this combination can one reach a true understanding of law. This trend initially saw comparative law as 'just another term for sophisticated legal analysis.'[17] as 'local or national science of law is a contradiction in adjecto';[18] 'in this sense comparative law is another name for legal science'.[19] It has been suggested that 'comparative law should provide the opportunity to study the internal structures of legal knowledge'[20] and contribute to jurisprudence by helping to 'construct a range of different "ontological" models through the institutional deconstruction and reconstruction of case law and doctrinal analysis from a range of different legal systems.'[21] So here the legal theorist wants to employ the services of comparative law for legal theory, since comparative law 'can go far in testing each system's construction of its perceived social reality.'[22] Yet, it is also claimed that,

---

[14] R. Sacco, 'Legal Formants: A Dynamic Approach to Comparative Law (Installment I of II)' (1991) 39 *American Journal of Comparative Law*, 1 at p. 26.

[15] R. Sacco 'Legal Formants: A Dynamic Approach to Comparative Law (Installment II of II)' (1991) 39 *American Journal of Comparative Law*, 343 at p. 388.

[16] D. Roebuck, 'The Past is Another Country: Legal History as Comparative law' (1994) *2 Asia Pacific Law Review (Special Issue)*, pp. 9-23.

[17] B. Kozolchyk, 'Trends in Comparative Legal Research: Apropos Dainow's the Role of Judicial Decisions and Doctrine in Civil Law and Mixed Jurisdictions' (1976) *24 American Journal of Comparative Law*, 100 at p. 111

[18] H.Yntema, 'The American Journal of Comparative Law' (1952) 1 *American Journal of Comparative Law*, 1 at p. 15; and L.J. Constantinesco, *Traité de Droit Comparé: La Méthode Comparative* (Paris, Libraire Générale de Droit et de Jurisprudence, 1974), pp. 306-310.

[19] H. Yntema, 'Comparative Legal Research – Some Remarks on Looking out of the Cave' (1956) 54 *Michigan Law Review*, 902.

[20] G. Samuel, 'Comparative Law and Jurisprudence' (1998) 47 *International and Comparative Law Quarterly*, 817 at p. 833

[21] *Ibid.*, p. 836 and G. Samuel, 'Comparative Law as a core subject' (2001) 21 *Legal Studies*, 444.

[22] Ibid. Also see W.J. Kamba, 'Comparative Law: A Theoretical Framework' (1976) 23 *International and Comparative Law Quarterly*, 494.

'Comparative law of this kind does provide the concrete basis for discussion of a general theory of law, and for a more illuminating theory to be developed. In this way, comparative law has lessons for legal theory'[23] But, if comparative legal research were there exclusively to test theories, then, comparative law would not be a subject in its own right.[24]

The combination of comparative law and culture took the form of 'law and society studies' in the 1970s, and 'law and popular culture' in the 1980s. At the present time, its main aim is to provide better understanding of multi-culturalism and integration. There is growing and impressive literature here with anthropologists and sociologists querying the complexities and problems arising. It is among scholars interested in culture that we find the majority of the so-called 'contrarian challenge' supporters. It is they who are most concerned with the clash of cultures surviving under monolithic value systems imposed by legislatures.[25] A 'mild' form of 'law and culture' studies will only enhance comparative law by providing the tools for 'deep level' understanding of legal phenomena, but an 'extreme' form of this post-modernist cultural relativism can prove to be counterproductive and lead comparative lawyers to the impasse of 'incommensurability'.

The combination of comparative law and economics becomes appealing as economists try to establish a blue print by which systems can choose the most efficient solution to global problems from the pool of solutions offered by competing systems as an alternative to harmonization and codification. Their belief is that a *ius commune novum* in European private law will develop through the competition of legal rules and the eventual emergence of the most efficient or 'best' rule.[26] The prerequisites for achieving harmony will not be necessarily similarity or regularity only, but will also be difference and diversity. This comparative law and economics approach aims to build models for efficient legal institutions and then compare them with the world alternatives provided by different legal systems, and offer explanations for the reasons and the mode of the departure.[27]

---

[23] J. Bell , 'Comparative Law and Legal Theory' in W. Krawietz, N. MacCormick and G. Henrik von Wright (eds.), Prescriptive Formality and Normative Rationality in Modern Legal Systems: Festschrift for Robert Summers (Berlin, Duncker & Humblot, 1995), p. 31.

[24] See I. Ward, 'The Limits of Comparativism: Lessons from UK-EC Integration' (1995) 2 *Maastricht Journal of European and Comparative Law*, 23 at p. 31.

[25] See for instance, L.A. Obiora, 'Toward an Auspicious Reconciliation of International and Comparative Analyses' (1998) 46 *American Journal of Comparative Law*, 669 and G.P. Fletcher, 'Comparative Law as a Subversive Discipline' (1998) 46 *American Journal of Comparative Law*, 683.

[26] J.M. Smits, 'A European Private Law as a Mixed System' (1998) *5 Maastricht Journal of European and Comparative Law*, 328; J.M. Smits, 'How to Take the Road Untravelled? European Private Law in the Making: A Review Essay' (1999) 6 *Maastricht Journal of European and Comparative Law*, 25 pp. 40-41 and also A. Ogus, 'Competition between National Legal Systems: A Contribution of Economic Analysis to Comparative Law' (1999) 48 *International and Comparative Law Quarterly*, 405.

[27] U. Mattei, 'Efficiency in Legal Transplants: An Essay in Comparative Law and Economics' (1994) 14 *International Review of Law and Economics*, 3.

In all the above, there will be tangible results and intellectual vigour will carry the discourse further. In this way the market value of comparative lawyers' work will increase as long as comparative law retains its independent character and is not replaced by 'comparative jurisprudence', 'historical comparative law', 'comparative cultural studies', 'comparative law and economics', or any other kind of 'comparative law and ...'. Comparative law must preserve its separate and distinctive position in the titles of such perspectives, although such combinations can produce additional benefits.

Comparative law is extensively used within the European Union and its prime task is in 'new *ius commune*' studies where it is asked to facilitate integration and make the case for reciprocal influence as the basis for convergence. Its related task is to find ways of reconciling civil law and common law and to aid the creation of European Codes. A more specific task is to act as a tool for construction in national and European courts.

Away from home, Europe sees comparative law as a tool for the export of legal ideas and institutions and aiding law reform. Competing models of Western European legal systems are put on convincing display with the help of comparative lawyers - this is yet another task.

There is renewed interest in research and teaching in comparative common law and in the USA there is concern that comparative law has grown in the shadow of Europe and that it must develop its own agenda if it is to be taken seriously.[28] Furthermore, in England there is a strong desire to keep English law intact within the European Union by stressing the view that legal systems of our day should remain flexible and realistic and therefore uncodified. Even the Privy Council now acknowledges the diversity of the legal systems and legal cultures in the Commonwealth: the 'unity of the common law' is changing.[29]

The eighth point concerns the assertion that 'globalization', the catchword of the new century, will diminish the value of comparative law. This is a mistaken view. In fact the reverse is proving to be the case. There is an increasing interest in localization. Both the local and those who study the local, feel the need to assert localization. The trend to integrate moves the focus to the different and its value. Thus comparative law will become indispensable in the globalization movement since in the effort to create universalist standards, interest in localized exceptions will also flourish. In addition, as William Twining says: 'processes of globalisation stir up old nationalisms, exacerbate cultural conflict, and encourage post-modern scepticism about the universality of values and ideas'.[30] To facilitate co-existence

[28] M. Reimann, 'Stepping Out of the European Shadow: Why Comparative Law in the United States Must Develop Its Own Agenda' (1998) 46 *American Journal of Comparative Law*, 637.

[29] R. Martin, 'Diverging Common Law – Invercargill goes to the Privy Council'(1997) 60 *Modern Law Review*, 94.

[30] W. Twining, 'Comparative Law and Legal Theory: The Country and Western Tradition' in I.D. Edge (ed.), *Comparative Law in Global Perspective* (New York, Transnational Publishers, 2000), p. 21.

and harmony, comparative law will be essential for the understanding of this diversity.

For those comparative lawyers who are engaged in comparative law within the boundaries of Europe, one of the most serious questions of the century will be: How will the 'new *ius commune*' for Europe be achieved and fare in the twenty-first century? 'Unity or harmony in diversity' is easier to achieve than 'convergence and integration by eliminating diversity'. The 'new *ius commune*' can be achieved by appreciating differences and 'transpositions' rather than looking for 'similars'. Here too, a more limited focus and realistic vision must be built upon the 'similarities' between 'differents', and by the accommodation of the 'differents' in harmony.

The ninth point is related to the controversial quest to find the 'better law' or the 'better solution'. What is the 'better law' approach, what is its value and is it workable? Within the context of Europe, is this an area where comparative lawyers should be at work? In any attempt to harmonize law, those involved in such projects have a number of choices. One is to keep the *status quo*; not to harmonize but hope that in time convergence may come as changing social, religious and economic conditions world-wide push localisms towards globalism and sporadic transplants take place. A second option is to strive towards a 'common core'. Here, though the ideal would be pitched at the highest common denominator, either the lowest common denominator or the average solution might be acceptable. However, the most innovative and progressive option is the 'better law' approach which entails the replacement of existing solutions by a solution offered by one of the jurisdictions - the most 'progressive' or 'modern' in the eyes of the harmonizers - or by a newly engineered solution to produce the desired result. For example, in the case of child law, it can be said that the 'best interest of the child' test is the result of one such attempt.

Together with others, the comparative lawyer's role is invaluable here. Nevertheless, in all this activity the main obstacle, even more important than any resistance on the part of localisms, is the legitimacy of, and therefore the justification for, the move. The 'better law' approach leaves room for creativity in drafting but may have to face the question of, for example, democratic deficit. When such exercises are academic, new ideas are easier to sell based on specific 'academic reputation', since the question of 'bindingness' does not arise.[31] Jonathan Hill observes that, 'the approach adopted by "better solution" comparatists fails to consider a more fundamental question, namely whether the function which the rule or institution serves is a worthwhile one'.[32] This is something that must be seriously considered.

The ideological dimensions of many answers and the 'cultural constraints' argument have to be weighed against claims to 'shared notions of human rights,' 'common tradition of shared values' or that 'the cornerstone principles have universality'. The real hope is that in the long term utilitarian pragmatism and

---

[31] This is not the search for the 'best solution' which is utopian.

[32] J. Hill, 'Comparative Law, Law Reform and Legal Theory', (1989) *Oxford Journal of Legal Studies*, 105-115, at p. 104.

cosmopolitanism will prevail. How can such a suitable receptive environment be created? In the field of harmonization, the answer may lie in the creation of, for example, Europe-wide standards to run parallel with, but not replace, national legislation. 'A workable starting point would be to keep culturally specific aspects aside at first, to harmonize the rest and then incrementally try to cover the field.'[33] However, what must be kept in mind at all times is that 'uniform legal standards at the level of Europe will not by themselves build effective legal systems. A high level of voluntary compliance with the legal rules is vital.'[34]

Finally, the future of comparative law will be tied theoretically and practically to appreciation of diversity, while striving for commonality where possible. A central point must be reiterated here. There is certainly nothing wrong with looking for similarities between legal systems. And the more different the systems are the more intriguing it is to discover similarities. To find similarities between similar legal systems is useful in efforts to harmonize and further, to unify laws, in grouping legal systems and in building theories of convergence. Such efforts can provide a pool of models to be used when looking for solutions to newly emerging problems. In addition, finding similarities between legal systems that are not similar may help in developing theories with wider application and help in future transpositions. At the same time, there is certainly nothing wrong with looking for differences between legal systems, and the more similar the systems are, the more intriguing it is to discover difference. Such discoveries can be used to test theories on the relationship of law and culture, that is, enhance our understanding of the impact of culture on law and law on culture, and to show the futility of efforts to build on assumed convergence where it does not exist. As comparative law must get involved in the search for and an explanation of divergences, especially between the seemingly similar with the aim of enhancing our understanding of law and legal and social cultures, this work is vital. To this end, we must concentrate on 'extraordinary' places and how mismatches between law and culture may be resolved. We must also be actively involved in reciprocal influence and transposition as these will dominate the twenty-first century. What is wrong is to look only for similarities and overlook differences or look only for differences and overlook similarities.

To summarize then: the comparative lawyer must develop an interest in fields other than private law and systems other than the normative-legal, in context, in mixing systems, in systems in transition and in the making, in looking beyond Europe and into both 'ordinary' and 'extraordinary' systems, in transpositions and the role of the tuners of the law, in the 'better law' approach, in the deconstruction of classifications and building of other approaches to legal systems such as the 'family trees' approach, in 'comparative law and …' studies and in deciphering the intricacies of the 'similar' and the 'different' - all demanding tasks.

---

[33] E. Örücü, 'A Family Law For Europe: Necessary, Feasible, Desirable?' in K. Boele-Woelki (ed.), *Perspectives for the Unification and Harmonisation of Family Law in Europe* (Antwerp-Oxford-New York, Intersentia, 2003), p. 571.

[34] *Ibid.*, p. 572.

In the past century we were told that comparative lawyers enjoyed privileges 'to the envy of other colleagues'. At the beginning of the new century we find that we have moved even further ahead and the popularity of our subject has indeed increased. It is important to reiterate once again that comparative law is no longer simply a way of contrasting and comparing civil law and common law in an effort to resolve the dichotomy between them, or to stress an impasse. Neither is it merely a sophisticated tool of private lawyers. The question: 'What is comparative law?' may still receive a startling range of replies, the meaning of both 'law' and 'comparison' being far from settled since, as in the past, comparative law remains essentially a 'contested project'. 'Comparative law', either as word or concept, may remain difficult to define acontextually, but this does not mean that it should be defined only according to its uses.

If the comparative law of tomorrow can provide an 'angle from which deformed images can be corrected and distortions in the perspective can be clarified',[35] then its contribution to an enriched understanding of the phenomenon of law and society in all its complexity will be great.

---

[35] E. Örücü, *Critical Comparative Law: Considering Paradoxes for Legal Systems in Transition*, Nederlandse Vereniging Voor Rechtsvergelijking No: 59 (Deventer, Kluwer, 1999), p. 132.

CODA

This Coda, the tail piece, is added to round off the work. It is added to emphasize how shifting horizons of comparative law in the twenty-first century reveal ways of appreciating diversity as well as aiding convergence. Shifting horizons also indicate that euphony and harmony can be achieved through both 'integrative' comparative law studies and 'contrastive' comparative law studies; and that harmony can indeed be found in diversity. As long as communication and conversation are continued through comparative legal endeavour, there will be cross-fertilization and horizontal transfers, and this can only enhance study and research in comparative law and our deeper understanding of laws. Our age is one of communication and conversation, and we should have harmony not just here and there, but everywhere.

'Traditional', 'conventional' or the so-called 'mainstream' comparative law will be supplemented, if not replaced, by 'critical comparative law'. The 'traditional' has slipped down either side of the pairs of Variations on the sub-themes of the theme 'Comparative Law'. 'Critical comparative law' must remain at the vantage point commanding all views; comparative lawyers must approach their subject not as a monophonic or even a homophonic texture, but as the polyphonic texture that it is. What actually exits must be analyzed and emphasized, be it similarity, difference, convergence or divergence. The value of comparative law for academics, students and practitioners can only increase in our century.

Systems covered cannot merely be the 'ordinary' as hitherto engaged with by 'mainstream' comparative lawyers, with the rest of the 'extraordinary' world left to regionalists to decipher. Globalization will reinforce localism with all its overlaps and mixtures. Diversity must be appreciated and preserved, yet commonality sought. Beyond 'Europeanization', the future requires the 'internationalization' and 'globalization' of the way the legal profession, the judges and legal scholars think. Comparative law will be the natural bridge to this.

A new approach to system classification is essential, the existing one having outlived its usefulness. The setting up of a convincing 'family trees' approach with all its overlaps is fundamental.

In 1983 Hans Baade said that in the USA, a typical and perennial complaint of the academic teacher of comparative law was: 'Colleagues are not interested in foreign law; students are ethnocentric boors; the bar consists of monolingual hicks; deans won't finance foreign travel; nobody will take Comparative Law.'[1] He then went on to say that all this was true somewhere but none true everywhere, and that

---

[1] H.W. Baade, 'Comparative Law and the Practitioner' (1983) 31 *American Journal of Comparative Law*, 499 at p. 508.

the picture was changing. The optimistic message today is that things can only get better.

This work should end on a cautionary note. Though our new century will be an 'era of comparative law', we must remember that comparative law is not a panacea. Nevertheless, it is imperative that the world of law is approached by comparative lawyers, dedicated to understanding, interpreting and re-presenting both similarity and diversity, not as a cacophonous world but as a euphonic and polyphonic whole.

BIBLIOGRAPHY

Aitkenhead, M., Burrows N., Jagtenberg R. and Örücü, E. *Law and lawyers in European integration: A compareative analysis of the education, attitudes and specialisation of Scottish and Dutch Lawyers* (Medelingen van het Juridisch Instituut van de Erasmus Universiteit Rotterdam No: 43, 1988)

Ajani, G. La circulation de modèles juridiques dans le droit Post-Socialiste' *Revue internationalle de droit comparé* –4 (1994), 1087-1105

Alexy, R.'The Nature of Arguments about the Nature of Law', in L.H. Meyer, S.L. Paulson and T.W. Pogge (eds.), *Rights, Culture, and the Law* (Oxford, Oxford University Press, 2003), 3-16.

Allison, J.W.F. *A Continental Distinction in the Common Law: A Historical and Comparative Perspective on English Public Law* (Oxford, Clarendon Press, 1996)

Ancel, M. *Utilité et methodes du droit comparé* (Neuchatel, Editions Ides et Calendes, 1971).

Antokolskaia, M. 'The "Better Law" Approach and the Harmonisation of Family Law' in K. Boele-Woelki (ed*) Perspectives for the Unification and Harmonisation of Family Law in Europe* (Answerp-Oxford-New York, Intersentia, 2003)

Appadurai, A., 'Disjuncture and Difference in the Global Cultural Economy', (1990) 2 *Public Culture,*

Arın, C., 'Femicide in the Name of Honor in Turkey', (2001) 7 *Violence Against Women*, 824.

Attwooll, E.M.M., *The Tapestry of the Law: Scotland, Legal Culture and Legal Theory*, (London, Kluwer Academic Publishers, 1997)

Ault H.J. and Glendon, M.A. 'The Importance of Comparative Law in Legal Education: United States – Goals and Methods of Legal Comparison', in N.J. Hazard and W.J. Wagner (eds) *Law in the USA in Social and Technological Revolution* (Brussels, Bruylant, 1974)

Baade, H.W. 'Comparative Law and the Practitioner' (1983) 31 *American Journal of Comparative Law*, 499 at p. 508.

Banakas, E.K. 'Some Thoughts on the Method of Comparative Law: The Concept of Law revisited', (1981) LXVII *Archiv fur Rechts- und Sozialphilosophie*, 289; and a suggestion by R.P. Schlesinger (ed) *Formation of Contracts: a Study on the Common Core of Legal Systems* (Dobbs Ferry, Oceana, 19681, 70.

Bankowski, Z., and Christodoulidis, E., 'The European Union as an Essentially Contested Project', (1998) 4 *European Law Journal*, 341

Baxi, U. *The Future of Human Rights*, (Oxford, Oxford University Press, 2002)

Bell , J. 'Comparative Law and Legal Theory' in W. Krawietz, N. MacCormick and G. Henrik von Wright (eds.), Prescriptive Formality and Normative Rationality in Modern Legal Systems: Festschrift for Robert Summers (Berlin, Duncker & Humblot, 1995)

Bell, J. 'Comparing Public Law' in Harding & Örücü (eds)

Bell, J. 'Mechanisms for Cross-fertilisation of Administrative Law in Europe' ch. 11 in J. Beatson and T. Tridimas (eds) *New Directions in European Public Law* (Oxford, Hart Publishing, 1998)

Bell, J.S. 'English Law and French Law – Not So Different?', (1995) 48 *Current Legal Problems* (Oxford, Oxford University Press, 1995) 63-101

Berkowitz, D. Pistor K. and Richard, J-F. 'Economic Development, Legality, and the Transplant Effect', *Law and Development Paper* No 1, CID Working Paper No 39, March 2000, Center for International Development at Harvard University at http://www.cid.harvard.educidwp/039.pdf p.5.

Berlin, I on Pluralism, <http://www.cs.utexas.edu.users/vt/notes/berlin.html>. Also in (1998) XLV *New York Review of Books*

Bernal, M., *Black Athena: The Afroasiatic Roots of Classical Civilisation*, 2 vols., (New Jersey, Rutgers University Press, 1987, 1991).

Berry, D.S. 'Interpreting Rights and Culture: Extending Law's Empire' (1998) IV *Res Publica – A Journal of Legal and Social Philosophy*, 1

Bingham, J. 'There is a World Elsewhere: The Changing Perspectives of English Law' (1992) 41 *International and Comparative Law Quarterly*, 527.

Blanc-Jouvan, X. 'Centennial World Congress on Comparative Law: Closing Remarks' (2001) 75 *Tulane Law Review*, 1235

Boele-Woelki K. (ed) *Perspectives for Unification and Harmonisation of Family Law in Europe* (Antwerp-Oxford-New York, Intersentia, 2003)

Bogdan, M. *Comparative Law* (Göteborg, Kluwer Tano, 1994)

Bussani, M. 'Current Trends in European Comparative Law: The Common Core Approach' (1998) 21 *Hastings International and Comparative Law Review*, 785.

Bussani, M., '"Integrative" Comparative Law Enterprises and the Inner Stratification of Legal Systems', (2000) *European Review of Private Law*

Cappelletti, M. *Judicial Review in the Contemporary World* (Indianapolis, Bobbs-Merrill, 1971).

Carey-Miller D.L and Zimmermann R., (eds), *The Civilian Tradition and Scots Law: Aberdeen-quicentenary essays* (Berlin, Duncker & Humbolt, 1997).

Carey-Miller, D.L. 'The Great Trek to Human Rights: The Role of Comparative Law in the Development of Human Rights in Post-reform South Africa, in Örücü (ed), 201-228.

Chang, R. 'Comparison and the Justification of Choice' (1998) 146 *University of Pennsylvania Law Review*, 1569.

Chiba, M, *Legal Pluralism: Towards a general theory through Japanese legal culture* (Tokyo, Tokai University Press, 1989).

Chiba, M., (ed.), *Asian indigenous law in interaction with received law*, (London, KPI, 1986)

Clark, D.C. 'Nothing New in 2000: Comparative Law in 1900 and Today' (2001) 75 *Tulane Law Review*, 871

Clark, D.S. 'The Use of Comparative Law by American Courts', (Supp. 1994) 42 *American Journal of Comparative Law*, 23

Clive , E., 'Scottish Family Law' in J.P. Grant (ed) *Independence and Devolution: The Legal Implications for Scotland* (Edinburgh, Green, 1976), 162

Clive, E.M. 'Scottish Family Law', in J. Grant (ed) *Independence and Devolution: The Legal Implications for Scotland* (Edinburgh, Green, 1976), 162

Coing, H. 'The sources and characteristics of the ius commune', (1986) 19 *Comparative and International Law Journal of Southern Africa,* 483-489

Constantinesco, L.J. *Traité de Droit Comparé: La Méthode Comparative* (Paris, Libraire Générale de Droit et de Jurisprudence, 1974)

Copland, A. *What to Listen for in Music*, Revised ed. (New York, Toronto, London, McGraw-Hill Book Co., 1957)

Cotterrel, R. 'Seeking Similarity, Appreciating Difference: Comparative Law and Communities', in A. Harding and E. Örücü (eds), *Comparative Law in the 21st Century* (London, Kluwer Law International, 2002)

Curran V.G., 'Dealing in Difference: Comparative Law's Potential for Broadening Legal Perspective', (1998) 46 *American Journal of Comparative Law*, 657

Curran, V.G. 'Cultural Immersion, Difference and Categories in U.S. Comparative Law', (1998) 46 *American Journal of Comparative Law,* 43

Curran, V.G. 'On the Shoulders of Schlesinger: The Trento Common Core of European Private Law Project' Vol. 2 [2002] No.2 Aricle 2 *Global Jurist Frontier* (The Berkeley Electronic Press)

David R. and Brierley, J.E.C., *Major Legal Systems in the World Today, An Introduction to the Comparative Study of Law,* 3rd ed. (London, Stevens and Sons, 1985).

de Cruz, P. *Comparative Law in a changing world,* 2nd edn. (London, Cavendish Publishing Limited, 1999)

de Cruz, P. 'Legal Transplants: Principles and Pragmatism in Comparative Family Law', in: Harding & Örücü (eds)

de Groot, G.R. 'The quality of bilingual dictionaries' 7 *Maastricht Journal of European and Comparative Law* 4 (2000) 331-335

de Sousa Santos, B., *Toward a New Common Sense: Law, Globalization, and Emancipation,* 2nd edn., (London, Butterworths, 2002

della Cananea, G. 'Beyond the State: The Europeanization and Globalization of Procedural Administrative Law' (2003) 9 *European Public Law*, 563

Demleitner, N.V. 'Challenge, Opportunity and Risk: An Era of Change in Comparative Law', (1998) 46 *American Journal of Comparative Law*, 647.

Drobnig, E. 'The Use of Comparative Law by Courts', in U. Drobnig and S. van Erp (eds), *The Use of Comparative Law by Courts* (The Hague, Kluwer Law International, 1999)

du Plessis, J. ,'The promises and pitfalls of mixed legal systems: The South African and Scottish Experiences' (1998) 3 *Stellenbosch Law Review*, 338.

Dupré, C. *Importing the Law in Post-Communist Transitions: The Hungarian Constitutional Court and the Right to Human Dignity* (Oxford, Hart Publishing, 2003)

Ehrlich, E. *Fundamental Principles of the Sociology of Law*, trans. W.L. Moll, (Cambridge, Mass., Harvard University Press, 1912, 1936)

Ehrmann, H.W. *Comparative Legal Cultures* (New Jersey, Prentice Hall, 1976)

Eörsi, G., 'Convergence in Civil law?', in Szabo and Péteri (eds) *A Socialist Approach to Comparative Law* (Leyden, Budapest, 1977) 45-94

Eörsi, G., 'On the Problem of the Division of Legal Systems', in M. Rotondi (ed) *Inchieste di diritto comparato 2. Buts et méthodes du droit comparé* (Padova, New York, 1973), 179-210

Evans-Jones, R., 'Mixed Legal Systems, Scotland and the Unification of Private Law in Europe', in J. M. Smits (ed) *The Contribution of Mixed Legal Systems to European Private Law* (Groningen, Intersentia, 2001), 39

Ewald, W. 'Comparative Jurisprudence (1): What Was it Like to Try a Rat?' (1995) 143 *Pennsylvania Law Review*, 1889

Ewald, W. 'Comparative Jurisprudence (1): What Was It Like to Try a Rat?' (1995) 143 *Pennsylvania Law Review*, 1889

Farmer L. and Veitch, S., (eds), *The State of Scots Law: Law and Government after the Devolution Settlement*, (Edinburgh, Butterworths, 2002).

Featherstone, M., *Undoing Culture: Globalization, Postmodernism and Identity* (London, Sage, 1995).

Feldbrugge, F.J.M. 'Sociological Research Methods and Comparative Law' in M. Rotondi (ed) *Inchieste di Diritto Comparato*, Vol 2: *Aims and Methods of Comparative Law* (New York, Oceana Publications, 1975)

Fitzpatrick P, 'Globalisation and the Humanity of Rights' (2000) (1) *Law, Social Justice and Global Development*, http://elj.warwick.ac.uk/global/issue/2000-1/fittzpatrick.html. 1-18

Fletcher, G.P. 'Comparative Law as a Subversive Discipline' (1998) 46 *American Journal of Comparative Law*, 683.

Fontana, D. 'Refined Comparativism in Constitutional Law' (2001) 49 *UCLA Law Review*, 539

Friedman, L.M.. 'Is There a Modern Legal Culture?' (1994) 7 *Ratio Juris,* 117

Ganado, J.M., 'Malta: A Microcosm of International Influences' in Örücü, Attwooll and Coyle (eds), 225-247.

Gerber, D.J. 'Globalization and Legal Knowledge: Implications for Comparative Law' (2001) 75 *Tulane Law Review*, 949

Gessner, V., 'Global Legal Integration and Legal Cultures', (1994) 7 *Ratio Juris,* 132

Gibbon, B. J.L and Caldeira, G.A., 'The Legal Cultures of Europe', (1996) 30 *Law and Society Review*, 1996), 55

Glendon, M.A. *Rights talk: The Impoverishment of Political Discourse* (New York, Free Press, 1991)

Glenn, H.P. *Legal Traditions of the World* (Oxford, Oxford University Press, 2000).

Glenn, H.P., 'Are Legal Traditions Incommensurable?' (2001) 49 *American Journal of Comparative Law*, 133

Glenn, H.P., *Legal Traditions of the World* (Oxford, Oxford University Press, 2000).

Gordley, J. 'Comparative Law and Legal Education', (2001) 75 *Tulane Law Review*, 1003

Gordley, J. 'Is Comparative Law a Distinct Discipline?' (1998) 46 *American Journal of Comparative Law*, 607.

Gordley, J. 'Is Comparative Law a Distinct Discipline?' (1998) 46 *American Journal of Comparative Law*, 607

Gordon, W.M. 'The Place of Legal History in the Teaching of Comparative Law and in the Education of Comparative Lawyers', in J.W. Bridge (ed), *UK Law For the Millennium*, United Kingdom Comparative Law SeriesVol: 19, 2nd edn., (London, UKNCCL/BIICL, 2000), 286-297

Graziadei, M. 'The Functionalist Heritage', Chapter 5 in P. Legrand and R. Munday (eds), *Comparative Legal Studies: Traditions and Transitions* (Cambridge, Cambridge University Press, 2003)

Grief, N. 'The Pervasive Influence of European Community Law in the United Kingdom', in T.G. Watkin (ed), *The Europeanisation of Law*, United Kingdom Comparative Law Series Vol: 18 (London, UKNCCL, 1998), 110.

Griffith, J. 'What is Legal Pluralism?', (1986) 24 *Journal of Legal Pluralism*, 1.

Griffiths, J., 'What is legal pluralism?' (1986) 24 *Journal of Legal Pluralism and Unofficial Law*, 1-56

Grossfeld, B. *The Strength and Weakness of Comparative Law*, trans. T. Weir (Oxford, Clarendon Press, 1990)

Grossfeld, B. *The Strength and Weakness of Comparative Law*, trans. T. Weir (Oxford, Clarendon Press, 1990)

Gutteridge, H.C. 'The comparative aspects of legal terminology', (1938) 12 *Tulane Law Review*, 401-411

Gutteridge, H.C. *Comparative Law,* 2nd edn., (London, Cambridge University Press, 1949; reprint, London, Wildy & Sons, 1974)

Hall, J. *Comparative Law and Social Theory* (Louisiana, Louisiana State University Press, 1963)

Hannerz, U., 'Cosmopolitans and Locals in World Culture', in M. Featherstrone (ed.) *Global Culture: Nationalism, Globalization and Moderity* (London, Sage, 1990)

Harding A. and Örücü, E. 'Preface' in id (eds) *Comparative Law in the 21st Century* (London, Kluwer Law International, 2002)

Harding A. and Örücü, E. 'Preface' in id. (eds) *Comparative Law in the 21st Century* (London, Kluwer Law International, 2002),

Harding, A. 'Comparative Public Law: Some Lessons from South East Asia' in Harding & Harding & Örücü (eds)

Harding, A., 'Global Doctrine and Local Knowledge: Law in South East Asia', (2002) 51 *International and Comparative Law Quarterly*, 36

Hartlief, T. 'Towards a European Private Law? A Review Essay', *Maastricht Journal of European and Comparative Law* 1 (1994), 166

Heringa, A-W. ' Towards a European Law School! A Proposal for a Competitive, Diversified Model for Transnational Co-operation', in: M. Faure, J. Smits & H. Schneider (eds.), *Towards a Ius Commune in Legal Education and Research* (Groningen, Metro: Intersentia, 2002), 3-13.

Heuschling, L. 'Comparative Law and the European Convention on Human Rights in French Human Rights Cases' in Örücü (ed) 23-48.

Hilf, M. 'The role of comparative law in the jurisprudence of the Court of Justice of the European Communities" in: *The Limitation of Human Rights in Comparative Constitutional Law* (Cowansville, Les Edition Yvon Blais, 1986)

Hill, J. 'Comparative Law, Law Reform and Legal Theory', (1989) *Oxford Journal of Legal Studies*, 105-115

Hondius, E. 'Towards a European Ius commune: The Current Situation in other Fields of Private Law' in: Boeke-Woelki (ed) 118-140

Hondius, E., 'The Supremacy of Western Law' in L. de Ligt. J. de Ruiter, E. Slob, J.M.Tevel, M. van de Vrugt and L.C. Winkel (eds) *Viva Vox Iuris Romani: Essays in Honour of Johannes Emil Spruit*, (Amsterdam, J.C. Giben Publisher, 2002)

Hope, D., Foreword to Derek Manson-Smith, *The Legal System of Scotland* (Edinburgh, HMSO, 1995)

Howard, R.E., 'Cultural Absolutism and the Nostalgia for the Community', (1993) 15 *Human Rights Quarterly*, 315-338.

Hyland, R. 'Comparative Law', in D. Patterson (ed) *A Companion to Philosophy of Law and Legal Theory* (Oxford, Blackwell, 1996), 193-197.

Ibbetson, D.J. 'A Reply to Professor Zimmermann', in T.G. Watkin (ed) *The Europeanisation of Law*, United Kingdom Comparative Law Series No: 18 (London, UKNCCL, 1998), 224

Ibbetson, D.J., A Reply to Professor Zimmermann', in T.G.Watkin (ed) The *Europeanisation of Law*, United Kingdom Comparative Law Series:18 (London, UKNCCL, 1998), 224

Jamieson, N. 'Source and Target-Oriented Comparative Law', (1996) 44 *American Journal of Comparative Law*, 121.

Jones R. and. Gnanapala, W.,*Ethnic Minorities in English Law* (Stoke-on-Trent, Trentham Books, 2000).

Kahn-Freund, O. 'Comparative Law as an Academic Subject', (1966) 82 *Law Quarterly Review*, 40-41.

Kamba, W.J. 'Comparative Law: A Theoretical Framework' (1976) 23 *International and Comparative Law Quarterly*, 494.

Kaminski, I.C. 'The Power of Aspiration: The Impact of European Law on a non-EU Country', in M. van Hoecke and F. Ost (eds), *The Harmonisation of European Private Law* (Oxford, Hart Publishing, 2000), 239-252.

Karameus, K.D. 'Comparative Law and Comparative Lawyers: Opening Remarks', (2001) 75 *Tulane Law Review*, 859-870

Kearns, P. 'United Kingdom Judges and Human Rights Cases', in Örücü (ed), 63-83.

Kennedy, D. 'The methods and the politics', in P. Legrand and R. Munday (eds), *Comparative Legal Studies: Traditions and Transitions* (Cambridge, Cambridge University Press, 2002), 345-433.

Klami, H.T. 'Comparative Law and Legal Concepts' in *Oikeustiede Jurisprudentia,* ((1981) XIV Suomalaisen Lakimiesyhdistyksen Uosikirya (Vammala 1981)

Koopmans, T. 'Comparative Law and the Courts' (1996) *International and Comparative Law Quarterly*, 545

Koopmans, T. 'Towards a New "Ius Commune"', in: B. de Witte and C. Forder (eds.), *The common law of Europe and the future of legal education* (Deventer, Kluwer; Metro, 1992)

Kozolchyk, B. 'Trends in Comparative Legal Research: Apropos Dainow's the Role of Judicial Decisions and Doctrine in Civil Law and Mixed Jurisdictions' (1976) *24 American Journal of Comparative Law*, 100

Kozyris, P.G. 'Comparative Law for the Twenty-First Century: New Horizons and New Technologies' (1994) 69 *Tulane Law Review*, 165.

Krislov, S., 'The Concept of Families of Law' in Podgorecki, Whelan & Khosla (eds.), 25-34.

LaPalombara, J. 'Parsimony and Empiricism in Comparative Politics' in Holt and Turner (eds)

Lask S. and Urry, J., *Economics of Signs and Space* (London, Sage, 1994) , p. 312.

Lasser, M. de S. –O, - l'E 'The question of understanding' in P. Legrand and R. Munday (eds) *Comparative Legal Studies: Traditions and Transitions* (Cambridge, Cambridge University Press, 2003)

Lawson, F.H. 'Comparative Law as an Instrument of Legal Culture' in F.H. Lawson, *The Comparison, Selected Essays*. V. II (Amsterdam, New York, Oxford, North-Holland Publishing Co., 1977)

Legrand P. and Munday R. (eds), *Comparative Legal Studies: Traditions and Transitions* (Cambridge, Cambridge University Press, 2003).

Legrand, P. 'Against a European Civil Code' (1997) *Modern Law Review*, 44.

Legrand, P. 'How to compare now' (1996) 16 *Legal Studies* 232, also in P. Legrand, *Fragments of Law-as-Culture* (Deventer, W.E.J. Tjeenk Willink, 1999) as 'A Redemptive Programme', 1-13.

Legrand, P. 'Legal Traditions in Western Europe : The Limits of Commonality', in: R. Jagtenberg, E. Örücü and A. de Roo (eds.), *Transfrontier Mobility of Law* (Deventer, Kluwer Law International, 1995), 63-84..

Legrand, P. 'The Impossibility of "Legal Transplants"', 4 *Maastricht Journal of European and Comparative Law* (1997), 111

Legrand, P. 'The same and the different', Chapter 9 in P. Legrand and R. Munday (eds), *Comparative Legal Studies: Traditions and Transitions* (Cambridge, Cambridge University Press, 2003), 240-311.

Legrand, P. 'What "Legal Transplant"?' in D. Nelken and J. Feest (eds), *Adapting Legal Cultures* (Oxford, Hart Publishing, 2001), 55-69.

Legrand, P. *Fragments on Law-as-Culture* (Deventer, W.E.J. Tjeenk Willink, 1999)

Lenaerts, K. 'Interlocking Legal Orders in the European Union and Comparative Law', (2003) 52 *International and Comparative Law Quarterly*, 873-906

Lewis, X. Europeanisationof the common law', in R. Jagtenberg, E. Örücü and A. de Roo (eds.) *Tranfrontier Mobility of Law* (The Hague, Kluwer Law International, 1995), 47.

Lord Goff, 'The Future of the Common Law', (1997) 46 *International and Comparative Law Quarterly*, 745

Macridis, R.G. *The Study of Comparative Government* (New York, Doubleday, 1955).

Mahoney, P 'The Comparative Method in Judgments of the European Court of Human Rights: Reference back to National Law', paper delivered at the BIICL Conference 'Comparative law Before National and International Courts' on 21 February 2003 (unpublished) which is an updated version of an article P Mahoney, 'The Role of Comparative Law in the Emergence of European Law, 2000 (a publication of the Swiss Institute of Comparative Law)

Malmström, A., 'The System of Legal Systems, Notes on the Classification in Comparative Law', (1969) 13 *Scandinavian Studies in. Law*, 127

Markesinis, B. 'Comparative law – A Subject in Search of an Audience' (1990) 53 *Modern Law Review*, 1

Markesinis, B. *Foreign Law and Comparative Methodology* (Oxford, Hart Publishing, 1998)

Martin, R. 'Diverging Common Law – Invercargill goes to the Privy Council'(1997) 60 *Modern Law Review*, 94.

Mattei, U. 'Efficiency in Legal Transplants: An Essay in Comparative Law and Economics' (1994) 14 *International Review of Law and Economics*, 3.

Mattei, U., 'Three Patterns of Law: Taxonomy and Change in the World's Legal Systems', (1997) XLV *American Journal of Comparative Law*, 1.

McCrudden, C. 'Human Rights and Judicial Use of Comparative Law', in Örücü (ed), 1- 22.

Menski, W.F., 'Muslim Law in Britain' (2001) *Journal of Asian and African Studies,* 127-163.

Menski, W.F., *Comparative law in a global context: The legal systems of Asia and Africa* (London, Platinum, 2000).

Merryman, J.H. 'Comparative Law and Scientific Explanation' in J.N. Hazard and W.J. Wagner (eds), *Law in the U.S.A. in Social and Technical Revolution* (Brussels, Bruyland, 1974)

Merryman, J.H. *The Civil Law Tradition: An Introduction to the legal Systems of Western Europe and Latin America*, 2nd ed. (California, Stanford University Press, 1985)

Merryman, J.H. *The Loneliness of the Comparative Lawyer* (The Hague/London/Boston, Kluwer Law International, 1999

Moccia, L. 'Historical Overview on the Origins and Attitudes of Comparative Law', in: Witte & Forder (eds.)

Monateri, P.G. 'Everybody's Talking'; The Future of Comparative Law' (1998) 21 *Hastings International and Comparative Law Review*, 825.

Monateri, P.G., ' The "Weak" Law: Contaminations and Legal Cultures' in *Italian National Reports to the XVth International Congress of Comparative Law*, Bristol 1998 (Milano, Giuffrè editore, 1998) 83- 110

Monateri, P.G., 'Black Gaius / A Quest for the Multicultural Origins of the "Western Legal Tradition"', (2000) 51 *Hastings Law Journal*, 479-555.

Moore, S., *Law as Process* (London, Routledge, 1978)

Moore, S., *Social Facts and Fabrications* (Cambridge, Cambridge University Press, 1986)

Müller-Graff, P.C. 'Common Private Law in the European Community', in B. de Witte and C. Forder (eds.), *The common law of Europe and the future of legal education* (Deventer, Kluwer, Metro, 1992),

Munday, R. 'Accounting for an Encounter', in P. Legrand and R. Munday (eds), *Comparative Legal Studies: Traditions and Transitions* (Cambridge, Cambridge University Press, 2002)

Nelken, D. 'Disclosing/Invoking Legal Culture: An Introduction' (1995) 4 *Social and Legal Studies*, 435-452

Newmark, P.P. 'Twenty-three restricted rules of translation', (1973) 12 *Incorporated Linguists*, 12.

Oba, A.A. 'Islamic Law as Customary Law: The Changing Perspective in Nigeria', (2002) 51 *International and Comparative Law Quarterly*, 817-850.

Obiora, L.A. 'Toward an Auspicious Reconciliation of International and Comparative Analyses' (1998) 46 *American Journal of Comparative Law*, 669

Ogus, A. 'Competition Between National Legal Systems: A Contribution of Economic Analysis to Comparative Law', (1999) 48 *International and Comparative Law Quarterly*, 405.

Ogus, A. 'The Contribution of Economic Analysis of Law to Legal Transplants', in: J.M. Smits (ed.), *The Contribution of Mixed Legal Systems to European Private Law* (Groningen, Intersentia, 2001), 27-37.

Örücü , E,. 'Mixed and Mixing Systems: A Conceptual Search', in E. Örücü, E. Attwooll and S. Coyle (eds) *Studies in Legal Systems: Mixed and Mixing* (London, Kluwer Law International, 1996

Örücü E. (ed) *Judicial Comparativism in Human Rights Cases*, United Kingdom Comparative Law Series Vol: 22 (London, UKNCCL/BIICL, 2003).

Örücü, E. ,'An Exercise on the Internal Logic of Legal Systems'. (1987) 7 *Legal Studies*, 310.

Örücü, E. ' Method and object of comparative law' in: H.W. Blom and R.J. de Folter (eds.), *Methode en Object in de rechtswetenschappen* (Zwolle, W.E.J. Tjeenk Willink, 1986)

Örücü, E. 'A Family Law For Europe: Necessary, Feasible, Desirable?' in K. Boele-Woelki (ed.), *Perspectives for the Unification and Harmonisation of Family Law in Europe* (Antwerp-Oxford-New York, Intersentia, 2003)

Örücü, E. 'Approaching Public Law as a Mixed System' (2002) *Juridical Review*, 131-142.

Örücü, E. 'Comparative Law in British Courts', in U. Drobnig and S. van Erp (eds) *The Use of Comparative Law by Courts* (The Hague, Kluwer Law International, 1999)

Örücü, E. 'Teaching Comparative Law and Comparative Law Teaching in the UK' in J. Bell (ed) *Studies in UK Law 2002*, United Kingdom Comparative Law Series Vol: 21, (London, UKNCCL/BIICL, 2002), 3- 30.

Örücü, E. 'The Turkish Experience with Judicial Comparativism in Human Rights Cases' in E. Örücü (ed), 131-158.

Örücü, E. 'Turkey Facing the European Union – Old and New Harmonies' (2000) 25 *European Law Review*, 57-71.

Örücü, E. 'Unde Venit, Quo Tendit Comparative Law', in Harding & Örücü (eds),

Örücü, E. 'Whither Comparativism in Human Rights Cases?' chap. 11 in E. Örücü (ed) *Judicial Comparativism in Human Rights Cases*, United Kingdom Comparative Law Series Vol: 22 (London, UKNCCL/BIICL, 2003), 229-242.

Örücü, E. *Symbiosis Between Comparative Law and Theory of Law – Limitations of Legal Methodology* (Mededelingen van het Juridisch Instituut No 16, 1982, Erasmus Universiteit Rotterdam),

Örücü, E., 'A Theoretical Framework For Transfrontier Mobility of Law', in R. Jagtenberg, E. Örücü and A. de Roo (eds) *Transfrontier Mobility of Law* (The Hague, Kluwer Law International, 1995) 5-18.

Örücü, E., 'Comparatists and extraordinary places' Chapter 13 in P. Legrand and R. Munday (eds), *Comparative Legal Studies: Traditions and Transitions* (Cambridge, Cambridge University Press, 2003, 467-489.

Örücü, E., 'Family Trees for Legal Systems: Towards a Contemporary Approach' Chapter 18 in M.

Örücü, E., 'Law as Transposition', (2002) 51 *International and Comparative Law Quarterly*, 205.

Örücü, E., 'Turkey: Change Under Pressure', in E. Örücü, E. Atwooll and S. Coyle (eds.) *Studies in Legal Systems: Mixed and Mixing*, (London, Kluwer Law International, 1996).

Örücü, E., 'Waar wet en cultuur elkaar ontmoeten: Cultureel pluralisme, juridisch pluralisme en pragmatisme, in 5 02 *Culturele diversiteit*, Justitiele verkenningen, Ministerie van Justitie WODC (Deventer, Kluwer, 2002).

Örücü, E., *Critical Comparative Law: Considering Paradoxes for Legal Systems in Transition,* Nederlandse Vereniging voor Rechtvergelijking No: 59, (Deventer, Kluwer, 1999) also in (2000) 4 *Electronic Journal of Comparative Law*, 2

Packer, J., 'On the Definition of Minorities', in J. Packer and K Myntti (eds) *The Protection of Ethnic and Linguistic Minorities in Europe* (Turku, Abo Akademi University Press, 1993), 23.

Palmer, V.V. 'Insularity and Leadership in American Comparative Law: The Past One Hundred Years' (2001) 75 *Tulane Law Review*, 1093

Palmer, V.V., *Mixed Jurisdictions Worldwide: The Third Legal Family*, (Cambridge, Cambridge University Press, 2001).

Peters A. and Schwenke, H. 'Comparative Law Beyond Post-modernism' (2000) 49 *International and Comparative Law Quarterly*, 800

Pfersmann, O. 'Le droit comparé comme interprétation et comme théorie du droit', (2001) *Oxford University Comparative Law Forum* 4 , p. 1 at ouclf.iuscomp.org; also in (2001) 53 *Revue international de droit comparé*, 275-288.

Podgorecki, A., 'Social Systems and Legal Systems – Criteria for Classification', in A. Podgorecki, C.J.Whelan and D. Khosla (eds), *Legal Systems and Social Systems* (London, Croom Helm, 1985)

Podgorecki, A., Whelan, C.J., and Khosla, D. (eds), *Legal Systems and Social Systems* (London, Croom Helm, 1985)

Prott, L., 'Cultural Rights as People's Rights' in J. Crawford (ed) *The Rights of Peoples* (Oxford, Clarendon Press, 1988), 91-101

Raz, J. 'On the Authority and Interpretation of Constitutions: Some Preliminaries', in I. Alexander (ed), *Constitutionalism: Philosophical Foundations* (Cambridge, Cambridge University Press, 1998), 152

Raz, J. 'On the Nature of Law', *Archives for Philosophy of Law and Social Philosophy*, 82 (1996), 1-25

Raz, J. *The Concept of a Legal System: An Introduction to the Theory of Legal Systems*, (Oxford, Oxford University Press, 1973)

Réaume, D.G., 'The Legal Enforcement of Social Norms: Techniques and Principles' (unpublished paper)

Reid K. and Zimmermann R. ,(eds), *A History of Private Law in Scotland* (Oxford, New York, Oxford University Press, 2000)

Reid K. and Zimmermann, R. 'The Development of Legal Doctrine in a Mixed System', in Reid & Zimmermann (eds)

Reid, E., 'Comparative Law: Perspective from a Mixed Jurisdiction', in *HLS Cahier Nr.2 Methodology and its application* (Groningen, Facilitair Bedrijf, 2001)

Reimann, M. 'Beyond National Systems: A Comparative Law for the International Age' (2001) 75 *Tulane Law Review*, 1103

Reimann, M. 'Stepping Out of the European Shadow: Why Comparative Law in the United States Must Develop Its Own Agenda' (1998) 46 *American Journal of Comparative Law*, 637.

Renfrew, C., *Archeology and Language: The Puzzle of Indo-European Origins*, (London, Jonathan Cape, 1987

Riggs, F.W. 'The Comparison of Whole Political Systems' in R.T. Holt and J.E. Turner (eds), *The Methodology of Comparative Research* (New York, The Free Press, 1970), 77.

Roberts, G.K. *What is Comparative Politics?* (Macmillan, Essex, 1972

Robertson, R., 'Globalization: time-space and homogeneity-heterogeneity' in M. Featherstone et al. (eds.) *Global Modernities* (London, Sage, 1995)

Robertson, R., *Globalization: Social Theory and Global Culture* (London, Sage, 1992)

Rodger. A., 'Thinking about Scots law' (1996) 1 *Edinburgh Law Review,* 3.

Roebuck, D. 'The Past is Another Country: Legal History as Comparative law' (1994) *2 Asia Pacific Law Review (Special Issue*), 9-23.

Roger of Earlsferry, 'Preface' in Farmer and Scott Eds)

Rosen, L., 'Beyond Compare', in: Legrand & Munday (eds.), 493-510

Sacco R. 'Legal Formants: A Dynamic Approach to Comparative Law (Installment II of II)' (1991) 39 *American Journal of Comparative Law*, 343.

Sacco, R. 'Legal Formants: A Dynamic Approach to Comparative Law (Installment I of II)' (1991) 39 *American Journal of Comparative Law*, 1

Sacco, R. 'One Hundred Years of Comparative Law', (2001) 75 *Tulane Law Review*, 1159

Samuel, G. 'Comparative Law and Jurisprudence' (1998) 47 *International and Comparative Law Quarterly*, 817

Samuel, G. 'Comparative Law as a core subject' (2001) 21 *Legal Studies*, 444.

Samuel, G. 'Epistemology and Comparative Law: Contributions from the Sciences and Social Sciences' in M. Van Hoeche (ed) *Epistemology and Methodology of Comparative Law* (Oxford, Hart Publishing, 2004).

Schauer, F. 'The Politics and Incentives of Legal Transplantations' *Law and Development Paper* No: 2. CID Working Paper No: 44, April 2000, Center for International Development at Harvard University, http://www.cid.harvard.edu/cidwp/044.htm , p.2, 18.

Schlesinger, R.B. 'The Past and Future of Comparative Law', (1995) 43 *American Journal of Comparative Law*,. 477

Schlesinger, R.B. (ed), *Formation of Contracts: a Study on the Common Core of Legal Systems* (Dobbs Ferry, Oceana, 1968).

Schmidt, F. 'The need for a multi-axial method in comparative law' in J.C.B. Mohr (ed), *Festschrift für Konrad Zweigert* (Tübingen, Paul Siebeck, 1981), 525-536.

Schmitthoff, M. ' The Science of Comparative Law' (1939) 7 *The Cambridge Law Journal*, 94-110

Schwartze J. (ed) *Administrative Law under European Influence* (London, Sweet & Maxwell, 1996)

Schwartze, J. 'Towards a Common European Public Law' (1995) 1 *European Public Law*, 232.

Sellar, W.D.H., 'Scots law – mixed from the very beginning? A tale of two receptions' (2000) 4 *Edinburgh Law Review*, 3

Slaughter, A.M. 'A Typology of Transjudicial Communication' (1994) *University of Richmond Law Review*, 99.

Smits J.M., (ed*) The Contribution of Mixed Legal Systems to European Private Law* (Groningen, Intersentia, 2001*)*.

Smits, J.M. 'How to Take the Road Untravelled? European Private Law in the Making: A Review Essay', 6 *Maastricht Journal of European and Comparative Law* 1 (1999), 25-46

Smits, J.M. 'Introduction: Mixed Legal Systems and European Private Law', in J.M. Smits (ed) *The Contribution of Mixed Legal Systems to European Private Law* (Groningen, Intersentia, 2001) 9

Smits, J.M. 'Systems Mixing and in Transition: Import and Export of Legal Models: The Dutch Experience' in E. Hondius (ed), *Nederlands Reports to the Fifteenth International Congress of Comparative Law* (Antwerp, Groningen, Intersentis Rechtswetenschappen, 1998).

Smits, J.M. 'The Harmonisation of Private Law in Europe: Some Insights from Evolutionary Theory', (2002) 31 *Georgia Journal of International & Comparative Law*, 79-99.

Smits, J.M., 'A European Private Law as a Mixed Legal System, (1998), 5 *Maastricht Journal of European and Comparative Law*, 328-340

Smits, J.M., *The Making of European Private Law: Towards a Ius Commune Europaeum as a Mixed Legal System*, (Maastricht, Metro 2002*)*

Snijders, W. *Building a European Contract Law; five Fallacies and two Castles in Spain*, Ius Commune Lectures on European Private Law No: 9 (Maastricht, Metro, 2003)

Tamanaha, B. *A General Jurisprudence of Law and Society* (New York, Oxford University Press, 2001), pp. xi-xii. William Twining reviews this book and cites this example in this recent review article, 'A Post-Westphalian Conception of Law' 37 *Law and Society Review* (2003)

Teubner, G. 'Legal Irritants: Good Faith in British Law or How Unifying Law Ends Up in New Divergencies', (1998) 61 *Modern Law Review*, 11

Tur, R.H.S. 'The Dialectic of General Jurisprudence and Comparative Law' (1977) *Juridical Review*, 238.

Twining, W. 'A Post-Westphalian Conception of Law: Review essay' (2003) 37 *Law and Society Review*

Twining, W., 'Comparative Law and Legal Theory: The Country and Western Tradition' in I.D. Edge (ed) *Comparative Law in Global Perspective* (New York, Transnational Publishers, 2000)

Twining,W., *Globalisation and Legal Theory* (London, Butterworths, 2000).

van Gerven, W., Lever J. and Larouche P. (eds.), *Tort law, Common Law of Europe Casebooks* (Oxford, Hart Publishers, 2000); H. Schulte-Nölke, R. Schulze and J. Jones (eds.), *A Casebook on European Consumer Law* (Oxford, Hart Publishers, 2000).
van Hoecke (ed), *Epistemology and Methodology of Comparative Law* (Oxford, Hart Publishing, 2004), 359-375.

van Hoecke M. and Ost, F., 'Legal Doctrine in Crisis: towards a European Legal Science' (1998) 18 *Legal Studies*, 197

van Hoecke, M., 'Deep Level Comparative law' in M. Van Hoecke (ed), *Epistemology and Methodology of Comparative Law* (Oxford, Hart Publishing, 2004)

van Hoecke, M., and Warrington, M., 'Legal Cultures and Legal Paradigms: Towards a New Model for Comparative Law', (1998) 47 *International and Comparative Law Quarterly*, 495.

van Niekerk, G. 'The convergence of legal systems in Southern Africa' (2002) XXXV *Comparative and International Law Journal of Southern Africa*, 308-318.

van Reenen, T.P. , 'Major theoretical problems of modern comparative legal methodology (3): The criteria employed for the classification of legal systems' (1996) XXIX *Comparative and International Law Journal of Southern Africa*, 71-99.

Varady, T. 'Notes on Ideological Precepts as Formants of Private Law in Central-East European Countries', (2002), Vol: 2, No 2, *Global Jurist Frontier,* 1-18.

Walker, D. M., *The Scottish Jurists* (Edinburgh, Green, 1985)

Ward, I. 'The Limits of Comparativism: Lessons from UK-EC Integration (1995) 2 *Maastricht Journal of European and Comparative Law*, 23[1] *Ibid.*

Watkin, T.G. *The Europeanisation of Law*, United Kingdom Comparative Law Series Vol: 18, (London, UKNCCL/BIICL, 1998)

Watson A., 'A Common Private Law for Europe?' 9 *Maastricht Journal of European and Comparative Law* 4 (2002

Watson, A. 'A Common Private Law for Europe?' *9 Maastricht Journal of European and Comparative Law* 4 (2002)

Watson, A. 'Aspects of reception of law' (1996) 44 *American Journal of Comparative Law*, 345.

Watson, A. 'Legal Transplants and Law Reform', (1976) 92 *Law Quarterly Review*, 94.

Watson, A. *Legal Transplants: An Approach to Comparative Law* (Edinburgh, Scottish Academic Press, 1974).

Watson, A., *Legal Transplants and European Private Law*, Ius Commune Lectures on European Private Law (2000 METRO, Institute for transnational legal research)

Watson, A., *The Making of the Civil Law* (Cambridge, Mass. and London, Harvard University Press, 1981)

Weatherill, S. 'Can There be Common Interpretation of European Private law', (2002) 31 *Georgia Journal of International & Comparative Law*, 139

Weir, T., 'Divergent legal systems in a single member state' (1998) 6 *Zeitschrift fur Europaisches Privatrect,* 56

Weiss, N. 'The Impact of the European Convention on Human Rights on German Jurisprudence' in Örücü (ed), 49-62..

Werro, F. 'Notes on the Purpose and Aims of Comparative Law' (2001) 75 *Tulane Law Review*, 1225

Weston, M. *An English Reader's Guide to the French Legal System* (New York / Oxford, Berg, 1991)

White, D. 'Some problems of a hybrid legal system: a case study of St. Lucia' (1981) 30 *International and Comparative law Quarterly*, 862-881.

Yntema, H. 'Comparative Legal Research – Some Remarks on Looking out of the Cave' (1956) 54 *Michigan Law Review*, 902.

Yntema, H. 'The American Journal of Comparative Law' (1952) 1 *American Journal of Comparative Law*, 1

Zimmermann, R. 'Savigny's legacy: Legal history, comparative law, and the emergence of a European legal science', (1996) 112 *Law Quarterly Review*, 557

Zimmermann, R. *The Law of Obligations, Roman Frontiers of the Civilian Tradition* (Oxford, Clarendon Press, 1996).

Zweigert K. and Kötz, H., *An Introduction to Comparative Law*, 3rd edn., trans. T. Weir (Oxford, Clarendon Press, 1998), pp. 63-67. Also see M. Bogdan, *Comparative Law* (Göteborg, Kluwer Tano, 1994), pp. 82-91.

Zweigert, K. 'Methodological Problems in Comparative Law', (1972) 7 *Israel Law Review*, 466.

INDEX

Made in United States
Orlando, FL
02 January 2025

56818688R00139